DATE DUE

Faith in Sports

Steve Hubbard

Faith

in Sports

Athletes
and Their Religion
on and off the Field

DOUBLEDAY

New York London Toronto Sydney Auckland

PUBLISHED BY DOUBLEDAY
a division of Bantam Doubleday Dell Publishing Group, Inc.
1540 Broadway, New York, New York 10036

DOUBLEDAY and the portrayal of an anchor with a
dolphin are trademarks of Doubleday, a division of
Bantam Doubleday Dell Publishing Group, Inc.

Biblical excerpts taken from the Holy Bible, New International Version R. Copyright 1973, 1978, 1984 by International Bible Society. Used by permission of Zondervan Publishing House. All rights reserved.

The publishers have generously given permission to use extended quotations from the following copyrighted works. From *Fourth and One*, by Joe Gibbs. Copyright © 1991 by Joe J. Gibbs and Jerry B. Jenkins. Reprinted by permission of Thomas Nelson, Inc., Publishers. From *Holyfield: The Humble Warrior*, by Evander and Bernard Holyfield. Copyright 1996 by Evander Holyfield and Bernard Holyfield. Reprinted by permission of Thomas Nelson, Inc., Publishers. From *Living the Dream*, by Hakeem Olajuwon. Copyright © 1996 Hakeem Olajuwon. Used by permission of Little, Brown and Company. From *Giant Steps*, by Kareem Abdul-Jabbar. Copyright © 1985 Kareem Abdul-Jabbar. Used by permission of Bantam. From *How to Raise an MVP*, by Ambrose and Freda Robinson with Steve Hubbard. Copyright © 1996 by Ambrose and Freda Robinson. Used by permission of Zondervan Publishing House.

Library of Congress Cataloging-in-Publication Data

Hubbard, Steve (Steve A.)
Faith in sports: athletes and their religion on and off the field by Steve Hubbard. — 1st ed.
p. cm.
1. Athletes—United States—Religious life. 2. Sports—Religious aspects. 3. Sports—
Religious aspects—Christianity. I. Title.
BL625.9.A84H83 1998
200'.88'796—dc21 97-29262
CIP

To
Julie, Katie, and Zack,
the wife and children whose
love comforts and inspires me daily

Acknowledgments

This book could not have been written without the help of a lot of wonderful people to whom I am eternally grateful.

Thanks to all the athletes, coaches, fellowship leaders, and ministers who took time out of their busy schedules to share their faith, and to the aides who arranged those interviews. Thanks to the publishers and writers whose works were excerpted and the photographers whose pictures enliven the words. Thanks to David and Fritz Rushlow for sharing their comments. Thanks to writers Joe Frisaro, Dana Scarton, Kelly Carter, and Ken Abraham, who shared their expertise. Thanks to Bill McCartney and Promise Keepers, for letting me attend and describe a gathering. Thanks to my agent, Scott Waxman, for helping to get this book in print. And thanks to my editor, Mark Fretz, whose vision spawned and molded this book and made it immeasurably better. May these stories encourage you in times of trouble.

Contents

Introduction

Green Bay wins Super Bowl XXXI and a string of Packers, led by the Reverend Reggie White, thank God. The New York Yankees win the World Series, and a tearful Wade Boggs thanks the Lord for a second chance. Baseball's Mike Piazza and basketball's Glen Rice are named MVPs of their All-Star games and thank God.

Tiger Woods wears a gold Buddha charm around his neck and tells a nationwide television audience he prayed walking up the eighteenth fairway during his record 1997 Masters victory. Steve Jones wins the 1996 U.S. Open and Ernie Els the 1997 U.S. Open and they thank the Lord in their first two or three sentences. Jeff Gordon wins the 1997 Daytona 500, stock-car racing's most prestigious event, and says God answered his prayers during the race. Evander Holyfield says God miraculously healed a hole in his heart and helped him pull off one of the greatest upsets in boxing history, the Christian beating the newly converted Muslim, Mike Tyson.

Danny Wuerffel clasps his hands in prayer after every touchdown pass, kneels in prayer after every game, wins the 1996 Heisman Trophy and immediately hugs his father the chaplain and thanks God and advises the nation to have a living relationship with Jesus. Sprinter Gwen Torrence and basketball stars Ruthie Bolton and Jennifer Azzi praise God when they win 1996 Olympics medals. Olympic wrestling champion Kurt Angle and U.S. figure skating champion Nicole Bobek are photographed on their knees, crying and praying, in newspapers across the world.

Magic Johnson says the Lord has reduced the AIDS virus in his body to undetectable levels. David Robinson and Hakeem Olajuwon win National Basketball Association MVP awards and fervently try to spread their Christian and Muslim faiths. Mahmoud Abdul-Rauf creates a nationwide controversy when he refuses to stand for the national anthem because of his Islamic beliefs, and Dennis Rodman sparks another when he insults Mormons with an obscenity.

John Smoltz wins the 1996 National League Cy Young Award, Andy Pettitte nearly wins the American League version, and both reach baseball's pinnacle, the World Series, where a third Christian pitcher, John Wetteland, wins Most Valuable Player honors, prays on the mound, and applauds Jesus to millions of viewers.

"God is moving," Wetteland tells *Sports Spectrum,* one of the magazines devoted to this new sensation, the devout athlete. "You see the World Series with me, Andy, and John. You see Danny Wuerrfel and Florida winning the national championship in college football. You see Reggie White and the Packers winning the Super Bowl. Before, so much of the time, you didn't see it. You just didn't see it. But now, God is moving. He is raising up people to share his message, and one way he is doing it is through sports."

In ever expanding numbers, athletes are turning to faith for answers and making that faith public. They express their convictions on television and radio, in newspapers, magazines, and books, at speaking engagements that often sound like sermons. They spread their religion religiously in hopes of converting others. They say God gave them their athletic ability and visibility so that they might minister to millions.

Reggie White is the NFL's all-time sack leader and maybe the greatest defensive end in history, but he believes spreading God's word is his true mission in life. White, an ordained minister and already one of America's most influential black religious leaders, says he uses his football fame to attract a broader audience. His celebrity status draws them in. His humor keeps them listening. And then, he hopes, his message sticks. The Minister of Defense is on a twentieth-century crusade: sack the quarterback, praise the Lord, and save the children and churches.

White organizes prayer meetings for players and fans alike. He speaks to hundreds of students and preaches to his congregation in Knoxville, Tennessee. He builds churches and subsidizes banks to help the impoverished help themselves. He credits his unbelievable recovery from a torn hamstring, which was supposed to end his season and require surgery, as a miracle from God. He blames racists for burning down his church and leads the charge as America examines why a spate of black churches were torched, and how far away we still are from racial equality. He spearheads a drive that leads to hundreds of thousands of dollars in donations to rebuild the church.

Hakeem Olajuwon, dubbed Michael Jordan's successor as the NBA's best player when Jordan retired briefly and Hakeem The Dream led the Houston Rockets to consecutive NBA titles, is not as evangelical, but he feels it his duty to wipe out America's perception of Muslims as terrorists and extremists. He has shared his Islamic faith in his autobiography, in long stories in *Sports Illustrated*, on HBO's "Real Sports," and with reporters all over the country, particularly when he explains why he fasts during the holy month of Ramadan.

Bill McCartney won a college national championship and built a football powerhouse at the University of Colorado, only to give it all up to focus on his faith, family, and Christian men's organization. Since McCartney founded the Promise Keepers, its audiences have multiplied from 4,200 men in 1991 to 1.1 million in 1996, making it one of America's most powerful religious movements.

While the sins and crimes and corruption of big-time sports

draw headlines, the numbers of sports figures who have found religion are also growing, and whereas once they were shy about it, now they shout about it. Faith in sports has come out of the closet, onto the field, and into the nation's consciousness.

As recently as the 1970s and early 1980s, talking publicly about faith was not all that common among athletes. Other athletes and the media sometimes ridiculed the religious as too-good-to-be-true God Squad Jesus freaks. Hard-driving lifestyles were viewed as macho. Christians were described as soft and wimpy. Muslims, Buddhists, and those committed to other religions were seen as weirdos.

But today athletes are turning to faith for answers to their questions about their riches, their temptations, and their stresses. As they have recognized the consequences of alcohol, drugs, tobacco, food, and unprotected sex on their bodies and their multimillion-dollar careers, many have found faith and fulfillment.

Encouraged by their religions to evangelize, they have used their sports stardom as an opportunity to share their testimony. At the same time, newspapers, magazines, books, television, radio, and the exploding multimedia information age are delving into sports as never before. Their in-depth coverage and search for new angles have increasingly led them to sports figures' faith.

Where once religion was ridiculed, now it's in vogue, and religious athletes are finding support in one another.

Membership in the Fellowship of Christian Athletes is rising rapidly, from 413 colleges in 1990 to more than 500 by 1996. FCA has about 6,000 college, high school, and junior high chapters, or huddles, and 450 adult huddles. FCA has sessions at all the national coaching conventions, and 13,000 attended its youth camps in 1996 alone.

Athletes in Action, the sports arm of Campus Crusade for Christ International, says it is busier than ever. Professional Athletes Outreach draws hundreds of athletes and their families to its conferences. Other Christian sports groups include Sports Outreach America, Champions for Christ, Hockey Ministries International, Run to Win Outreach, and Sports Family Outreach. Many of these organizations and even some athletes have their own web sites and magazines, both online and print. Almost every pro sports team has a chapel coordinator, regular chapel programs, and team prayers before and/or after games. Chaplains accompany the men's and women's golf tours and the men's tennis tour.

The sports programs at the University of Notre Dame and Brigham Young University have always helped attract interest toward the Catholic and Mormon churches. The Reverend Jerry Falwell wants to design a sports program at Liberty University that is second to none in hopes of spotlighting the university and attracting people to Christianity. He fired a successful football coach and hired a former pro coach, Sam Rutigliano, to boost the program's visibility, and almost miraculously, it worked.

"The image of Christianity in America used to be that it was for a bunch of old ladies," said Ralph Drollinger, long active with Athletes in Action and Sports Outreach America. "Now athletes are being Christians. That is saying it's cool to be a Christian."

Some athletes were introduced to religion at an early age and never wavered. Some, like David Robinson, went to church as children but abandoned the practice as soon as their parents stopped hovering over them, then returned to faith with a new-found zeal to fill the empy spot in their souls. Many were swayed by teammates or even coaches.

Some found in faith an answer to dealing with their fame, loss of privacy, and growing wealth. Others found it helped them handle the tremendous highs and lows of a very public occupation. Some found it helped them deal with adversities ranging from slumps to drugs to alcohol to cancer. Others simply have gone along with the crowd, not committing themselves entirely but attending chapel services or mouthing team prayers in hopes their "faith" would be a magical good-luck charm to avoid injuries and increase the chance of victory.

"The word is getting out a little more," said Chris Hull, FCA's associate director of programs in 1996. "For a long time, it was a best-kept secret. Now we're getting more visibility. As the numbers of religious athletes grow, they can pull in others. As visible as athletes have become, you see a lot of people talking about religion and God. A lot of people see religion as an alternative to the drug rate, the crime rate, and all the other problems we have as a society. The need is there."

If you read this book because you like sports, you might be surprised at the names and number of famous athletes and coaches who are religious, be they Christian, Muslim, Buddhist, Jewish, or whatever. You will gain insights into what led them to faith, what drives them, what fulfills them.

If you read these pages because you are into religion, you will examine hard questions about faith in sports. You will see how religion has helped sports stars cope with their personal and professional lives, their advantages and adversities.

Chapters 1 through 3 will give you the basics: who, what, when, where, how, and why faith has permeated sports. We will give you names and incidents to reveal how faith has become a bigger part of sports. Then we will launch into the real meat of the book: how and why our sports figures' faith developed, how they share it now, how they use it to deal with the ups and downs of their lives and careers, how religious issues affect the games they play and how the games they play impact their faith.

No matter your interests, you will explore answers to society's largest questions. How can we succeed in life? How can we balance faith, family, and career? How can we not only survive but thrive?

1

Many Faiths and Many Sports

Every test confirmed the doctors' worst fears: Reggie White's hamstring was torn, torn so badly he needed surgery to repair it, torn so badly he could not possibly play again that season.

Twelve days before Christmas 1995, the Green Bay Packers announced the sad news, and The Minister of Defense went home to seek solace. But, playing with his children, White thought the hamstring felt surprisingly good. He called the team's strength and conditioning coach, Kent Johnston, and they headed to the training facility, where they put the injured tendon through strength-testing exercises—and were astonished to see how much stronger it was.

They drove directly to coach Mike Holmgren's house. It was almost midnight. Holmgren was just turning out his Christmas lights and heading to bed when the doorbell rang. "I thought it was Santa," he recalled, smiling.

Ho, ho, ho! He had one of the all-time greats to unwrap before

Christmas. The next day White practiced. Three days later he played—and played well. Played so well he helped the Packers to the National Football Conference championship game, their first since 1967.

White, an ordained minister, said there was no logical explanation except one: it was a miracle from God. "The Lord took all the pain away," he said.

"Everybody's saying how the Lord healed Reggie," said Anthony Morgan, a teammate and close friend. "It's not that. It's just Reggie's heart. It's the way Reggie approaches the game. For him to come out there and play on the injury . . . we feed off stuff like that because we're walking around here with a nagging injury and you see a legend like Reggie White playing hurt."

"Maybe I have to disagree with Anthony," White replied. "I know it's nothing but God, because I'm not supposed to be walking, let alone running around. It's been a blessing."

A miracle from God? Or the power of White's heart?

"Probably it was both," Holmgren said. "Reggie told me it was a miracle. I believe him. His spirit and the type of athlete he is helped control that situation. It was a little mind-boggling. He's so inspirational. He's like Lazarus. He always comes back and rises from the dead."

With God's help, of course. White returned in 1996 to spearhead the Packers to victory in Super Bowl XXXI, their first in twenty-nine years. White set a Super Bowl record with three sacks.

And the surgery he was supposed to need? Never had it. Never needed it.

OREL HERSHISER'S surgeon, Dr. Frank Jobe, who had revived more pitchers' careers than any other man, looked at the Dodger pitcher's tests and all he could say was, "I'm sorry."

He thought Hershiser's career was over. He could try surgery, but this procedure had never been attempted, let alone succeeded, on a major-league pitcher before. Hershiser, who had won the Cy Young Award and World Series MVP honors two years before, in 1988, wanted to try. After surgery, after months of grueling therapy and rehabilitation, the pain was still severe. The Dodger with the bulldog heart, the man who had fought through every adversity, told his wife he could not take it anymore. It was time to retire.

Jamie reminded him of Bible verses James 5:14–16, which call upon Christian friends to surround one who is hurting, anoint him with oil, and pray for him. They gathered friends and their pastor in their home. All prayed for Hershiser. They asked God to relieve his pain.

"From that day forward," Hershiser said, "I never had any pain in my arm."

Hershiser won the Comeback Player of the Year Award in 1992, and he came back for more postseason heroics while pitching for Cleveland in 1995 and 1997. He was the 1995 American League Championship Series MVP and is 8-3 lifetime in the postseason.

BRETT BUTLER, star outfielder for the Dodgers, was in such severe pain from his tonsillectomy he could not sleep for eight straight days. He barely had strength to get out of bed. Every swallow and sneeze was excruciating. He pleaded for pain pills, begged his wife to shoot him and let him die. The surgery had revealed a rare form of cancer, and he talked constantly of dying, whether he wanted to be buried or cremated, what kind of funeral he wanted. His wife told him to write down the instructions, seal them in an envelope, and then start thinking positively and remembering God.

Two days before he would have fifty lymph nodes removed from his neck to determine the cancer's spread, the Butlers went through a scene similar to the Hershisers' a few years before. Their minister and ten friends gathered in the Butlers' home to pray. Each read Scripture. They prayed for the family for two and a half hours. They dipped their fingers in olive oil to anoint Butler, rubbing his forehead and the incision from the tonsillectomy.

"I was brought to the point of peace," he recalled. "I no longer questioned 'Why me?' I was no longer afraid to die."

Cancer was found in just one lymph node. Less than four months after a doctor told him a comeback was impossible, Brett Butler returned to Los Angeles, got on base twice, and scored the winning run to lift the Dodgers into first place. Every Dodger called it a miracle.

DAVID ROBINSON was six months old when an accident almost cost him his life. After a crying spell, his mother thought he was sleeping peacefully. She did not think much of it. But a couple of minutes later, something drew her to his room to double-check.

And she could not find her little boy! She scurried around the house, asking her brother-in-law and nieces and nephews if they had picked him up. They had not. Frantic, she scurried back to the bedroom, and finally she spotted the top of his head. He had rolled off the edge of the bed and was scrunched so tightly between the mattress and wall, his nose and mouth were mashed shut. He had stopped breathing so long, his body had turned blue.

"He's dead!" she screamed. "My baby is dead!"

Her sister ran in the room and said, "Stop it! Look, he *will* be dead if you don't give him CPR."

Freda was deathly afraid. She had never done mouth-to-mouth on anything but a mannequin. "Lord," she wailed, "don't let my child die!"

She brought him to, but the doctors said a child could suffer brain damage within minutes, and since they did not know how long David had gone without breathing, they could only wait and see if his mind turned out all right. She agonized for years until, at age three, David began to read. Not only was he not behind, he was ahead of speed. She was convinced God had answered her call and delivered a miracle, and something special lay ahead.

That story was shared in a 1996 book, *How to Raise an MVP*, cowritten by Freda and Ambrose Robinson and this book's author. David Robinson had grown up to become the 1995 NBA MVP, and, his parents think, God has even bigger plans for him when he leaves basketball. David already donates millions to charity and spreads his faith and good deeds to thousands.

ERNIE IRVAN was struck by something that Nascar chaplain Max Helton said. It was July 1994, the Sunday morning of the big auto race at Pocono—a day that changed Irvan's life forever.

They say there are no atheists in foxholes, and maybe that is also true in NASCAR, when thirty or forty men play bumper cars at 150–200 mph. Irvan asked how he could have a personal relationship with Jesus Christ, and that day he made the commitment.

"It was the biggest thing I ever did," he said. "When I gave myself to Christ, it was like taking out an insurance policy."

Little did he know how quickly he would need it. Only a few weeks later, Irvan's Thunderbird crashed into a wall at 170 mph, cracking his skull, damaging his lungs, and battering him so severely, one rescuer was sure he was dead. The doctors were not much more comforting. He was nine times more likely to die than to live.

Kim Irvan, told she likely would become a widow, prayed fervently at her comatose husband's side. NASCAR fans and racers prayed too. Rival Darrell Waltrip said he and his wife got down on their knees and prayed, "Lord, Ernie is developing a relationship with you. This is an opportunity for you, Lord, to heal him and bring him back."

Ernie Irvan came back . . . not only to live, but to race again. And to win again, at the same race and same track (the Miller 400 at Michigan Speedway) where he crashed. "The thoughts of what happened at this racetrack were going through my mind," Swervin' Irvan said after winning on Father's Day 1997. "It's probably not the best thing to do, because I was getting a little teary-eyed. It's pretty hard to drive a race car with tears in your eyes."

Not all prayers are answered in such dramatic fashion. Nor is this meant to suggest that the sole measure of faith in sports is to work miracles in an athlete's lifetime. No, the true believers say faith influences every aspect of their lives and careers.

And there are a lot of true believers. The sheer numbers might surprise you because:

• Not all religious athletes spend a lot of time publicly discussing their faith.

• Even if they do, their faith is not always shared by today's secular media, which are not quite comfortable or consistent in dealing with what can be a hot-potato issue.

• Just as in the rest of society, the problem children in sports generate more headlines than the people who live honest, faithful lives.

And yet finding religion in sports should come as no surprise, because by one recent estimate 289 million people in North America call themselves religious and only 23.9 million are nonreligious, with just 1.4 million considering themselves atheists. The overwhelming majority, 246.3 million, are Christians, with 5.9 million Jewish, 5.5 million Muslims, 1.3 million Hindus, and 559,000 Buddhists. It is only natural for faith to spill over into sports.

Likewise, America's religious athletes are mostly Christians. But here is the difference between sports and society at large: Muslim pro athletes probably outnumber those of Jewish and all other non-Christian faiths. While there were several big-name Jewish stars in the past—e.g., Sandy Koufax, Mark Spitz, Sid Luckman, Max Baer, and Hank Greenberg—they are not as widely known today, perhaps because Jewish athletes are less strident in spreading their faith, perhaps because pro sports are dominated by African-Americans, and there are few black Jews. Rare is the religious American coach or athlete who is neither Christian nor Muslim. Even though Chicago Bulls coach Phil Jackson has incorporated a nontraditional mix of Zen Buddhism, Taoism, and Lakota Sioux teachings into his Christian Pentecostal upbringing, he calls himself a Zen Christian.

Perhaps because female athletes are not as famous as their male counterparts and are not interviewed as often or as in depth, not as many women athletes express their faith. Ice skating is the most popular women's sport on television, but none of today's best figure skaters is staunchly religious. However, a few female tennis players and a significant number of women's golfers are Christians.

When faith and sports conflict, sport often wins. Koufax, a Jewish pitcher for the Los Angeles Dodgers, caused a furor when he refused to pitch the opening game of the 1965 World Series because it was Yom Kippur. Muhammad Ali, the world heavyweight boxing champion, gave up his title and career when he refused to join the Army because of his Black Muslim beliefs. Jonathan Edwards, an Anglican triple jumper from Great Britain, did not compete on Sundays for several years, but set the world record when he changed his mind. Eli Herring, a devout Mormon who was drafted into the NFL by the Oakland Raiders even though he said he could not compete on the Sabbath, gave up potential millions for his beliefs.

But Koufax, Ali, Edwards, and Herring are the exceptions. Even devout Christians such as David Robinson play on Christmas and Easter, and strict Christians and Mormons such as Reggie White and Steve Young play on Sundays, rather than taking them off as days of rest. They will turn the other cheek in Sunday morning chapel and smite their brother's cheek on Sunday afternoon gridirons. They believe God wants them to compete, to win, to use their sports celebrity as a platform to spread their faith and give glory to him.

America's most noted current Muslim athlete, Hakeem Olajuwon of the Houston Rockets, faithfully practices the five pillars of Islam: he believes Allah is the only God and Muhammad is his prophet; he prays five times a day while facing Mecca; he donates a portion of his earnings to charity; he fasts during the day in the holy month of Ramadan; and he has made a pilgrimage to Mecca.

Christians, Mormons, Muslims, and Jews—religions that are influenced by the Bible—believe there is but one god; Hindus worship a pantheon of deities. All those faiths believe in some forms of heaven and hell, good and evil, with the Bible-based religions identifying evil with the Devil.

"If there wasn't a Devil, there wouldn't be any evil," said Terrell Buckley, a Christian cornerback for the Miami Dolphins. "So I think the Devil *is* out there. The Lord doesn't stand for bad, so there is something evil out there. I think the Devil tests us. That's where your faith in the Lord comes in. If you get tested by the Devil and put your beliefs in the Lord, good always wins over evil."

Faith in Sports

Muslim athletes are often given new names by their imam, or spiritual leader, during the shahadah commitment ceremony. Cassius Clay became Muhammad Ali. Bobby Moore became Ahmad Rashad. Chris Jackson became Mahmoud Abdul-Rauf. Keith Wilkes became Jamaal Wilkes. Lew Alcindor became Kareem Abdul-Jabbar. Sharmon Shah became Karim Abdul-Jabbar.

Several black athletes have converted from Christianity to Islam because they found more answers from Allah, but Tunch Ilkin found meaning in Jesus Christ.

"I grew up as a Muslim," said Ilkin, a former Pro Bowl lineman for the Pittsburgh Steelers who was born in Turkey and moved with his parents to the United States when he was two and a half.

"Ninety-nine-point-nine percent of Turkey is Muslim. When I was a kid, my parents shared their perception of God, and it was a God I could not believe in. The God of Islam is a fickle and I would say an unjust God, not like Jesus. You live a good [Muslim] life, you may or may not be rewarded. So I became an atheist or at least an agnostic," until watching and talking to several Steelers who convinced him to convert to Christianity.

By contrast, Kareem Abdul-Jabbar rejected Catholicism and took college classes and pored over books on everything from existentialism to Buddhism, Taoism, Hinduism, and Zen before choosing Islam. Why did he feel the need for any religion? Because, he wrote in his autobiography, *Giant Steps,* Malcolm X taught him "that some central philosophy was necessary in order to live a meaningful life."

What attracts other athletes to faith? The answer is as old as time. Religion helps explain the unexplainable and comfort the uncomfortable. "If God did not exist," Voltaire said more than two centuries ago, "it would be necessary to invent him."

Or, as today's sports sage Phil Jackson says, religion is a "technique" to get through life, a set of beliefs and principles that are comforting, that bring us together as a community. Or, as one minister told David Robinson, the Bible is an instruction manual for how to live life.

"The overriding feeling that my faith provides in times of struggle is that God has a plan for me," golfer Loren Roberts said.

"When I struggle, I know it's for a reason. When I succeed, I know it's for a reason. Whether God is trying to teach me something or trying to show me that's not the way to go, I always pray for the Lord to give me guidance.

"It's the overriding feeling in the back of my mind: things are happening for a reason, whether I want it or not. God has ordained it. That doesn't mean I throw up my hands and say, 'I let you run my whole life.' God gave us the right to make decisions, whether the decision is to follow Him, to become a Buddhist or an atheist or whatever."

These are just a few of America's most notable sports figures who put faith in faith. The list is not all-inclusive—it would fill books—but the names are familiar:

MUHAMMAD ALI, former heavyweight boxing champion. When Cassius Clay became a Black Muslim, changed his name, and refused induction into the U.S. Army because of his religious beliefs, he became one of the world's and his era's most important spokesmen for civil rights, black power, and religious freedom. His resolute stand for religious rights made him an icon far transcending sports.

EVANDER HOLYFIELD, three-time heavyweight boxing champion. Holyfield said with the help of a faith healer named Benny Hinn, he "prayed away" the hole in his heart that doctors told him they could not repair. They forced him to retire from boxing, and he did for a while, until Mayo Clinic tests gave him a clean bill of health. "My faith is what's going to take me through this," Holyfield said.

"What people don't realize is that it's not like Jesus just jumps out of the sky and helps you. His spirit works through people. It's like if you were stranded, and somebody comes by to pick you up, you're not gonna say, 'Well, I'm waiting for Jesus.' The Lord works through people."

GEORGE FOREMAN, former heavyweight boxing champion. The meanest, toughest fighter around, Foreman gave it all up because he felt fighting conflicted with his Christian ministry. Yet he returned to boxing a decade later, saying the money he could raise and the platform he could preach from were more valuable to the children and poor folks he was trying to help.

MIKE TYSON, former heavyweight boxing champion. Insisting he was innocent of rape charges even after his conviction, the troubled boxer converted to Islam while in prison. When he was released, he went straight to a mosque to pray. But some skeptics question how true a believer he is. He bit off part of Holyfield's ear in their 1997 rematch and was charged with harassing a woman in a nightclub. One moment he's talking of giving up all his riches and the next he's buying more houses, cars, and expensive toys.

OSCAR DE LA HOYA, welterweight boxing champion. When he won a gold medal during the 1992 Barcelona Olympics, he knelt on one knee in prayer for his deceased mother and draped the gold medal around her photograph. He still prays to his mother, Cecilia, before every title bout.

BARRY SANDERS, NFL's Detroit Lions. One of the top two running backs today, Sanders could set the all-time NFL rushing record before he is through. He is a strong and humble Christian who tithes to the church.

EMMITT SMITH, NFL's Dallas Cowboys. Today's other top runner, Smith makes an annual list of goals. First on his list: "Keep Jesus Christ #1 in my life."

STEVE YOUNG and BRENT JONES, NFL's San Francisco 49ers. Two of the nicest men in sports, Young is a devout Mormon and Jones a devout Christian. Young earned bachelor's and law degrees from Brigham Young University, the Mormon school named after his great-great-great-grandfather. He ranks among football's greatest quarterbacks. He has won five passing titles, owns the top passer rating in history, and is one of only five NFL players ever voted

Most Valuable Player twice. The sure-handed Jones went to four straight Pro Bowls as one of the league's premier tight ends.

"I'm not sure a lot of people know just how involved Steve Young is with the Mormon Church in the off season," said Lynn Stiles, a faithful Mormon and former 49ers assistant coach. "He's a great ambassador for the church and school, constantly doing firesides and benefits. Brent Jones overcame injuries and worked himself up from our fifth tight end to the Pro Bowl. He's unique: a great person, a great human being, really a competitor, very much an overachiever."

CRIS CARTER, NFL's Minnesota Vikings. Carter credits former Philadelphia Eagles teammates Reggie White and Keith Byars with helping him become a Christian. But it was only after being released by the Eagles and wandering aimlessly with the Vikings that he made a full commitment to faith and family, whereupon he gave up drugs, alcohol, and red meat, cut down his sweets, boosted his workouts—and set NFL receiving records. He was ordained as a minister during the 1996 off season.

JIM HARBAUGH, NFL's Indianapolis Colts. Harbaugh experienced a religious awakening in 1990, but after his release from the Chicago Bears, he did not fully resurrect his life and career until he came off the Indianapolis Colts' bench in 1995. He says he felt like he was a loser living a country-western song—lost his job, lost his girl, even lost his dog—yet he persevered. Buoyed by his faith in God and his teammates' faith in him, he won three games in the fourth quarter to earn the nickname "Captain Comeback," the league passing title, the Pro Bowl, and an appearance in the conference championship game, where he came within one dropped "Hail Mary" pass of making the Super Bowl. He gave praise to God every time a TV camera rolled live.

DENNIS BYRD, NFL's New York Jets. Told he would never walk again after suffering a crippling spinal injury, Byrd vowed he would, and he has succeeded thanks to his Christian faith, indomitable spirit, and physical therapy.

MIKE SINGLETARY, NFL's Chicago Bears. A surefire future Hall of Famer, this former great linebacker now is one of the top motivational speakers in the country, mixing sports with a strong Christian message.

CURTIS MARTIN, NFL's New England Patriots. Even his friends called him a knucklehead—and worse—for turning pro early after an injury-marred college season. But Martin said he prayed to God and was told it was time. The guy who was supposed to have a lame brain and brittle body merely led the American Football Conference in rushing as a rookie, then carried the Patriots to the Super Bowl his second season. He credits his faith for helping him avoid gangs, drugs, and violence in the Pittsburgh ghetto where he grew up.

ISAAC BRUCE, NFL's St. Louis Rams. Bruce came into 1995, his second pro season, as an unknown—and emerged with one of the best receiving seasons in history. Because he wants to be a Pentecostal minister when he retires, just like his mother, teammates call him Reverend Ike. ESPN's Chris Berman calls him "The Rev." Opponents call him unstoppable. In just his second season, he had more receiving yards than all but one player in NFL history.

IRVING FRYAR, NFL's Philadelphia Eagles. The first pick in the 1984 draft says he's "lucky to be alive" after struggling with drugs, drinking, and the law. But "divine intervention" saved him, and he devoted his life to God, becoming an ordained Pentecostal minister in 1992 and counseling addicts with the wisdom of his ordeal. He turned around his life and his career, emerging as a Pro Bowl receiver for a perennial Super Bowl contender. "The Reverend Fryar is a wonderful wide receiver, but I think he's an even better preacher," says the Reverend Robert Stanley.

DARRELL GREEN, NFL's Washington Redskins. Just five feet eight, Green used his Christian faith and 4.3 speed to overcome his lack of height and become a regular Pro Bowl cornerback and potential future Hall of Famer.

ROBERT JONES, NFL's St. Louis Rams. When the middle linebacker was struggling for Dallas in 1994, he looked in the Bible and saw Nimrod was the best athlete but could not understand why until he read about Samson, "and decided that was me. Before the first game of the year, against Pittsburgh, I decided not to cut my hair, and I wound up getting a game ball." The pattern kept repeating itself until a big game against Philadelphia. "That was an extra-big game, so I let my hair go for an extra week—and I had the best game of my life."

BRUCE SMITH, NFL's Buffalo Bills. A two-time NFL Defensive Player of the Year and runner-up to Reggie White for the league's all-time sack record, Smith says he prays every night and before each game. "I thank God each and every day for his son, the Lord Jesus Christ, for blessing us, for giving us life, for saving us from our sins," Smith said.

DEION SANDERS, NFL's Dallas Cowboys and baseball's Cincinnati Reds. The 1995 NFL Defensive Player of the Year, "Prime Time" is one of the best cornerbacks in NFL history, plus one of baseball's best base stealers. He announced in 1997 that his pending divorce had led to introspection and such a Christian rebirth that he hoped to become an evangelist or pastor. "I've been born again and I'm not only showing it, I'm living it," he said. "Being alone without my wife and kids gave me a chance to look within myself. I fornicated and had sex outside my marriage and I'm opening the door for Jesus. Now I have peace in my life."

ZACH THOMAS, NFL's Miami Dolphins. Runner-up for Defensive Rookie of the Year, the middle linebacker is the product of a Catholic family so devout, they have a cross twenty-one stories high near their home. It is visible for miles in the Texas flatlands.

EDDIE GEORGE, NFL's Tennessee Oilers. Asked to name his most memorable moment, the 1995 Heisman Trophy winner and 1996 NFL Rookie of the Year replied, "Being saved by Jesus Christ. That's my biggest moment. I put every game in the Lord's hands."

ROGER STAUBACH, NFL's Dallas Cowboys. Roger "The Dodger" was a Hall of Fame quarterback and one of the first players identified strongly with the Fellowship of Christian Athletes. He's now a successful businessman.

TOM LANDRY, NFL's Dallas Cowboys. A retired Hall of Fame coach known for his character and honesty, Landry is heavily involved in the FCA and focused on religion in his autobiography. When Dallas was America's Team, Landry was dubbed God's Coach.

DON SHULA, NFL's Miami Dolphins. Shula retired in 1996 as the winningest coach in NFL history. A devout Catholic, he attended Mass each morning at six-thirty before starting his workday as an iron-jawed, iron-willed but fair coach.

JOE GIBBS, NFL's Washington Redskins. Gibbs won three Super Bowls and shared his faith every chance he could get. His autobiography and his Hall of Fame induction speech both dealt more with faith than with football. Now an NBC commentator and race-car owner, he's working on another book, and he offers a personal pamphlet and video that spread his faith.

DAN REEVES, NFL's Atlanta Falcons. Reeves has gone to half a dozen Super Bowls as a player and coach. One of the league's most intense coaches, he overcame crippling childhood diseases and is a staunch Christian like his mentor, Landry.

TONY DUNGY, NFL's Tampa Bay Buccaneers. Only the fourth black coach in modern NFL history, Dungy was often interviewed for vacancies for a decade but never chosen as a head coach until 1996. Some say he was blackballed because of his race, but Dungy, a strong Christian, persevered and finally got his chance.

VINCE TOBIN, NFL's Arizona Cardinals. Another man who made his head coaching debut in 1996, Tobin grew up in Burlington Junction, Missouri, a little farming town with more churches (three) and grain elevators (three) than stoplights (none). The Tobins went to church every Sunday even if snowstorms made the roads nearly impassable. Sometimes they made it and the pastor did not. "I grew up as a Catholic, with very strong Christian values. There was always a right way and a wrong way to do things and in order to get ahead, you had to work. There was no shortcut," said Vince, whose brother Bill built the Bears into Super Bowl champions and the Colts into conference finalists. Vince considered the priesthood but chose coaching, which he believes is about quiet teaching, not screaming rhetoric. "Vince does his talking on his knees," says his cousin Pat, a Catholic priest.

DAN ROONEY, NFL's Pittsburgh Steelers. The owner of the Steelers is known as one of the league's best and most influential owners, brokering deals when it seemed the NFL was at an impasse. Like his late father, Art, Sr., the beloved founder of the team, Dan shuns material displays, gives freely, and attends Mass almost every morning. He might be the NFL's only owner to drive his own low-priced American car and wear fifteen-year-old suits and ties.

MAHMOUD ABDUL-RAUF, NBA's Sacramento Kings. One of college basketball's leading scorers as Chris Jackson when he played at Louisiana State, he changed faith and overcame Tourette's syndrome to become an NBA star. His brief refusal to stand for the national anthem because of his Muslim beliefs was one of the biggest sports stories of 1996.

SHAWN BRADLEY, NBA's New Jersey Nets. NBA teams were so infatuated with the seven-foot-six beanpole's rare height and shot-blocking ability, he was the second pick in the 1993 draft despite playing only one year of college ball at BYU and missing two years on a Mormon mission. His faith and beliefs were not readily accepted in Philadelphia, and he began to bloom as a player only after his trade to New Jersey in 1996.

A. C. GREEN, NBA's Dallas Mavericks. One of the league's most durable and intense competitors, Green wrote a book about his strong faith and his desire to become a minister once he retires. But does his faith always jibe with what some say is occasional dirty play on the court?

KEVIN JOHNSON, NBA's Phoenix Suns. Maybe the league's fastest point guard, Johnson carries his Bible with him at all times and is frequently seen reading it on the team plane.

AVERY JOHNSON, NBA's San Antonio Spurs. Waived numerous times by several teams, Johnson called on his Christian faith to help him deal with the adversity and has persevered to become a Spurs leader and one of the league's better point guards.

SAM PERKINS, NBA's Seattle Supersonics. A superb outside shooter for a big man, Perkins is an NBA veteran and a Jehovah's Witness.

SHAREEF ABDUR-RAHIM, NBA's Vancouver Grizzlies. The Pacific 10 Conference's leading scorer as a freshman, Abdur-Rahim chose the University of California partly because of its Muslim studies program, and drew further attention to his faith when, like Olajuwon, he fasted during the month of Ramadan. One of the first picks in the 1996 draft, he's expected to become a big-time star in the NBA.

DAVE DRAVECKY, baseball's San Francisco Giants. The left-handed pitcher made a heroic comeback after a surgeon removed a tumor and half the muscle from his pitching shoulder, only to break his arm twice and eventually lose his career and arm to cancer. He and his wife have written six books, have their own video and nonprofit support group for cancer patients, and he's a popular Christian inspirational speaker.

JIM EISENREICH, baseball's Florida Marlins. His eyes blinked, his muscles twitched, and he released guttural, snorting sounds and involuntary curses. The stress of being a big-league outfielder aggravated a condition that Eisenreich had endured since the age of six. Doctors finally discovered he had a rare neurological disorder called Tourette's syndrome, but Eisenreich struggled with it, struggled as fans and opponents mocked him, and after two seasons of agony he retired. He stayed out of baseball for two years before deciding he would rely on God and medication to help him deal with his illness.

"I was convinced God would bring something good out of all this," he said, and returned to the majors in 1987. A high-average hitter, he helped the 1993 Phillies to the World Series, but had to wait until 1997 to win it all with the Florida Marlins. "Today God has given me the ability to talk about the disorder on behalf of the Tourette Syndrome Association. I don't run from reporters anymore, and I am aware of how crucial it is for kids with Tourette to have a role model. Until there is a cure, I will always suffer some symptoms. But I believe that God will never give me more than I can handle."

GARY GAETTI, baseball's St. Louis Cardinals. Gaetti was a leading hitter and party person when the Minnesota Twins won the World Series in 1987. But he converted to Christianity in August 1988 while recuperating from knee surgery, and both his batting average and the Twins' winning percentage declined. When he became a Bible-reading, gospel-preaching, fire-and-brimstone Christian, some of his teammates resented the change and some of the media blamed his faith for his declining performance. They said he was too complacent about baseball, seeing everything as God's will. The complaints did not bother Gaetti, who said he was "a walking dead man" and "would have gone to hell" if he had not changed. He returned with several good seasons, including a thirty-five-homer, ninety-six-RBI year for Kansas City in 1995, and a game-winning homer for St. Louis in the 1996 playoffs.

GREG MCMICHAEL, baseball's New York Mets. McMichael missed two years of high school sports because of a rare knee condition, and even after two surgeries his doctor advised him to give up all sports. He gave up all except baseball, and he became a top high school and college player. But he struggled in minor-league baseball and was released by Cleveland, which might have had base-ball's worst pitching staff at the time.

"I was a AAA pitcher being shellacked by Class A hitters," he said. "I asked God, 'Do you really want me to do this?' I did a lot of praying. I was trying to decide whether God was telling me to hang it up, or was this a gut check?" It was a gut check. The Atlanta Braves gave him a second chance, and he made the most of it. He joined the best staff in baseball, the team closest to his hometown so his parents could watch him play, and became a part-time closer and full-time World Series champion.

JOHN SMOLTZ, baseball's Atlanta Braves. Smoltz had a great arm, but his results were merely good until he developed faith in God and confidence in himself in 1996, and won the Cy Young Award as the National League's best pitcher.

PEDRO MARTINEZ, baseball's Boston Red Sox. The 1997 National League Cy Young winner, for the Montreal Expos, Martinez also is deeply religious. Before games, he scrawls *Dios camina commigo* on the instep of his shoes. "It means 'God walks with me,' " he explained. "I believe that with every step I take, here or on the baseball field, I have got to thank God."

JOE CARTER, baseball's Toronto Blue Jays. A perennial All-Star and one-hundred-RBI hitter, Carter will forever be remembered for his dramatic three-run homer run in the bottom of the ninth inning to win game six and the 1993 World Series. As fireworks exploded inside Toronto's dome, Carter made an ecstatic, leaping tour around the bases, only the second time in the eighty-nine-year history of the fall classic that a series had ended on a home run. Forced to go to church as a child, he did not commit to Christianity until his college roommate had to give up the sport he loved, football, and yet still had peace of mind because of his faith. Carter committed himself and found his faith helped him deal with failure, which comes seven out of ten at-bats for even the best hitters. "One thing I always say when I talk to kids is that you're going to have trials and tribulations," Carter said. "The one thing that God always promised us is victory in the end."

PAUL MOLITOR, baseball's Minnesota Twins. A high-average hitter throughout his career, Molitor joined the 3,000-hit club, which virtually guarantees a spot in the Hall of Fame once he retires. Injuries slowed Molitor when he was in his prime. Old age was supposed to stop him in 1996, when he turned forty. Instead, he was as good as ever, hitting .341 while driving in 113 runs and scoring 99. "The Lord means everything to me," he said. "I don't know how anyone can face each day not having that foundation."

JEFF BRANTLEY, baseball's St. Louis Cardinals. Relief aces are supposed to scowl and intimidate batters, but Brantley said he is "the closer who goes to church on Sunday." No one saved more games in 1996, when he won the National League's Rolaids Relief Man Award. He has pitched in the All-Star Game and the World Series. Not bad for a guy who was told he was too little to play . . . get this . . . Little League. A guy cut from his ninth-grade baseball team. A guy cut by the San Francisco Giants just three years before. A guy who says he's the shortest pitcher in the big leagues. A guy who, instead of being nasty, gave teammate Jeff Shaw a $10,000 gold Rolex watch as thanks for his setup work in 1996.

MARY JOE FERNANDEZ, tennis. Her Catholic faith has helped Fernandez, a two-time Olympic doubles champion, cope with the lows of endometriosis, asthma, pneumonia, and a string of minor illnesses. "I really would have lost it by now if I didn't have my faith," she said. "I just know God is using these tough times to make me stronger."

MEREDITH MCGRATH, tennis. When her coach and parents were in separate towns, McGrath, alone and battling injuries, was welcomed into the home of Bob and Maggie Charlton. They became her adopted family and taught her to place Jesus Christ at the center of her life. Buoyed by her new family, faith, and health, she won seven doubles titles in 1995 alone, including her first Grand Slam event.

MICHAEL CHANG, tennis. Chang has praised God faithfully since he became a Christian in 1988, the same year he turned pro at age fifteen. He's finished most years in the world's top ten rankings, winning several Grand Slam events despite his slight size, and winning fans with his never-say-die effort. Chang's brother is his coach, and his parents and sister-in-law usually travel with them. He devotes time each morning and evening to Bible study, often with the whole family, and prays throughout the day.

TOM EDGER, hockey. Edger retired from the NHL's Pittsburgh Penguins to devote full time to the ministry.

BETSY KING, golf. A Hall of Fame golfer and the leading money winner in LPGA history, King says she prays at various times for everything from peace to patience to performing well enough to honor God. And yes, sometimes she prays for victory. But she says her faith in a higher power—and her realization that she should not judge her worth based on her score—gave her the perspective to succeed on and off the course.

CHRIS JOHNSON, golf. She played on the LPGA tour for seventeen years before winning her first major in 1997—right about the time she discussed her faith on Robert Schuller's "Hour of Power" television show.

TIGER WOODS, golf. The hottest name in golf and perhaps all of sports—with the possible exception of Michael Jordan—Tiger was the 1996 *Sports Illustrated* Sportsman of the Year and could dominate the PGA Tour for years to come. Some jealous PGA Tour players derisively called him "Buddha" because of the Buddha charm that hangs around his neck and because his father predicted Tiger would be more influential in world history than Buddha. Earl Woods told *Sports Illustrated* that Tiger was "the Chosen One" with "the power to impact nations."

PAUL AZINGER, golf. When Azinger won the 1993 PGA Championship on the second hole of sudden death, he leaped into the air and thanked the Lord, just as he always promised to do when he won a major. But when he raised the trophy, he felt a sharp pain in his right shoulder, and the pain would not leave. By late November he was barely able to operate the stick shift in his car. When doctors said it was cancer, he thought, "Dear Lord, help me. I'm scared to death!" He rushed into a bathroom and threw up. He cried out for God to save him. He had considered himself a Christian for eight years, but now he realized golf, not God, had been his priority. He decided to put his full faith in God, and when he overcame cancer and told his story over and over, including his 1995 autobiography, *Zinger,* he became an inspiration for America.

TOM LEHMAN, golf. Lehman flunked out of his first stint on the PGA Tour and spent years working his way back, barely scraping by on mini-tours. When he finally made it back to the PGA in 1992, he began to make big money—but also suffer heart-wrenching defeats in three majors in three years before finally winning his first, the 1996 British Open. He led the 1996 tour with a record $1.78 million in earnings, became PGA of America Player of the Year, and won the Vardon Trophy for lowest scoring average. He's an active speaker for FCA, Athletes in Action, Executive Ministries, Campus Crusade, and Youth for Christ, sharing his testimony, telling them never to get down, to realize true meaning in life is found not in your golf score but your walk with Jesus Christ.

STEVE JONES, golf. Like his friend Tom Lehman, Jones went through a lot of adversity before winning his first major, the 1996 U.S. Open. A dirt-bike accident nearly ended his career, forcing him off the tour for several years, forcing him to change to an unconventional grip so he could hit the ball without pain.

LOREN ROBERTS, golf. Roberts won just $16,659 his first three years on the PGA Tour. He bounced on and off the tour, forced to requalify for five years before finally making it for good in 1987. Even then, he did not break through totally until 1994, when he won his first tour event and became one of six members to earn $1 million that year. He says he turned his life and career around when he fully committed to Christianity in 1983.

COREY PAVIN, golf. The little golfer who could, Pavin harnessed his emotions and won the 1995 U.S. Open. Pavin's Christian faith so impressed David Robinson, he named his son Corey.

JEFF GORDON, auto racing. Gordon finished first or second in the 1995, 1996, and 1997 Winston Cup race, which goes to the stock-car driver who scores the most points during the NASCAR season. Known as "Boy Wonder" because of his youth, good looks, and instant success, he and his wife pray together every day, and he says his Christian faith helps him appreciate life and gives him peace and contentment. "It's just amazing the attitude that you get when Christ is in your life," Gordon said. "You just have a whole new attitude about life, because you know that there is a far better place than where we're at."

DARRELL WALTRIP, auto racing. Waltrip won back-to-back Winston Cup titles and won three Driver of the Year awards before wrecking at Daytona in 1983. He realized it was a miracle he was not killed because his car stopped right in front of traffic, but he had drifted from the faith instilled as a child. He sometimes went to church to keep his wife happy, but it was not until her pastor came to see him, unannounced, that he began to reevaluate his life. The minister complained about Waltrip being sponsored by a beer company. He had received similar complaints from mothers and DWI accident victims. He realized that, to be a true Christian, he had to walk the walk. His wife had endured three miscarriages, but they still wanted children. What kind of man did he want his child to look up to? He prayed about it and chose another sponsor. The next year they had their first child. They remain active in NASCAR ministries.

MICHAEL SHMERKIN, figure skating. Shmerkin represented the Soviet Union four times in junior championships, but he could not skate as a Jew in his native Russia until his mother remarried and immigrated to Israel. He competed in the 1996 world championships to the music of "Easter Parade."

MICHELLE KWAN, Olympic and pro figure skating. The 1997 U.S. and World figure skating champion is a Buddhist.

MARY LOU RETTON, Olympic gymnastics. America's sweetheart, the 1984 Olympic champion, touches on her Christian faith in her second career as a public speaker and endorser, but believes in keeping her religion fairly private.

JIM RYUN, Olympic track. When the former Olympic runner and world record holder in the mile wrote a Christian-oriented essay on courtship for the magazine *Focus on the Family,* Democrats circulated it and tried to use it against the Republican candidate for Congress in 1996. Ryun wrote that any young man who wants to date his daughters must talk and pray with the father before he decides whether the youngsters can begin dating.

GWEN TORRENCE, Olympic and pro track. Torrence is so competitive, the great sprinter has not always been received warmly by other athletes or portrayed glowingly by the media. But her Christian faith helped her mellow and accept her fate when a thigh injury forced her to miss the 1996 Olympics 100-meter race. And when she took a bronze medal in the 200, she did not complain about finishing third. Instead, she was gracious and praised God when the cameras focused on her.

RUTHIE BOLTON, Olympic and pro basketball. A member of the United States women's basketball team that won the gold medal in the 1996 Olympics, Bolton gave thanks for her Christian faith in interviews and in an album of seventeen gospel songs recorded with several brothers, sisters, nieces, and nephews. The daughter of a Baptist preacher, Bolton schooled teammate Nikki McCray to sing gospel songs, and they did duets and sometimes led the whole busful of players on renditions such as "Work It Out," hitting the chorus, "Jesus will work it out!"

When Bolton made the team, she shouted, "Praise the Lord!" Still, she said basketball is just "background music" because "the most important thing is to do right and please God." She has gone by her married name, Bolton-Holifield, since joining the Sacramento Monarchs for the debut season of the Women's NBA.

JENNIFER AZZI, Olympic and pro basketball. Like Bolton, Azzi gave up a lucrative foreign contract to compete for $50,000 on the women's version of the Dream Team. Unlike Bolton, Azzi didn't become a true Christian until she joined an Athletes in Action team in 1991. Now the former NCAA champion and Player of the Year says God is her "rock." She spent the 1996–97 season as a player and commentator for the new American Basketball League. "It's basically taken all of me to get here—physically, mentally, and especially spiritually," she said. "I think my spiritual life has matured over the last few years, and that's kind of what was missing before. It has helped me to make it to the next level."

LISA LESLIE, Olympic and pro basketball. One of the top centers in the world, Leslie was another member of the gold-medal team who started workouts and meals with prayers. One of several who found peace in reading the Bible, she joined the WNBA's Los Angeles Sparks.

NANCY LIEBERMAN-CLINE, Olympic and pro basketball. One of the greatest players in women's basketball history, Lieberman-Cline was inducted into the basketball Hall of Fame in 1996 and then made a comeback, at age thirty-eight, with Athletes in Action and then the Phoenix Mercury of the WNBA. "Lady Magic" led Old Dominion University to a pair of college titles, has played in four pro leagues, and has written two books.

MICHELLE AKERS, Olympic and pro soccer. The all-time leading goal scorer for the U.S. men's and women's national team programs, Akers captained the United States to the 1996 Olympic gold medal. Akers, who has played professionally in Sweden, tells her dramatic life story in speeches for Campus Crusade for Christ and the Fellowship of Christian Athletes, plus her web site, plus her autobiography. She overcame her parents' divorce, her own failed marriage, eleven knee operations, and chronic fatigue and immune dysfunction syndrome (CFIDS) after recommitting herself to Christ in 1994. "I've finally learned he is the only one who is never going to let me down. Everything else has failed me," she wrote in *Face to Face with Michelle Akers.*

GENE STALLINGS, college football. Stallings won Super Bowls as a Dallas Cowboys assistant and a national championship as Alabama's coach. But the father of a handicapped son has always made faith and family the top two priorities in his life.

NOLAN RICHARDSON, college basketball. Richardson was raised by his grandmother from the age of three after his parents died. "Ole Mama" was struggling to raise the last four of her eleven kids in a tiny shotgun house in El Paso, Texas, but still she took in Nolan and his two sisters.

"And every Sunday we were expected to be up and scrubbed for church," he said. "That was the most important rule in her house: 'Don't do anything without asking the Lord to help you,' she would say. She taught me about faith and determination, and those lessons have stood me in good stead during some difficult times, especially when my wife Rose and I lost our daughter Yvonne to leukemia in 1987. Today, whenever the Razorbacks win a game, I look up from courtside to heaven and say to Yvonne, 'Baby, we got you another one.' I like to think Ole Mama is up there next to her looking down. And I ask the dear Lord every chance I get to help me make those two women proud."

TOM OSBORNE and BOBBY BOWDEN, college football. Two of the nation's winningest and most respected coaches, each has won national championships, Osborne at Nebraska and Bowden at Florida State. The day before every game, Bowden huddles his team, reads a Bible verse, and tells a story relating to the verse before he ever mentions the opponent or the game plan.

SAM RUTIGLIANO, college football. Rutigliano became a Christian in 1962 after he fell asleep at the wheel of his car, causing an accident that killed his four-year-old daughter Nancy. He looked to religion for support and found it. He was the Cleveland Browns' head coach and an NBC commentator, but he's found more fulfillment coaching a Baptist college.

"The view from the top [of the NFL] isn't nearly as exhilarating as the climb," he said. "I got all the way to the top and when I got there I said, 'Is that all there is? There's got to be more to life.' As a Christian coach, there is."

2

A History of Separation

It was game six of the 1986 World Series. The Boston Red Sox led the New York Mets by two runs in the bottom of the tenth inning. The Red Sox were one out away from their first World Series victory since 1918. The so-called Curse of the Bambino—they had not won it all since trading away Babe Ruth—was about to end.

Until God stepped up to the plate to pinch-hit for Mets catcher Gary Carter.

Or at least that's the way Carter sees it.

"When I was in the on-deck circle, a lot of people might have been wondering what was going on in Gary Carter's mind," recalled Carter, one of the great catchers of all time. "What was going through my mind was, I was praying. I just remembered the many days I was in my back alleyway, dreaming up situations like bases loaded, bottom of the ninth inning of the World Series. In those dreams, I was facing someone like Sandy Koufax or Whitey Ford or someone like that."

This time it was Gary and God vs. Calvin Schiraldi.

Not a good match-up for the BoSox.

"I just said, 'God, this is your at-bat. I don't want to make the last out. I know you're right here with me. I'd love to be able to come through and keep the game alive. And I just want to be a trivia question. I just want to go up there and do my very best.' That's what I prayed about," Carter continued.

"God was right there with me. I just truly felt a presence. I just felt like I wasn't the one swinging the bat, that our good Lord was with me. I got things started with the hit to left field. Kevin Mitchell and Ray Knight followed with hits. And then Mookie Wilson hit the ball between Bill Buckner's legs. In a matter of ten minutes, we had come back and won the game. I think there was shock throughout all Red Sox fans and their team that we had come all the way back.

"I just know those prayers were answered. Maybe God was a Mets fan that year. We were a team of destiny. We were meant to be."

They beat the stunned Sox in game seven and won the World Series. Buckner, who let the routine ground ball go between his legs, was painted as one of history's all-time worst goats. Years later he was still so reviled in Boston, he felt the need to move out of New England for his family's safety and sanity.

So what about Bill Buckner? Was God punishing him?

"I don't know how strong Bill Buckner's faith was," Carter replied, "but also, if you look back at the replay, I'm not so sure Bill Buckner would have beaten Mookie Wilson to the bag on that play. Bob Stanley was not covering. He was late. It was going to be a foot race. With Buckner's bad ankle and all, he looked up momentarily—and that's what cost him as the ball went through his legs. I'm sure that was going through his mind, a slow-hit ball, Mookie's speed. He knew it was going to be a close play. Was he to blame for that entire series? Absolutely not."

Was God to credit?

"I always believed something good was going to happen as long as you put it in God's hands, let God take over, and he will produce. That's my philosophy," said Carter, who'll probably make the Baseball Hall of Fame once he's eligible. "Whenever you try to take things upon yourself, they never seem to get done. In my lifetime, my career, I just know my faith was strong."

In his lifetime, he has seen a great change. Carter became a Christian in his first training camp, as an eighteen-year-old with the 1973 Montreal Expos, and when he made the majors for good in 1975, not many athletes were very religious. Or at least not many talked about it.

Faith and sports were almost always separated. Teammates, coaches, and the media did not view religious athletes with reverence. Just the opposite.

"Back then," Carter said, "proclaiming yourself a Christian and trying to stand up for your beliefs might have been a little bit more ridiculed and not as accepted. There were few Christians. I was sort of considered a too-good-to-be-true type of guy.

"If someone asked if you gave praise to God, people shut you off. It wasn't an open forum to talk about. It was not really well received. It was kind of taboo. Now, it's kind of a given, and it's appreciated by a lot of people, and they know what kind of an influence an athlete can be on people in other walks of life."

The attitude began to change in the eighties, as more athletes turned to faith and were strongly encouraged by religious leaders to share their testimony. The media did not always spread the word, but as television, radio, and multimedia competition expanded, as print reporters also sought human-interest stories to separate themselves from TV and radio (where the fans had already heard the news and the game), the stories have been told more and more often.

"I'm glad athletes are speaking out more," Carter said. "When I first came to the big leagues, I was one of the first to take that stance. I was the president of our chapel services. If I'd say a curse word, the first thing the [non-Christian teammates] would say was, 'Oh, yeah, you're a real strong Christian guy!' or something like that. They were more apt to pick on little slip-ups rather than look at themselves in the mirror. There might have been three or five or maybe a half dozen guys that would go.

"But now you're seeing half the team goes to chapel services and

I think it's because there's a need and certainly a search by a lot of today's players. They're wondering about their futures and what they want out of life. I think there is apprehension: 'Is this the lifestyle that I want to lead?' They realize there are a lot of bad things happening—a lot of wars and drugs and confusion about this world. Where do people always turn in times of trouble or in bad health? They always turn to God, right? It's like they're realizing where their passions should be.

"And that's why you are seeing more people come out more vocally about what God means in their lives. A lot of players know they've been given a gift. These days they're not afraid to share with everybody where they've gotten their strengths from and where they've gotten their gifts from and where they've gotten their blessings from.

"If you're being recognized in this game—not only baseball but every athletic forum—it's a great opportunity to share with so many other people."

You could trace the history of religious athletes back to David slaying Goliath with his slingshot—still the greatest sports upset of all time. Or you could think of the Roman chariot races or the original Olympic Games. But let's stick to the twentieth century.

Eric Liddell, a British sprinter and devout Congregationalist, refused to run the 100 meters on a Sunday at the 1924 Olympics, even though he was favored to win. Liddell instead won the 400, and his story—along with that of 100-meters champion Harold Abrahams—formed the basis for the Oscar-winning 1981 movie *Chariots of Fire.*

Ruth Langer, Judith Deutsch, and Lucie Goldner refused to participate in the 1936 Olympics for both religious and political reasons. The swimmers were Austrian but also Jewish, and Langer said it would have been "unthinkable to compete in the games in Nazi Germany where my people were being persecuted" by Adolf Hitler. Langer's refusal led Austria to ban her from competition and strip her of her titles. (She moved to Italy and then to Britain, becoming the British women's long-distance swimming champion, but the games were canceled in 1940 and 1944 because of World

War II. By the 1948 Olympics in London, Langer had retired from competition. Not until 1995 did Austria apologize and restore her titles.)

Hitler allowed Jews to compete for the German Olympic team because (1) he did not want to lose the games and (2) he hoped to humiliate them. He made Jews compete at a horrible Jews-only stadium with his special police standing nearby, shouting crude anti-Semitic insults. German star Margaret Bergmann equaled the national high-jump record—at the same height that would win the Olympics—only to be told she could not compete. (Hitler also tried to disgrace blacks, only to have American Jesse Owens embarrass him with a stunning performance.)

Another track star of the era, mile recordholder Glenn Cunningham, quietly shared his faith with fellow runners. But faith in sports went public in the 1940s. Gil Dodds, the world indoor mile champion who was nicknamed "the Flying Parson," ran a lap around the Soldier Field track before sharing his Christian testimony with 65,000 at a youth rally in 1945.

In 1952, when Sir Edmund Hillary became the first to scale Mount Everest, the world's highest mountain at 29,028 feet, he buried a cross in the snow at the peak and his guide Tenzing placed a small offering of food to the Gods of Chomolungma, which all devout Buddhists believe to inhabit this mountain's summit. "Strange companions, no doubt, but symbolical at least of the spiritual strength and peace that all peoples have gained from the mountains," Hillary wrote in *High Adventure*.

Billy Graham began using athletes in his crusades in 1947, and the movement gained further momentum when the Fellowship of Christian Athletes was founded in 1954. The FCA used pro athletes to attract youths to summer camps and workshops. Bobby Richardson, the second baseman for the longtime World Series champions, the New York Yankees, appeared with Graham during many rallies in the 1960s and later became baseball coach at Jerry Falwell's Baptist college, Liberty University.

In the NFL in the 1960s, Bill Glass of the Lions and Browns and Buddy Dial of the Steelers and Cowboys organized fellowship meetings among players. Norm Evans, a tackle for the Dolphins from 1966 through 1975 and a member of their unbeaten 1972 team and Silver Anniversary team, turned informal fellowship meetings into Professional Athletes Outreach in 1971. Roger Staubach and Tom Landry became noted as FCA members when Dallas was going to the playoffs every year and becoming known as America's Team in the seventies.

Walt Hazzard was among the first NBA players to convert to Islam when he played in the sixties, and Sandy Koufax of the Los Angeles Dodgers created a stir for all Jews when he refused to pitch the opening game of the 1965 World Series because it coincided with Yom Kippur.

But the sixties' defining moment for religion in sports—and maybe in all American society—was Muhammad Ali's controversial decision to oppose the Vietnam War. He was at the forefront of the most contentious social causes of the decade: civil rights and the war.

Fighting under his birth name of Cassius Clay, he won the heavyweight boxing gold medal at the 1960 Rome Olympics. But when the "Louisville Lip" returned home, he found he was still persecuted because of the color of his skin. Denied a meal by a restaurant owner and harassed by a motorcycle gang, he threw his precious gold medal into the Ohio River.

Increasingly angry at the slow progress of civil rights in America, he joined the Black Muslims, who were preaching racial separation at a time when Martin Luther King, Jr., was preaching integration. When his promoter heard the news, he nearly canceled Clay's fight with heavyweight champion Sonny Liston. On February 26, 1964, the day after Clay's stunning upset of Liston, he announced he had joined the radical Nation of Islam. A few months later he announced he was rejecting his "slave name" and adopting his Muslim name, Muhammad Ali.

Ali's announcements prompted death threats and hate mail, and even though he flunked his military physical and said he would not fight in Vietnam because war was against his religion, he was reclassified in 1966 and in 1967 ordered to report by the President himself, Lyndon B. Johnson.

Forced to choose between the laws of the United States or the principles of the Nation of Islam, Ali chose faith, and became an instant hero for an eclectic group of blacks, the persecuted, anti-war demonstrators, and religious and civil rights leaders. But to most of white America he was a villain. He was stripped of his boxing titles and his boxing licenses, and the State Department took away his passport so he could not fight overseas. He was convicted of a felony, and though he was not jailed, he was placed on the FBI subversives list, was tailed by agents, and had his phone bugged.

When he was finally allowed to box again after a three-and-a-half-year exile, he dodged bullets by racists shouting, "You draft-dodging nigger!" and received phone calls snarling, "Nigger! If you don't leave Atlanta tomorrow, you gonna die!"

The U.S. Supreme Court overturned his draft-evasion charges in 1971, and as the war grew steadily unpopular and civil rights became law, Ali emerged not only as a heavyweight champion but as an American and even world icon. Even as he battles Parkinson's disease today, his legend grows. When he lit the Olympic flame and received a replica of his rejected gold medal at the 1996 games, he was greeted with tumultuous applause and hugs and kisses from even the most jaded athletes.

By 1971, Ali had become "the most commanding voice for and symbol of the decade's causes," *Sports Illustrated* wrote in a 1996 retrospective. And today? "Ali is as near to a cultural saint as any man of our era."

Four years after the world's greatest boxer rejected Christianity for the Black Muslims, college basketball's greatest center rejected Catholicism for Islam. Lew Alcindor changed names to Kareem Abdul-Jabbar, though he would not announce it until after he made his pilgrimage to Mecca in 1971.

Abdul-Jabbar chose Islam because he thought it answered his spiritual questions better than the Roman Catholicism of his youth and because it was shared by many members of the black race. Though he felt victimized by racism, he rejected what he called the "racist demonology" of the Nation of Islam (or Black Muslim) leader, Elijah Muhammad. He thought Elijah Muhammad had bastardized true Muslim faith and turned it into "mumbo-jumbo" and a "sham" religion, he wrote in *Giant Steps*.

When he boycotted the 1968 Olympics because he felt America was racist and because he wanted to graduate from college on time, Abdul-Jabbar had been deluged by hate mail calling him an "uppity nigger" and "a traitor." However, that did not prepare him for the trauma that lay ahead. He had bought a Washington, D.C., townhouse for his spiritual adviser, Hamaas Abdul-Khaalis, to spread the Islamic faith. But his mentor was denouncing the Black Muslims' faith, saying Elijah Muhammad's preachings were all wrong, and eight or nine Black Muslims were sent to kill Abdul-Khaalis. When they did not find him home, they slaughtered three sons, two grandchildren, his wife, and daughter in a bloody massacre January 18, 1973. Abdul-Jabbar received round-the-clock police protection for months, living in fear that the Black Muslims would hunt down him, his family, and his adviser.

The Muslims were not the only ones paying the ultimate price for their faith. A bevy of Israeli athletes were slaughtered at the 1972 Olympics in Munich, Germany. Swimmer Mark Spitz, an American Jew, survived the scare and set an Olympic record by winning seven gold medals.

Faith and sports did not always have such deadly conflicts, but the tension between faith and sports surfaced repeatedly in the 1970s.

Baltimore infielder Pat Kelly protested that manager Earl Weaver allowed the Orioles only fifteen or twenty minutes for a prayer service.

"Earl, don't you want us to walk with the Lord?" Kelly asked.

"Pat," Weaver replied, "I'd rather you walk with the bases loaded today."

Dick Williams, managing the Seattle Mariners, also set ground rules for Christian players when their chapel services began to interfere with team practices. There were times when they were supposed to be on the field but instead were attending chapel.

Devout Christians who played for the San Francisco Giants in

1977 and 1978 were criticized by not only the media but manager Dave Bristol and some teammates.

"For some of them, their faith seemed to take away their aggressiveness," third baseman Bill Madlock told the *Pittsburgh Press* in 1991. "The impression I got from some of them was that, if God meant for someone to pitch a shutout, he would pitch a shutout. And if God meant for us to win, we would win. I was mad. I didn't look at it that way. I think if you look at it that way, you don't go out there being aggressive enough."

Pitcher Bob Knepper was singled out by many critics. "He would get knocked out of the inning and he would go in and write letters in the clubhouse," Madlock said. "Other guys would get mad and upset when they lost. I think he did care, but the emotion just wasn't there. There's nothing wrong with taking part in those [Christian] things. It's when they start using it as an excuse not to hustle and not to try . . . that's when it becomes an excuse and a problem."

Faith in sports caused another stir in 1977 when heavyweight boxer George Foreman retired in his prime to lead his ministry in Houston. He did not return to the ring for a decade.

Even in the 1980s, religious sports figures were often ridiculed as members of the "God Squad." Gerry Faust was openly mocked for his public preachings and slavish devotion to Catholicism while at Notre Dame—probably because he was the one Fighting Irish football coach whose teams did not have much fight in them.

In 1986 golfer Larry Mize was dubbed Larry "Demize" after blowing a lead in The Players Championship. A year later he won the Masters—and suddenly he was a hero and everybody wanted to hear his story. He talked about golf . . . but he also made sure to talk about his faith in Jesus Christ.

In the 1980s we also began to see many signs of religion in the arena. Faith was no longer just something athletes talked about behind the scenes; now they demonstrated their faith right on the field. Many was the football player who knelt in prayer, crossed himself, and/or looked to the heavens to praise God after a touchdown or big play.

Signs bearing the biblical verse John 3:16 ("For God so loved the world that he gave his one and only Son, that whoever believes in him shall not perish but have eternal life") began to appear at numerous sporting events all over the country.

Sprinter Carl Lewis and two other Americans knelt on the track in unison after they won all three medals in the 200 meters at the 1984 Olympics. The next day a photograph of the finish-line prayer appeared in newspapers throughout the country.

When the Dodgers clinched the seventh game of the 1988 play-offs against the New York Mets, Orel Hershiser spontaneously sank to his knees on the mound and bowed his head in prayer. Again, newspapers across the country carried the glorification of God.

When Giants pitcher Dave Dravecky came back from cancer surgery to pitch in 1989, he credited faith as the source of his courage, and was hailed as an inspirational hero all across the country.

When Buffalo's Scott Norwood lined up for a 47-yard field goal that would win or lose Super Bowl XXV, cameras showed both the Buffalo Bills and New York Giants down on their knees, praying, hands clasped, looking to the heavens. Norwood's kick sailed just wide right. It was heartbreaking for some and heartwarming for others, yet players from both teams knelt in a circle at midfield and prayed.

Both prayer scenes were shown to the largest television audiences of the year. Were the Giants' prayers answered? Is God a good-luck charm? Does he care who wins or loses a game? Should we all emulate our football heroes and pray at work?

America had a lot of questions to answer.

Faith and sports mixed not just at the professional level but at the top college and amateur levels as well. Universities such as Brigham Young, Liberty, and Oral Roberts promoted religion through successful sports teams. Notre Dame attracted a nationwide group of "subway alumni" because of faith and sports. When Notre Dame played the University of Miami in the late 1980s, T-shirts promoted it as a morality play—"Catholics vs. Convicts"—more than a football game.

The local American Civil Liberties Union protested and stopped Colorado coach Bill McCartney from making his team engage in group prayer before and after games. He reluctantly conceded, but he still scheduled chapel service and made it available to anyone who wanted. He still used his platform to spread his religious ideals. He still told his players he was praying they would all become Christians. He eventually formed the Promise Keepers Christian men's organization.

In 1992, Boulder was one of three cities in Colorado to have a law promising fair treatment of gays in employment, housing, and public accommodations. McCartney publicly countered by attaching his name and coaching title to a group that wanted to wipe out gay rights laws in the state. The antigay ballot measure was approved by 53 percent of Colorado voters. (The law eventually was overturned by a 1996 U.S. Supreme Court ruling.)

University of Colorado president Judith Albino censured McCartney for using his high-profile public university job to push his religious cause. After a closed-door meeting with the president, he was supposed to say he would no longer use his platform to champion political issues. Instead, he launched into another antigay speech. Standing at a university lectern and wearing a team sweater, he called homosexuality "an abomination of God." He kept his job.

When the UCLA men's basketball team won the 1995 NCAA Final Four, many Bruins coaches and players (including MVP and future first-round pick Ed O'Bannon) dropped to their knees at midcourt, held hands, and prayed. Across America, it was becoming common to see athletes kneeling and giving thanks to God after scoring a touchdown or making a big play in their sport.

Florida quarterback Danny Wuerffel clasped his hands in prayer after each touchdown pass. Florida State quarterback Danny Kanell pointed to the heavens after each score. Southern California football players prayed at a November game. For a short while, religious football players faced penalties for praying in the end zone because the NCAA initially interpreted the demonstrations as violations of its new rules. But when Jerry Falwell's Liberty University took the matter to court, the NCAA said praying would not be penalized.

In the 1988 Olympic Games in Seoul, South Korea, American Joe DeLoach stepped into the blocks at the 200-meter final, glanced at Carl Lewis, his legendary teammate, and prayed, "Father, I need you to run this race with me." The prayer gave him peace. But Lewis beat him out of the blocks and had a big lead at the halfway point, until DeLoach felt "the strength of a lion" in his feet. He surged past Lewis and everyone else to win the gold medal. And when they put the medal around his neck and played the national anthem for him, he decided it really was for someone else.

"Thank you, Lord," he whispered.

When an injury kept DeLoach out of the 1992 games, he was heartbroken. He could not understand why God had done this to him. He asked God, he prayed to God, and he said God answered him directly: "The passion you feel for running is the passion I want you to feel for me."

DeLoach committed himself to the Lord and soon became an elder and youth pastor at Joy Tabernacle, helping youths in a troubled Houston ghetto. And then, instead of training to run in Atlanta, he trained to preach. He spoke at rallies sponsored by Lay Witnesses for Christ International.

That group was one of many at the summer games. Proselytizing has gone on at every Olympics since 1964, but never on the scale of the 1996 Atlanta games:

• About 100,000 volunteers joined thousands from the area for ministry work in Atlanta. Games Outreach ran sports clinics and festivals for inner-city youths, hosted vacation Bible camps for kids, and handed out Bible tracts at concerts.

• The American Bible Society printed more than five million items to hand out.

• Youth with a Mission, an international evangelism ministry, mobilized about five thousand people from one hundred countries.

• The Southern Baptist Convention planned to give away one

million plastic hospitality bags, each containing a six-page evangelistic message.

• Thirty local Christian denominations and groups joined to form Quest Atlanta '96.

Combine these groups with the FCA, Athletes in Action, Professional Athletes Outreach, Sports Outreach America, ministries and chapels for each pro sport, and you'll find a well-oiled, well-organized movement to add converts, teach them, and convince them to spread their faith. As one FCA piece of literature asks: "Why not utilize hero worship of the athlete to spotlight the greatest product of all: Christianity?"

Print and online magazines such as *Sports Spectrum, Sharing the Faith,* and *Christian Sports Flash* are devoted to stories about Christian athletes. Former minor-league pitcher Tom McGough hosts "Sportsweek," which mixes athletes' testimonies with highlights and previews, as one of the shows that Cornerstone TeleVision offers free to local stations. "The 700 Club," a popular evangelical talk show produced by the Christian Broadcasting Network, often features Christian athletes. A spate of books by religious athletes and coaches have been released in the past few years, including David Robinson, Reggie White, Kareem Abdul-Jabbar, Hakeem Olajuwon, Muhammad Ali, Evander Holyfield, Andre Dawson, Brett Butler, Paul Azinger, Dan O'Brien, Dennis Byrd, Phil Jackson, Joe Gibbs, Gary Carter, Tom Landry, Bill McCartney, and Dave Dravecky.

With so many athletes talking about God, many Americans have come to view sports and religion as working together, according to Wheaton College sociology professor James Mathisen.

In fact, the argument can even be made that sports have taken the traditional place of religion in America. Think about it. What takes up more pages in your newspaper—sports or religion? Which is more likely to be talked about at the water cooler on Monday morning? Which evokes more passion? Which is bigger business? Who excites our youth more—Michael Jordan or Jesus Christ?

Fresno State football coach Jim Sweeney says, "Football is a religion in the South." Radford University sports sociologist Steve Lerch says fans "worship Michael Jordan with much the same intensity as they worship religious figures."

"Sports has become our religion," said Dr. Drew Harvey, pastor at Mount Lebanon United Methodist Church in suburban Pittsburgh. "Religion and family were once the glue that bound civil society together. Now the family is under decay, and religion is, too. If you want civic pride in Pittsburgh today, what do you talk about? Whatever sport is in season.

"When you think about it, there are a lot of similarities. In religion, you have a center of devotions. In sport, it's winning. In religion, you have rituals. If I've ever seen anything ritualistic, it's baseball and football players. You see them wearing 'lucky' jerseys. Remember [former Pirates infielder] Richie Hebner? He'd touch every part of his body, in the same order every time, before he took a swing. Religion involves taking the individual and giving him a great source of identity. That's the same with the athlete and his team, or the fan and his favorite team. When the Steelers went to the Super Bowl, 'we' went to the Super Bowl.

"In Christianity, you often have mentors, spiritual guides. In sports, older athletes take people under their wing. The Methodists' founder, John Wesley, believed you could not do it alone. Every member was accountable to the rest of the class, otherwise known as the team," the Reverend Harvey continued.

"Religion has rivalries. The Steelers have the Cincinnati Bengals, the Pirates the Cincinnati Reds. Religion has a priest structure. A lot of times the sports columnists are our prophets and the broadcasters our high priests. When Myron Cope [the beloved Steelers radio announcer] waves his Terrible Towel to cast a spell on the Steelers' opponent, he waves it to the gods of football. The same thing goes for soccer overseas. We don't have anything like they do for mass hysteria, but when our team loses the big game, there's mourning. The god is dead."

So if sports and faith are intertwined, and sports can help attract people to faith, then Dr. Harvey will use both to his advantage. When the city of Pittsburgh was captivated by the Steelers' march into the playoffs and finally into the Super Bowl, the minister wore black and gold, the team colors, to every Sunday service. Each week, more and more people, especially youths, showed up, many wearing black and gold.

"Yes," the Reverend Harvey said, "I'm using sports. I'll use anything—within reason—to preach the gospel."

He is not alone. A Hail Mary is not found just in church anymore.

3

Front-Page News

If religion and sports once were separated, if they once intermingled only occasionally, those chasms were gone by 1996 and 1997.

Everywhere you turned in the last year and a half, religion and sports were intertwined:

JANUARY 7, 1996: "Captain Comeback" Jim Harbaugh helped the Indianapolis Colts score a stunning playoff upset in Kansas City against the Chiefs, owners of the NFL's best regular-season record but with a kicker who would miss three field goals this day. As soon as the game ended and the Colts headed to the American Football Conference championship game, Harbaugh started praising God for his miracle turnaround from second-string quarterback to Pro Bowl quarterback.

JANUARY 8, 1996: Inner City Community Church in Knoxville, Tennessee, where Reggie White of the Green Bay Packers is associate pastor, was burned. Arson investigators found nineteen Molotov cocktails and racist slurs on the walls and doors such as "Die nigger and die nigger-lovers" and "White is right." A week before the fire, White got a phone call warning of a possible attack. The church received a bomb threat, and police found a threatening letter purportedly written by a group called Skinheads for White Justice.

But investigators would go on to infuriate White by also looking into the church membership because the homemade bombs were found inside a locked church with no signs of forced entry and two gas lines were turned on, suggesting the arsonist knew where to look. They subpoenaed White's bank records and interrogated more than two hundred church members.

But, along with anger and sorrow, White also felt joy. "Lord," he said, "Satan must really be worried about what we are doing. Now he is trying to burn us out. We must be doing something right."

JANUARY 22, 1996: When the Long Beach State basketball team arrived in its locker room at New Mexico State, it found a slur directed at the faith of coach Seth Greenberg. Someone had written, "Seth, get ready for an ass-kicking, you Jew bastard," in red ink on a grease board normally used to diagram plays. Greenberg notified New Mexico State's athletic department and was still livid when he met the media after the game.

"There's something more important than basketball," he stormed. "There's something more important than basketball, all right? That's life and being a good person. When I hear my players being called the N word and my white guys being called white boys, that's a bad commentary on life. And that's a bad commentary on this university and this state. And there's no place for that.

"That is an insult to every human being that walks the earth. And for them to allow that to happen is sickening. For me to walk in that locker room and see an anti-Semitic remark and they don't have any security and don't know where it came from, that is sickening."

Late in the game, Greenberg had officials eject three students from the stands, accusing them of racial remarks. Big West Conference commissioner Dennis Farrell called it an "insidious and cowardly act," and ordered New Mexico State to investigate what happened. "This type of behavior will not be tolerated." But somehow New Mexico State officials seemed to think they were the ones slandered. College president J. Michael Orenduff expressed regret in a letter to Long Beach State president Robert Maxon but also criticized Greenberg: "His remarks impugned New Mexico State University and the entire state of New Mexico based on one anonymous piece of paper and alleged remarks that came from a very small number of people and which, in fact, were heard differently by persons close to the scene."

Greenberg called the letter "an insult" and was further angered by New Mexico State coach Neil McCarthy, who said Greenberg wanted attention and overreacted because of his father's recent death. "If people want to stick their heads in the sand up to their necks, that's up to them," Greenberg said. "I feel bad for Neil if he feels that way. Obviously, he has never been the object of a hate crime."

FEBRUARY 9, 1996: The *Chronicle of Higher Education* chronicled the ties between faith and sports in a story headlined "Devout Athletes: Public Displays of Religious Faith by Coaches and Players Raise Concerns." The NCAA had entered the debate about religious expression at sporting events.

FEBRUARY 17, 1996: The Associated Press distributed a story nationwide detailing Hakeem Olajuwon's decision to follow the Islamic fasting requirements during Ramadan. The Muslim holy month, which began in late January with the sighting of a new moon, celebrates the month in which God revealed the Koran, Islam's holy book, to the prophet Muhammad. Muslims are forbidden to eat or drink between sunrise and sunset during the holy month.

During Ramadan, Olajuwon typically rises at 5 A.M. for breakfast, then does not eat again until a light meal after sundown. He enjoys his main meal after the game. During the month, he will lose ten pounds. It is a special sacrifice for a professional basketball player, who could be weak with hunger during a game. Islamic law would actually give Olajuwon an out—travelers are not required to fast—but he demurs. He says that law was prescribed during ancient times when travel by camel over difficult terrain was a hardship. NBA travel is luxurious.

Besides, he said his game has never been better: "I feel much better. I feel lighter, faster, much more mentally focused. When God prescribes something, it is for your best interest. My role is very important because Islam has been misunderstood, especially in America [where people often associate the religion with terrorism]. You have to educate the people. Islam is a religion of peace . . . submission and obedience to the will of God. These are God-conscious people. They are dignified. They honor their word. The quality of a believer should reflect in their behavior."

But Olajuwon does not fast for himself or others. "Your main purpose in doing everything is for the pleasure of God, to please God regardless of what other people think." Olajuwon said he planned to extend his fast to Mondays and Thursdays year round. He says fasting cleanses his system of impurities and a smaller stomach means less back pain. "Your whole body goes through a change. It's like a rebirth."

People thought he would get weak from hunger and would be at a disadvantage. "If they only knew," he said, "they would be fasting."

MARCH 7, 1996: When Doron Sheffer scored a team-high nineteen points to lift the University of Connecticut into the Big East Conference semifinals, he said it was the only time all week he had not thought about the series of terrorist bombings in his native Israel that have killed sixty of his people. He had gone to elementary school with one victim. Sheffer grew up in Ramat Efal, a suburb of Tel Aviv, not far from the mall where a suicide bomber wrapped in explosives took the lives of at least fourteen people during the festive Purim holiday, Israel's Halloween. Sheffer served his three-year obligation in the Israeli military before coming to the United States to play basketball.

MARCH 12, 1996: Denver Nuggets guard Mahmoud Abdul-Rauf was suspended without pay by the NBA after he refused to stand during the playing of the national anthem. All season, he had stretched on court or returned to the locker room when "The Star-Spangled Banner" was played and he was suspended only after revealing his reasoning.

A star guard for Louisiana State and a first-round pick when known as Chris Jackson, Abdul-Rauf adopted the Islamic faith in 1991 and changed his name in 1993. He said he did not believe in standing for any nationalistic ideology. The Koran, he said, states that nothing should come between him and Allah. He could not worship any object but God. He claimed the American flag was "a symbol of oppression, of tyranny."

"You can't be for God and for oppression," he said. "My beliefs are more important than anything. If I have to give up basketball, I will."

Reaction was swift and strong. Ed Wearing, the state commander of the American Legion veterans organization in Colorado, suggested Abdul-Rauf renounce citizenship, that refusing to honor the flag "is tantamount to treason." Some columnists attacked his patriotism and questioned why it took him five years to take his stance. Most disagreed with his views but wrote he was entitled to freedom of speech and religion. Others wrote the NBA was within its rights to establish restrictive rules for employees.

MARCH 14, 1996: The NBA lifted its suspension of Abdul-Rauf after he said he was willing to stand and pray during the anthem. "I realize there is a better way," he said. "In Islam, if after making a decision you see that which is better, you do that." Abdul-Rauf said he was not sorry and not compromising a position that cost him one game check, or $31,707.

Fans would make his life miserable every time he played again in 1996. They would boo and curse and hold up nasty signs. They would taunt and chant. Abdul-Rauf said he thought he would have to leave the country to escape harassment, and after the season the Nuggets did trade him—not to one of the NBA's two Canadian teams, but to the Sacramento Kings.

MARCH 15, 1996: A *USA Today* story detailed how Mike Tyson was trying to regain his heavyweight title and find himself. "His conversion to Islam seems to have made him more reflective," Jon Saraceno wrote. "But he doesn't sound at peace with the one person he needs the most. Himself. For a fellow who within the last twelve months has had his freedom restored, undergone a spiritual awakening, become a father again, and has, according to promoter Don King's math, made $64 million since August, Tyson appears glum."

Released from prison March 25, 1995, after a three-year confinement for a rape conviction he still insists was wrong, Tyson attended a Muslim mosque and recently had invited former champion Muhammad Ali into his home to share their religion. He said prayer had not helped him much "because I don't believe in myself the way I truly should, about me as a man. I'm having pretty much a hang-up with that, with me, dealing with my life. I just don't believe anybody. . . . I had problems with life. It was just crazy. I was just killing myself—spiritually, physically, intellectually. I was just a mess."

APRIL 7, 1996: Paul Stankowski, who qualified for the Bell South Classic only when he won a minor-league tournament (the Nike Tour) the previous week, looked up to the heavens and thanked God when he won the PGA event. Stankowski, a three-time All-American at the University of Texas at El Paso, was an altar boy who attended Catholic private schools from first through eighth grades, and he was led closer to the Lord by his brother, friends, and the Fellowship of Christian Athletes, but not until some scary drinking episodes did he rededicate himself on March 9, 1991, at his brother's wedding.

APRIL 25, 1996: Aaron Walker, a student at Page High School in Franklin, Tennessee, was to receive his school's Fellowship of Christian Athletes Male Athlete of the Year award, only to have Tennessee FCA officials block the honor because he was a Mormon. Steve Robinson, the FCA's state director, said there are differences between Mormonism and traditional Christianity, and the organization had to "take a stand and not compromise on what our convictions are."

APRIL 29, 1996: *Sports Illustrated,* the nation's most widely read sports magazine, devoted not only its entire cover but ten full pages to David Robinson's born-again Christianity and the reigning NBA MVP's fight against the seven deadly sins.

APRIL 30, 1996: The *Washington Post* devoted a whopping fifty-four column inches to the story of the religious conversion of Sean Gilbert. The Redskins' new defensive tackle said he changed his life when he became a born-again Christian. "Before that, I had a master's degree in cussing, a bachelor's degree in deceiving and a PhD in psychology, playing mind games. I was doing wicked things."

He partied into the night, got into minor scrapes with the law, and fathered two children with Nicole Norman before finally marrying her. But on October 12, 1994, he woke up in the middle of the night alone and wondering if his world were coming to an end. He called then teammate David Rocker. "He came over and prayed the prayer of salvation with me and I received salvation that night," Gilbert said.

MAY 9, 1996: Danny Wuerffel, the Florida quarterback and 1996 Heisman Trophy winner, said he would not pose for *Playboy*'s All-America college preseason football team, citing his religious convictions. The son of an Air Force chaplain declined an invitation to be named the magazine's National Scholar Athlete of the Year. His decision cost him an expense-paid trip to a posh Phoenix resort.

"It didn't take any thought at all," said Wuerffel, who clasped his hands in prayer after each touchdown pass. "It wasn't a thing I had to waste much time thinking about. It would've been a lot of fun, and that's fine for some. I'm sure there's a good bit of the population out there that would think I'm silly for doing this. But there's also a good bit of the population that would understand that's not the type of person I would want to portray myself as."

MAY 13, 1996: For the second time in three weeks, *Sports Illustrated* devoted its longest story to faith in sports. Headlined "Leap of Faith: Once Sundays Were No Longer Sacrosanct, England's Jonathan Edwards Exploded into the Greatest Triple Jumper in History," the story detailed how Edwards emerged to break a ten-year-old world record in the triple jump and set an example for the ultracompetitive, ultraselfish track world. "It's a bit of a cliché to call someone nice," former track star Sebastian Coe said. "But Jonathan is a ray of light in athletics." And, said 1992 gold medalist Mike Conley, "I can't bring myself to get mad at Jonathan. I can only get mad at what he jumped."

The oldest son of an Anglican vicar, Edwards believed the Sabbath must be kept as a day of reflection and worship, so he never competed on Sundays. By 1988 he had become the second-best triple jumper in Great Britain and seemed certain to make the Olympic team for Seoul—except the national trials took place on a Sunday. Edwards chose not to compete and became an instant celebrity. Television crews showed up at his church the morning of the trials. He was named to the Olympics team anyway on the basis of his prior jumps, but in Seoul failed to qualify for the finals (as he would fail again in the 1992 Barcelona Olympics). In 1991 he faced the same conflict and did not go to the world championships in Tokyo because the triple jump finals were on a Sunday.

In the spring of 1993, after much study and contemplation, Edwards began competing on Sundays. It was a difficult, emotionally trying decision. His parents publicly supported him but struggled with the shift. "It made us evaluate our own thinking," his mother said. She imagined a thrashing by the British media: "I feared what people would say, with Jonathan changing his mind after taking this stand."

The decision "was very much between my conscience and God," said Edwards, who decided he should honor God by doing his absolute best. He began to work harder, to lift weights, add coaches and film study, and make subtle changes in his techniques. He won all fourteen of his meets in 1995, breaking the world record three times.

Postscript: NBC Sports also profiled Edwards during the Olympics, when American Kenny Harrison set Olympic and U.S. records to win the gold and Edwards won the silver medal.

MAY 14, 1996: *USA Today* columnist Bryan Burwell wrote about the debate over whether David Robinson of the San Antonio Spurs is too nice to win: "Everyone is seeking answers for what makes this talented, decent man tick. What makes his competitive fires burn? Do his competitive fires burn?" Coach Bob Hill defended Robinson, but Burwell observed, "But this is not a debate about his human character, which is certainly unassailable. This is a debate about Robinson's athletic heart and soul. Does he have what it takes to lead a team to an NBA title?"

Burwell pointed out that the same questions had been asked about Michael Jordan and Hakeem Olajuwon before they led the Bulls and Rockets, respectively, to six titles in the nineties. He concluded with a quote from Spurs guard Avery Johnson, another strong Christian: "It's not so much what you go through, it's how you handle the bad night, a bad season or a hard lesson you get in the playoffs. That's what makes not just great players but champions."

MAY 20, 1996: *Sports Illustrated* profiled Jim Harbaugh, writing that he had been a devout Christian since experiencing a religious awakening in 1990 and that when he spoke at a "Path to Profit" seminar, he urged listeners to "turn your life over to Jesus Christ." The same issue also profiled Brett Butler's battle with throat cancer, and quoted the Los Angeles Dodgers center fielder saying how God was helping him through adversity again.

But three pages after the Butler story, the magazine ran a less flattering portrait of faith in sports. The two-page photo showed the Cincinnati Reds' owner kneeling at her bedside, praying before she went to bed. But the headline was less than complimentary: "Heaven Help Marge Schott," with this subheading: "The Reds' owner, long ago reduced to a life of loneliness, has further isolated herself by her spiteful words and witless deeds." The story detailed Schott's slurs against blacks and Japanese, and helped lead to her suspension from baseball.

MAY 26, 1996: Utah Jazz owner Larry Miller did not attend the Jazz's big playoff game. He is a devout Mormon and does not attend games on Sundays.

MAY 27, 1996: Yet another *Sports Illustrated* cover story was devoted to faith in sports. "Phil Jackson and His Mystical Methods" detailed how the Chicago Bulls' coach called upon Christianity, Zen Buddhism, and even Lakota Sioux teachings to help the Bulls win more games than anyone in NBA history. Jackson's book, *Sacred Hoops: Spiritual Lessons of a Hardwood Warrior,* further explored his faith-in-sports connections.

JUNE 11, 1996: The cover story on the front page of *USA Today,* the national newspaper, was headlined "Faith on Deck: Baseball Star Brett Butler's Battle with Cancer" and "Family Turns to Prayer, Friends and Each Other."

The same day, the cover story on the paper's front sports page profiled Baltimore Orioles second baseman Roberto Alomar, who was flirting with baseball's first .400 season since 1941. It told of a nice Catholic guy who enjoys life, who says "God wants" him to excel at baseball, who invokes the Almighty frequently. Alomar, who still attends Mass on Sundays, credits his mother with instilling his faith. "God is the most important thing in life," Maria Alomar said. "When you walk with God, you don't feel worry about anything. Robbie is confident. God walks with him."

Postscript: Alomar's name would be sullied when he spit on an umpire in the heat of the 1996 pennant race. He would later apologize and pledge $50,000 to charity, saying, "I'm not a bad person. I made a mistake. God knows I didn't mean anything bad."

JUNE 16, 1996: Steve Jones won the U.S. Open by one stroke over his good friend Tom Lehman and Davis Love III. Lehman said he kept thinking of a Bible verse as he tried to win. He even shared it with Jones. "It was Joshua 1:9," he told reporters. " 'Be strong and courageous; be not dismayed; have strength.' "

Lehman was done in by three bogeys on the back nine, including the final hole after his drive took a bad bounce into a bunker.

That allowed Jones to win his first major with a one-foot putt. He bent over, picked his ball out of the hole, shook his fist, and leaned back and looked to heaven. He grabbed his little girl and then his boy in each arm—what a Father's Day present!—and kissed his wife.

The USGA president handed him the silver trophy and, live on national television, Jones said, "First of all, I thank the Lord Jesus Christ for changing my life. I couldn't have done it without God. My stomach was wrenching. Even with God, I was still nervous." At the mention of Jesus, the fans cheered wildly.

JULY 1, 1996: Tristam Coffin, a twelve-year-old soccer player, keeps his head covered whenever he goes out in public because he is a practicing Sikh. He wears a blue bandanna when he plays for the Franklin, Massachusetts, Cosmos, and though headwear is generally prohibited by youth soccer leagues, no one had objected in the three years he has played for the Cosmos or in the first four games of the Easton Classic.

But in the championship game, official Ron Quintiliani told coach John Peters that Tristam would have to remove the bandanna if he wanted to play. The coach explained the circumstances, but Quintiliani would not budge. Peters sent Tristam, bandanna-clad, to his usual midfielder's spot. The official ordered the preteen to the sideline, and he left, in tears. Peters pulled the rest of the team off the field. Quintiliani dropped the ball to signal the start of play, and after two Dudley players touched the ball—the second intentionally booting it out of bounds under coach's orders—the referee declared Dudley the victor by forfeit.

"Tristam was pretty shaken," Peters told *Sports Illustrated.* "I took the players aside and told them that some things are more important than soccer, that you have to stand up for things you believe in." Dudley coach Chet Dawidczyk thought so too. As the Cosmos watched the Dudley players receive their trophies, Dawidczyk took his over to Tristam. "This is for you," he said.

JULY 9, 1996: "God has blessed me and I'm very grateful," Mike Piazza said after hitting a home run and double and being named Most Valuable Player of the All-Star game.

JULY 17, 1996: "Gwen Torrence is a regular on Sundays at Mount Patmos Baptist Church in Decatur," *USA Today*'s story began. "You'll find her clapping, kneeling, praying, singing and, maybe, crying."

"Sometimes I just feel like shouting, I get so overjoyed," Torrence told the paper. "I feel so much better. I love saying, 'Thank you, Jesus.' I write down the things I've heard and want to keep in my head. I go to relieve the stress and strain. I become a person when I sit there."

JULY 18, 1996: Basketball star Shaquille O'Neal plays a genie in the movie *Kazaam*. "We all have genies in our lives," he said. "The genie is God. When I was little, I used to pray to God a lot: 'I wish I can do that. I wish I can do that.' Times are hard, times are rough, but I never gave up. Kids these days try something for a while, but when they think they aren't good enough, they quit. Nobody is born great."

JULY 24, 1996: Butch Reynolds, the world 400-meter track recordholder, said his two-year suspension in 1990, later overturned by American courts, was the most depressing period of his life. He said his faith and religious beliefs kept him going.

JULY 25, 1996: Alexander Popov of Russia completed back-to-back golden doubles, winning the 50- and 100-meter freestyle swimming events in both Barcelona and Atlanta. But he left reporters puzzled with enigmatic replies. "There's a saying in the Bible: 'If you want to know, I won't tell you. And if I told you, you wouldn't believe me,' " he said after one question. Asked the secret to his success, he replied, "It's probably a gift from God that I can control my technique all the way through. Perhaps you should ask him."

JULY 26, 1996: In hawk-everything-you-can Olympic Park, people sold an Italian sausage sandwich for four dollars, a Coke for two dollars, and Olympic pins for all sorts of money. But they could not sell Jesus. A band of ten young churchgoers from Fort Walton, Florida, drove to Atlanta to perform "street drama and dance to share in the gospel of Jesus Christ" only to be expelled, Jonathan Sansom told Reuters. Jeremy Bloom said a security officer ordered him to leave the park when he was holding Christian brochures. Jennifer Freeman was thrown out of the park for handing out booklets from a group called the Testament League. "We're supposed to have freedom of religion and freedom of speech, and I think we're being discriminated against," she said.

JULY 27, 1996: When he was enshrined in the Pro Football Hall of Fame, former Redskins coach Joe Gibbs repeatedly referred to the power of God in his speech before a national television audience. "For the last six months, I've been asking myself how I got in the Hall of Fame," said Gibbs, one of three coaches to win at least three Super Bowls. "The answer is that God picks very average men and women and what he does is give them a life, some talent, and surround them with great people."

JULY 28, 1996: San Francisco Giants relief pitcher Mark Dewey, a fundamentalist Christian, refused to join a pregame show of solidarity for homosexuality and wore his red AIDS ribbon sideways, making the looped ribbon resemble the Christian fish symbol. His actions drew so much criticism, he responded with an open letter:

> Much speculation has been made about my character, but very little is based on the intent of my heart. Everything I have done and said has been to express love and compassion for all people with AIDS, their friends and families, and those who have lost loved ones to the disease, without compromising the teaching of Scripture. I have no hatred or ill will toward homosexuals. I have concern for all who have AIDS, and I am not opposed to the search for a cure or action taken by people to raise money for research. I do, however, hate sin, and the Bible clearly teaches that sexual immorality (fornication, adultery, homosexuality, etc.) is sin.
>
> I could not be involved with the ceremonies because sexual immorality was condoned and in some cases encouraged. I altered the ribbon for the same reason. I wore the ribbon like a fish to show

my love and compassion for lives as well as for souls. All I did and said was out of a love for God and for people. The bottom line is this: The deadly "disease" we are battling is sin (it kills body and spirit). *All* have sinned. There is a cure—the shed blood of Jesus Christ.

JULY 30, 1996: Joe Frazier suggested God was punishing Muhammad Ali by making him suffer from Parkinson's disease, which has left the three-time heavyweight champion of the world walking haltingly and talking only in a mumble. "I think it was the hand of the Lord that touched him to slow him down, to show him no man can be *the*," Frazier said.

JULY 30, 1996: In jail for auto theft during the 1992 Olympics, Nate Jones assured himself at least a bronze medal as a heavyweight boxer with a victory this day, then told how God helped turn him around. "Man, I have come to realize that there is somebody upstairs," said Jones, whose sister had recently been released from the hospital after being seriously ill with meningitis. "I have a sister that almost died twice. I am here in the Olympics and I wasn't supposed to be here. Really, I ain't supposed to be living. So I'm just real glad to be here. It's something that no matter what I've done, nobody can ever take from me. And now I'm coming home for sure with a medal. I'm at peace with myself."

AUGUST 1, 1996: Emerson Fittipaldi called his death-defying crash "a message from the Lord" and said he would probably never race again. A two-time winner of the Indianapolis 500 and one of the world's best Formula One auto racers, Fittipaldi fractured the seventh cervical vertebra in his neck after crashing into a wall at 230 mph during the Marlboro 500 in Michigan on July 28. The crash cost him permanent loss of 15–18 percent flexibility in his neck.

AUGUST 2, 1996: Muhammad Ali was presented with a gold medal to replace the one he won at the 1960 Rome Olympics during the Atlanta games' men's basketball final. At halftime of the Dream

Team's gold-medal win over Yugoslavia, 35,000 strong rose to their feet to cheer "The Greatest."

When IOC president Juan Antonio Samaranch hung the medal around his neck, Ali kissed him on both cheeks and then kissed the medal, a replica of the one he tossed into the Ohio River in disgust after he and a friend had been chased away from an all-white restaurant. The Dream Team surged toward him and hugged him, and he burst into a wide smile of delight.

"I think when Mr. Ali came out, the emotions were shown for everything he did back then," Orlando Magic star Anfernee Hardaway said. "He got the applause he deserves for all the struggle he had to go through back there. He's still the greatest in our hearts." Added Indiana Pacers star Reggie Miller: "For African-Americans, he's a role model for a lot of guys on our team. To get to touch him gave me a lot of joy. He's the greatest champ of all time. To be within arm's reach was very special."

Ali's stands for religious and racial rights made him a symbol of black pride and a voice for the oppressed. "He's the most principled man I've ever met," coach Lenny Wilkens said. "He had the courage of his convictions in a very difficult time. People today recognize that and we're certainly very proud of him."

AUGUST 8, 1996: Hakeem Olajuwon was married to eighteen-year-old Dalia Asafi of Houston in an arranged union. "There is no dating process, no boyfriends and girlfriends in Islam," Olajuwon announced. "Families meet, talk, get to know one another. Then the marriage is arranged."

He said he had worshiped for years at the same Houston mosque as the bride's father. But since men and women are separated when praying, he did not encounter his future bride or her mother until a meeting was arranged. "In the Islam faith, it is customary for a girl to marry much younger than they do in America, at age fifteen or sixteen, for instance," he said. "Dalia may be eighteen in terms of age, but because of her background, beliefs and religious understanding, she, like many other Islamic young women, possesses a maturity, knowledge and wisdom beyond her years."

The thirty-three-year-old Nigerian native was raised as a Muslim and recommitted to his Islamic faith as an adult. Last month he signed a five-year, $55 million contract extension with the Rockets. He donates part of his salary to his own charity, The Dream Foundation.

AUGUST 9, 1996: When former Pro Bowl kicker Fuad Reveiz retired from the Vikings because of a painful left foot, he told reporters, "I want to thank God first, for the ability, how he's blessed me."

AUGUST 9, 1996: A suspected bomb found at the back door of Reggie White's community investment bank turned out to be an elaborate hoax eight months after White's church was firebombed. The bank is an offshoot of the Inner City Church, where White is an associate pastor. White helped create the Knoxville Community Investment Corporation about two years ago with a million dollars of his own money. "We are in this neighborhood to bring hope into a hopeless situation," the Reverend Jerry Upton said. "We are still praying that with God we can make a change in this community."

AUGUST 15, 1996: Andre Dawson announced he was retiring after twenty-one years as one of baseball's greatest talents. Only three other men in baseball history had three hundred home runs and three hundred steals: Willie Mays, Barry Bonds, and Bobby Bonds. An eight-time All-Star, "The Hawk" was such a dominant player in 1987, he was voted the National League's MVP even though his Chicago Cubs finished last. He never played in a World Series, and a dozen knee operations robbed him of a chance to be his generation's Mays or Bonds. Still, he had no regrets. "Thanks to God, I've been blessed with a wonderful career," he said.

AUGUST 17, 1996: Mark McGwire, who would go on to lead the majors in home runs with fifty-two in 1996 and fifty-eight in 1997, said: "I play the game because I enjoy the game and I play the game because I really believe God gave me the talent to play it."

AUGUST 18, 1996: Tim Puller, who would fight in Madison Square Garden in two days, calls himself "The Hebrew Hammer" and wants to be the first Jewish heavyweight champion. "There's Jewish promoters and Jewish managers in boxing, but there aren't many Jewish fighters. I want to show people that Jews can fight," said Puller, who hadn't proved it in his past two bouts, both losses.

Born in Israel to a Yemenite father and a Dutch mother who spent four years in concentration camps during World War II, Puller wore a tattoo on his left arm picturing a Star of David and a ring of barbed wire to honor his mother and Jewish survivors of the Holocaust. He also wore two large earrings, a Jewish star necklace, and boxing trunks decorated with a Star of David and the flags of Israel and the United States. "It's the entertainment business," said Puller, a six-foot-six, 225-pound part-time actor. "In boxing, you need a good gimmick."

SEPTEMBER 16, 1996: A *Sports Illustrated* story on Mike Tyson's easy defeat of Bruce Seldon discussed Tyson's conversion to Islam and how he "seemed to be much more serene than ever before, even pleased with himself."

SEPTEMBER 16, 1996: Fans held up a huge sign saying JESUS SAVES right behind the goalposts, every time the Pittsburgh Steelers and Buffalo Bills kicked field goals and extra points on "Monday Night Football," one of the nation's highest-rated shows.

SEPTEMBER 22, 1996: Brian Blades scored a touchdown in the Seattle Seahawks' 17–13 win over the Tampa Bay Buccaneers and knelt in the end zone and prayed.

SEPTEMBER 23, 1996: Two signs bearing the simple message JOHN 3:16 were seen often during another "Monday Night Football" game.

SEPTEMBER **29, 1996:** Phillippi Sparks of the New York Giants intercepted a Warren Moon pass, ran into the end zone, bowed to the crowd, then looked skyward and pointed a finger as high as he could to praise God. Sparks said two of his friends had been shot the previous week, one dying and the other being hospitalized in grave condition. "I was praying with all my heart and sincerity for my friend," he said. "It came out pretty good."

SEPTEMBER **29, 1996:** "We got some help from above," Chicago Bears coach Dave Wannstedt, who attends church every morning, said after his injury-depleted team nipped Oakland on a last-second field goal.

SEPTEMBER **30, 1996:** Ricky Watters broke a tackle of All-Pro safety Darren Woodson and scored standing up to give the Philadelphia Eagles a 10–0 lead over the defending champion Dallas Cowboys. He knelt in the end zone and crossed himself. And once again a prime-time national television audience saw the message JOHN 3:16 in big red letters behind the goalposts when the teams kicked extra points and field goals.

OCTOBER **6, 1996:** Cris Carter caught two touchdown passes to lead the Minnesota Vikings to victory, but instead of a wild me-first celebration, he simply knelt in the end zone, pointed his index finger to the sky, and looked to the heavens.

OCTOBER **14, 1996:** *Sports Illustrated* pictured Heisman hopefuls Danny Wuerffel of Florida and Peyton Manning of Tennessee and their teams praying together after a game. It headlined its Wuerffel profile "Answered Prayer" and told how reporters snooped around, trying to find his flaws, only to discover the chaplain's son didn't curse, drink, smoke, chase women, cut class, or even lose his temper. When they wrote that he chewed his fingernails, he promptly stopped. The magazine said he carried his Bible around campus, talked to God twice a day—and held the NCAA career passing efficiency record.

OCTOBER 16, 1996: Texas Tech supplemented its media blitz for another Heisman candidate, running back Byron Hanspard, with a separate page on its World Wide Web site. A licensed Pentecostal minister, Hanspard would finish sixth in the Heisman race after running for 2,084 yards, fifth in NCAA history.

OCTOBER 20, 1996: After three terrific years in Miami, wide receiver Irving Fryar was cast aside because the new Dolphins coach, Jimmy Johnson, feared he was too old at age thirty-four. Johnson signed a younger, far less accomplished receiver, Charles Jordan, for almost the same money Fryar wanted, and Fryar signed with Philadelphia. In his first game against his old club, Fryar caught a career-high four touchdown passes, and after each one he pointed to the heavens, then knelt and prayed. Jordan did not even play.

" 'Revenge is mine, sayeth the Lord!' " said Fryar, an ordained Pentecostal minister, and shook his fist in a postgame press conference. But then he dropped his fist and his voice. "So revenge comes from the Lord. I didn't feel any revenge. I just felt good about contributing today."

OCTOBER 26, 1996: New York Yankees third baseman Wade Boggs, one of the best hitters in baseball history, won the first World Series of his long career, perhaps a payback for his one other fall classic appearance, when the Mets beat his Boston Red Sox after Bill Buckner's error, one of the most infamous blunders in history. "Ten years ago, I said, 'Lord, give me one more chance'—and he gave it to me," a very teary and emotional Boggs said after the Yankees came from two games down to beat the Atlanta Braves.

NOVEMBER 1, 1996: Less than an hour after George Foreman weighed in for a fight in Tokyo, he appeared with his Bible in hand to perform a wedding ceremony. Foreman married his Los Angeles attorney, Henry Holmes, to Lorrie Beban in the kind of wedding only boxing could produce. Here was a Catholic (Holmes) being married to a Jew (Beban) by a Baptist minister (Foreman) in a country where Buddhism dominates. And it was all filmed in time to rush it to ABC's Tokyo offices to get it on ESPN's "Sports-Center" in hopes of boosting pay-per-view sales of the fight.

NOVEMBER 9, 1996: A major underdog, Evander Holyfield, warmed up for his World Boxing Association heavyweight title fight by dancing to the gospel song, "Mighty Man of War," in the minutes before the fight. Then he went out and upset the seemingly invincible Mike Tyson with an eleventh-round technical knockout. Holyfield joined Muhammad Ali as the only three-time heavyweight champions and cited his religious dedication as the reason for his success. "You can't choose against God," he said. "I did what it took to win. What the spirit leads me to do, I do."

Tyson's only other loss came against Buster Douglas in 1990, possibly the only greater upset in heavyweight boxing history. Oddsmakers had listed Tyson, the self-described "baddest man on the planet," as an overwhelming favorite, with odds ranging from 25–1 to 5–1. The conventional wisdom was that Holyfield had simply taken too many punches in too many tough fights to survive more than a couple of rounds with Tyson's power, let alone beat him. He was thirty-four years old, had won just four of his past seven fights, and almost didn't get licensed to fight in Nevada because of the hole discovered in his heart. Even his sparring partner beat him.

"So I prayed," Holyfield said. "I prayed a lot." He began small. First, he asked just to be able to survive the few rounds of sparring each day. Then he asked for the strength to make them competitive rounds. Then he asked to win. One day he started beating up his sparring partner. Holyfield credited prayer for a big part of the turnaround. The doctors at the Mayo Clinic might say otherwise, but he believes prayer was how the heart problem that forced his second retirement came to be mysteriously healed.

But he also was pragmatic. He trained sixteen weeks for Tyson instead of the usual six to eight. "You can pray all the time and I do," Holyfield said. "I'm not embarrassed to say that because I've been a praying man all my life. But nothing good comes without work."

NOVEMBER **14, 1996:** Evander Holyfield was cheered by several thousand fans during a parade in his hometown of Atlanta. Mayor Bill Campbell mentioned some memorable sports events he had watched: Cal Ripken breaking Lou Gehrig's consecutive games record, the Atlanta Braves winning the World Series in 1995, and sprinter Michael Johnson breaking the world 200-meter record during the Atlanta Olympics. But, Campbell said, "There has never been a more inspirational moment in sport than when Evander Holyfield won this title." And Holyfield again credited his faith for his victory. "I'm honored and I thank God for giving me the confidence and everything to get the job done," the fighter said.

NOVEMBER **18, 1996:** *Sports Illustrated* articles on Holyfield, hockey player Brendan Shanahan, and tennis superstar Steffi Graf all mentioned God.

NOVEMBER **24, 1996:** A Fort Lauderdale *Sun-Sentinel* story profiled Levon Kirkland. The Pittsburgh Steelers' star linebacker was the son of a very strict and demanding pastor but had not become deeply religious until 1996. In a conversation with his sister-in-law, Patricia Kirkland, herself a clergywoman, he was ruminating over his failure to win the MVP honors in Super Bowl XXX. She told him, "Levon, you could be a giant in this game. But God wants you to be his giant first."

Levon Kirkland took this religious revelation to his father and asked to be baptized at age twenty-seven. His father performed the ceremony and may have made a small statement to his son about waiting so long to get it done. "I thought he held me under the water a little too long," said Levon, who would go on to have his best year and earn his first Pro Bowl appearance.

NOVEMBER **30, 1996:** When Florida State guard Todd Fordham saw how pumped up star halfback Warrick Dunn was, he looked to the sky and offered a prayer and a plea. "I asked God to be with us. And I asked the coach to put the ball in Warrick's hands."

Coach Bobby Bowden, a devout Christian himself, heard the

plea, and Dunn answered the prayers. Dunn ran for 185 yards and the second-ranked Seminoles beat top-rated Florida, 24–21, to take over first in the college football polls. Afterward, Dunn held hands at midfield with his opponent but fellow Christian, Danny Wuerffel, for a gentle word and a postgame prayer. Florida State chaplain Clint Purvis clutched Wuerffel's shoulder.

Dunn's mother, a Baton Rouge police officer, was killed while escorting a store manager's night deposit in January 1993. A week later he made his recruiting trip to Florida State and decided to go there. This day he wrote on each taped wrist, "Mom." Below that he wrote, "Mr. T" for Chuck Tanner, an elderly man who befriended Dunn in Tallahassee and died before this season. "He was always there when I needed someone to talk to about my mom," Dunn said. "I think about them all the time. I'm glad they were upstairs watching this game." Dunn points to the sky after every touchdown he scores and says, "Did you see that, Mom?"

DECEMBER 14, 1996: Florida quarterback Danny Wuerffel won the Heisman Trophy as the nation's top college football player. When the award was announced in a nationally televised ceremony, the first thing Wuerffel did was hug his father, an Air Force chaplain. The first thing he said was, "First and foremost, I want to give thanks to God. He is the rock upon which I stand. I want to ask him to forgive me for my sins, because there are many." And the last thing he said: "The biggest blessing of all is having a living and loving relationship with Jesus. Thank you all."

Wuerffel won the Heisman Trophy, Maxwell and Walter Camp Awards as the nation's outstanding player, the Davey O'Brien and Johnny Unitas Awards as the top quarterback, the Honda and Draddy Awards as the top scholar-athlete. The Associated Press All-American set forty-seven school, conference, and NCAA records.

And he was more than just a one-dimensional jock. He was an Academic All-American with a 3.75 grade point average, including a perfect 4.0 his final two years. He graduated a semester early with a degree in public relations. He was president of the campus Fellowship of Christian Athletes. His fellow senior classmates voted him Outstanding Male Graduate. He played the trumpet, piano, guitar, and harmonica, and sang in the church choir. He prayed at bedside every night and led a Bible class in his room every Tuesday night.

"Every night when I say my prayers, I'm begging Jesus for forgiveness," Wuerffel said. "By no means do I ever want people to think of me as a model of perfection. I'm not even close. I'd rather point people to the only person who led a perfect life, and that's Jesus Christ. He's the only one who should be emulated."

DECEMBER 23, 1996: When *Sports Illustrated* named his son Tiger as its 1996 Sportsman of the Year, Earl Woods told the magazine he was "personally selected by God himself" to raise "the Chosen One" who will "transcend this game and bring to the world a humanitarianism which has never been known before."

Gary Smith wrote, "Every year near his birthday, Tiger goes with his mother to a Buddhist temple and makes a gift of rice, sugar, and salt to the monks there who have renounced all material goods. A mother-of-pearl Buddha given to Tiger by his Thai grandfather watches over him while he sleeps, and a gold Buddha hangs from the chain on his neck. 'I like Buddhism because it's a whole way of being and living,' Tiger says. 'It's based on discipline and respect and personal responsibility. . . . I believe in Buddhism. Not every aspect, but most of it. So I take bits and pieces. I don't believe that human beings can achieve ultimate enlightenment, because humans have flaws.' "

DECEMBER 1996: Shawn Bradley was called for a technical foul when he protested a call too heatedly. Referee Hue Hollins told New Jersey Nets coach John Calipari that Bradley had sworn at him. "He's a Mormon," Calipari replied. "He doesn't swear."

"I'm a Baptist," Hollins replied. "And I don't lie."

DECEMBER 30, 1996: Byron Hanspard, an All-American running back at Texas Tech and a Pentecostal minister, announced he would forgo his senior year of college and turn pro because the NFL offered a bigger platform to spread his faith. Hanspard, who won the Doak Walker Award presented annually to the nation's best running back, would be drafted in the second round by the Atlanta Falcons in April.

Hanspard, who often cited Bible passages when discussing football, said playing on Sundays wouldn't clash with his religion. "If the Lord felt that it would hurt me a lot, he wouldn't have told me to go to the NFL," he said. "I don't have to go to church on Sunday to worship."

Hanspard preached part time at Community Baptist Church on Lubbock's lower-income east side. After each home game he delivered a brief sermon to his teammates and coaches. He was a member of Lay Ministries for Christ International, a nationwide evangelical organization that counts Reggie White among its membership.

JANUARY 2, 1997: Florida State coach Bobby Bowden preached in a New Orleans church a few days before the Sugar Bowl, but in the rematch for the national college football championship, Florida won the game and the title thanks to quarterback Danny Wuerffel, son of an Air Force chaplain, and coach Steve Spurrier, son of a minister.

Wuerffel threw for 306 yards and three touchdowns and ran for a fourth touchdown to give Florida its first national championship in a century of football. "God smiled on the Gators, no doubt about it," Spurrier said.

JANUARY 4, 1997: The previous night, Jacksonville tackle Tony Boselli was vomiting repeatedly, sick to his stomach and complaining of a terrible headache. About nine-thirty, a handful of Jaguars teammates came into his room, surrounded his bed, knelt, and prayed for his recovery. Fourteen hours later, bingo! A healthy Boselli held one of the AFC's leading sack men, Alfred Williams, to no sacks and one tackle, and the Jaguars, two-touchdown underdogs, upset the Denver Broncos.

Both Jaguars interviewed on live national television mentioned the Lord. "We've got a bunch of guys who love the Lord and he's been with us," quarterback Mark Brunell said. Boselli said, "God actually healed me," and that his magical quarterback was "blessed by God."

Thirty of the fifty-three Jaguars were professed born-again Christians and not shy about telling the world. "We have a lot of guys on this team who love the Lord," Brunell said.

"I think it's great to have Christians like Mark on the team," tight end Rich Griffith said. "Not that non-Christians are bad, but you can pretty much bet a Christian isn't going to be out every night beating people up, using drugs, that stuff."

JANUARY 5, 1997: Two Patriots players and their owner were interviewed on live TV after beating Pittsburgh and all three mentioned their faith. Owner Robert Kraft begged God to let them win the AFC championship the next week. Running back Curtis Martin said he prayed God would help him channel his energy and he did. "Everything we prayed for came true. God truly blessed us." And fullback Keith Byars, before answering the first question, began, "First, I want to give honor to God, through whom all blessings flow." And he closed his comments by saying, "Sometimes the Lord closes one door and opens another. Hallelujah!"

JANUARY 8, 1997: Staff for the TV show "Hard Copy" arrived in Jacksonville to do a story on Christianity in sports. Mark Brunell sponsored a retreat in Texas during the off season attended by about twenty players. Offensive lineman Greg Huntington had a framed picture of Jesus, two prayer cards stuck in the frame, a bottle of holy water and a Bible in his locker. The group was so devout that it sometimes caused a subtle division in the locker room, some players becoming irked with what they deemed "fanatical" devotion. However, most of the talk came back to good-natured kidding. "I don't know what God thinks of winning and losing," Brunell said. "But I know he cares about people and football teams. I know he cares about this team and every team."

Before the Jaguars and Patriots played for the AFC title, a writer said to New England coach Bill Parcells, "From reading the papers, you'd think God is on both sides."

"No offense," Parcells replied, "but that seems to work best if your players are big and fast."

JANUARY 12, 1997: As the Patriots ran out the clock on a victory over the Jaguars and a trip to Super Bowl XXXI, the network cameras caught Keith Byars exclaiming on the Patriots' sideline: "Thank you, Jesus!" Patriots cornerback Otis Smith returned a fumble for the clinching touchdown and said on live TV afterward, "Glory be to God." And NBC showed Curtis Martin looking to the sky, holding his hands in thanks, and saying, "We thank God for this victory." And Willie Clay, who made the crucial endzone interception with Jacksonville on the precipice of tying the score, said, "I'd like to thank the Lord for all the time he's given me."

The same day, Green Bay won the NFC championship and the other berth in the Super Bowl, and Reggie White addressed the home crowd in the trophy ceremony afterward. "God brought me here for a purpose. I have to give glory to God," he said, nearly in tears. And he told reporters, "When I came here four years ago, I was asked if we had a chance of winning the Super Bowl. I said we did. Pretty much everything I said has come to pass. You can laugh all you want to, but I know what God said to me and it's all worked out the way he wanted it to work out."

JANUARY 19, 1997: Fasting from dawn to dusk while observing the Islamic holy month of Ramadan, Hakeem Olajuwon showed a nationwide TV audience how strong his faith and game were during a day game. Without eating anything or even taking a sip of water, he had thirty-two points, sixteen rebounds, five blocked shots, and four assists as the Houston Rockets upset the mighty Chicago Bulls. "Good thing I'm just a regular old Southern Baptist," teammate Charles Barkley said. "We can eat and drink whenever we want."

JANUARY 26, 1997: After Reggie White set a Super Bowl record with three sacks and won his first championship at any level, he joined Curtis Martin and other Patriots and Packers in a prayer circle seen by billions of viewers on worldwide television. And at the presentation of the Vince Lombardi Trophy, Reggie told the world, "I want to say thank you, Jesus." Teammates Andre Rison and Antonio Freeman also thanked God on live TV. And safety Eugene Robinson said of his trade from Seattle to Green Bay: "I really felt God was bringing me here. Don Beebe [a Packers receiver] and I both said we couldn't believe how spiritual this team was."

And White told reporters, "Now I can sit back with my son for years and watch highlights of this Super Bowl, and he can see Daddy getting three sacks. I thank God I was able to step up when I did. God sent me here [to Green Bay]. Some of you guys thought I was crazy four years ago. But now I'm getting a ring. How crazy do you think I am now?"

FEBRUARY 9, 1997: After Glen Rice led the East to a 132–120 victory in the NBA All-Star game, he was named Most Valuable Player, took the microphone, and in front of a sellout crowd and a national television audience, the first thing he did was thank God. He scored a record twenty points in one quarter, a record twenty-four points in one half, and twenty-six in the game.

FEBRUARY 10, 1997: Three separate *Sports Illustrated* profiles discussed athletes and their religion. NASCAR legend Bobby Allison was a profoundly Catholic man who struggled with his faith in the face of overwhelming adversity. Cleveland's Terrell Brandon was called a nice guy, the NBA's best pure point guard, and its best-kept secret. His father was an associate pastor in a Pentecostal church for twenty-four years and was recently promoted to assistant pastor. "People think I'm going to use my money to buy cars," Brandon said, "but I'd rather give it to my church, to my family, do something I can be proud of." And finally a story headlined, "Onward Christian Soldier," told about Tracy McGrady, who had gone from "an obscure Florida high school player to the brink of the NBA draft" when he went to a "Christian boot camp" called Mount Zion Academy.

FEBRUARY 16, 1997: Jeff Gordon became the youngest winner of the Daytona 500, nicknamed the Great American Race because it's the most prestigious stock-car race in the world. Gordon said he turned to prayer when he was nearly a lap down midway through the race. "I prayed to God, 'If I'm going to glorify you this day, you've got to give me a caution,' " he said. A few laps later, an accident brought out the yellow caution flag, and Gordon caught up right behind the leader.

That gave "the Wonder Boy" eighteen victories and $8 million in winnings the past two years. He led Rick Hendrick Motorsports teammates Terry Labonte and Ricky Craven to an unprecedented 1–2–3 sweep of the 500, and before he even got out of the cockpit he called the team owner on a cellular phone and congratulated him. Hendrick was back home in Charlotte, North Carolina, about to begin six months of chemotherapy in his life-threatening battle with leukemia. Hendrick called the dramatic sweep "the best medicine that the good Lord could give me."

FEBRUARY 23, 1997: Shortly after arriving in camp with the New York Mets, Carlos Baerga declared he had sworn off drinking alcohol and had become a born-again Christian in hopes of regaining his All-Star form. "I'm going to make a lot of adjustments," Baerga said. "I want the people in New York to see the real Carlos Baerga. I don't drink anymore. I've gone back to church. I've stopped doing a lot of things I was doing before. I want to be the player I was before."

MARCH 7, 1997: The cover story in *USA Today* Sports told how Hakeem Olajuwon was voted one of the fifty greatest players in NBA history and detailed his Islamic beliefs. David DuPree wrote of "the serenity of his eyes . . . the peace and guidance he gets from his Islamic religion. . . . Religion is at the center of everything for Olajuwon. He says it has taught him discipline and compassion and given his life balance."

The story told how Olajuwon actually played better during the month of Ramadan while abstaining from food and drink from dawn to sunset. The NBA's three most notable Muslims—

Olajuwon (25.4 points), Mahmoud Abdul-Rauf (14.1 points), and Shareef Abdur-Rahim (20.2 points)—all were effective despite fasting. "A lot of people talk religion, but very few people live it," Rockets teammate Charles Barkley said. "Hakeem lives it."

MARCH 20, 1997: A *Fort Lauderdale Sun-Sentinel* story on relief ace John Wetteland told how he had been nicknamed "Cosmic Cow" and used alcohol, drugs, and LSD before becoming a born-again Christian. Wetteland, who thanked God on national television when he was named Most Valuable Player of the 1996 World Series, signs his autograph now with a postscript: Psalms 9:10. One of baseball's top closers, he had forty-three saves for the New York Yankees in the regular season and seven more in the post-season before joining the Texas Rangers in 1997.

MARCH 21, 1997: The *Boston Globe* story began, "God is good. God is great. Got a problem with that? Just ask God himself and he'll tell you why it's true. 'No one at any program in the country is better than me,' says Providence College point guard God Shammgod. 'And next season, when I work on my shooting, I'll be even better.' Now, who's going to argue with God? Certainly not Marquette or Duke, a couple of NCAA Tournament teams who ran into and eventually away from Shammgod's Friars last week-end. . . . You don't think [Providence will win]? That would mean you don't believe in God. And right now, for Providence fans, that's heresy."

God Shammgod was named after his father, who wasn't around much when he grew up, so he went by his dad's last name and his mom's maiden name, Wells, and was known as Shammgod Wells while in high school. But when the son reconciled with his father, he resumed using his given name. Providence beat Tennessee-Chattanooga in the NCAA Sweet Sixteen, but God lost his chance to go to the Final Four when, despite his twenty-three points, the Friars lost to eventual national champion Arizona.

MARCH 23, 1997: Newspapers throughout the world ran a photo of figure skater Nicole Bobek kneeling on the ice and praying for her coach, Carlo Fassi, who died of a heart attack March 20. The 1995 U.S. champion was shaken by her coach's death and finished thirteenth in Lausanne, Switzerland, at the world championships, the most important event in figure skating in non-Olympics years. In truth, however, this was more a show of her emotion than her religion, because Bobek is not devout.

MARCH 27, 1997: Former British boxing champion Chris Eubank converted to Islam after knocking out Colombian Camilio Alacon in the fourth round. The thirty-year-old former World Boxing Organization middleweight and super-middleweight champion became a Muslim and changed his name to Hamdan after the technical knockout. He said he had been studying Islamism for two years and planned to start training the United Arab Emirates national boxing team.

MARCH 28, 1997: Minnesota coach Clem Haskins, who directed his basketball team to the NCAA Final Four, said he had put his life in perspective two years before, when he was lying on a hospital bed after a heart attack. "You can't move, and you're thinking this may be the last breath, so you start thinking about what's really important," he said. "God, family, job, in that order."

MARCH 31, 1997: A jury had found O. J. Simpson innocent of murdering Nicole Brown Simpson and Ron Goldman, but a civil trial found otherwise, and most of the public treated the former football hero as a pariah. Simpson invoked religion when he told *Sports Illustrated:* "I can take people's shots. The Bible says I'm going to get it back seven times. The deeper they get into me, the more I get back down the line."

APRIL 4, 1997: Doctors said powerful drugs had reduced the AIDS virus in Magic Johnson's body to undetectable levels, but cautioned he was not cured. Still, Magic suggested something more powerful than drugs had helped. "If it wasn't for the Lord's blessing, I wouldn't be as healthy as I am now," the former NBA superstar said.

APRIL 6, 1997: The *Miami Herald* sports section ran three stories dealing with faith and sports. Two detailed how the Miami Dolphins used Father Leo Armbrust to interview pro prospects because coach Jimmy Johnson thought the team priest had a good feel for judging players' character and intelligence. But not all the pros agreed. Oakland Raiders boss Al Davis snickered when he was introduced to the priest. "Father Leo can help you judge a player's character. You can put all those character guys into the game in the fourth quarter when you're losing," Davis told Johnson. Another story told how Father Leo interviewed Northwestern cornerback Hudhaifa Ismaeli, a Muslim who fasted for Ramadan. The Dolphins drafted him in the seventh round. And the third story followed three members of the Miami Heat into the basketball team's chapel service.

APRIL 9, 1997: After a jury found Cleveland Indians relief ace Jose Mesa innocent of all charges in a rape trial, he said, "God [caused] the jury to do this . . . because they knew I didn't do that stuff." And while his wife said the trial's revelations of Jose's actions hurt their marriage, her faith in God kept her going. "People make mistakes," Mirla Mesa said, "and you have to forgive."

APRIL 13, 1997: Tiger Woods became the first African-American and Asian-American to win the Masters, and media around the world reported on how he broke down racial barriers and influenced people of all colors to play or watch golf. His victory was monumental not just because he won in a record eighteen-under, or by a record twelve strokes over his nearest competitor, or even that he was the youngest winner of golf's greatest event. No, it was monumental because a black man was not allowed to play the Masters until 1975, a few months before Tiger was born, and that man, Charlie Sifford, flew from Pompano Beach, Florida, to Atlanta, then raced to Augusta, Georgia, on Sunday morning to hug and encourage Tiger.

"It means so much," Tiger told a national television audience. "I think of the pioneers, Charlie Sifford and Teddy Rhodes and Lee Elder. If not for them, I wouldn't be here. Coming up the eigh-

teenth fairway, I said a little prayer of thanks to all those guys."
And CBS's Jim Nantz concluded the broadcast, "Destiny's Child
. . . has claimed his first Masters."

MAY 18, 1997: Chris Johnson won her first major tournament in
seventeen years on the women's golf tour when she parred the
second hole of a playoff in the LPGA Championship in Wilming-
ton, Delaware. The thirty-nine-year-old said she struggled with her
career until deciding to modify her swing five years before.

"I could stay out here and have a good tournament now and
then, wait for that time when it's your week and everything goes
your way and God comes down and just says, 'Okay, you're going
to win this week.' And I said no, that's not what I want to do. If
I'm going to be away from my husband and if I'm going to travel
and if I'm going to come out here, it's not worth it to struggle."

JUNE 1, 1997: Utah Jazz owner Larry Miller's team was appearing
in the NBA finals for the first time in franchise history, but he did
not watch game one in person or even on television because he is a
devout Mormon who feels he should observe Sundays with his
family. "It's hard," Miller said. "But at the same time, I feel I have
to set an example and stay true to what I believe."

Utah's Karl Malone, voted the NBA's Most Valuable Player in a
controversial decision, missed two free throws with 9.2 seconds
left, and Chicago's Michael Jordan, revered as a god by millions,
hit a twenty-one-foot jumper at the buzzer to give the Bulls an 84–
82 victory, and once again, God was on Air Jordan's side.

JUNE 8, 1997: Miller again stayed away from game four—until the
final minutes, when he could take it no more. He listened on the
radio as he drove to the Delta Center, and he arrived just in time
to see Malone redeem himself by making two critical free throws
with eighteen seconds left. NBC interviewed him and showed him
celebrating when Jordan missed and Utah's Bryon Russell dunked
to close out a 78–73 Jazz victory. And then Malone told the national audience, "I thank God for giving us the energy we needed
at the end."

JUNE 13, 1997: The Bulls won the NBA title in six games, and Jordan won his fifth championship and fifth NBA finals MVP award in seven years. And, for the rare time on national TV after a big sporting event, no mention was made of God. However, religion was at the forefront of the pregame show, when Chicago's Dennis Rodman apologized for two earlier profanities he used to denigrate Utah's large Mormon population. He claimed he did not realize he was offending an entire religion, but the NBA did not believe his excuse. The league fined the flamboyant forward a record $50,000. Though the Mormon Church offered no comment, the Anti-Defamation League harshly criticized Rodman's vulgar comments, and one Chicago columnist called upon the Bulls to release Rodman immediately.

"I feel sorry for him," Jazz president Frank Layden said. "I pray for him. And I'm not a Mormon, I'm a Catholic. Because I think what we are seeing is nothing but a tragedy in that guy's life. . . . I think someday we'll pick up the paper and we are going to see 'Rodman Dead.' "

JUNE 15, 1997: Ernie Els edged another strong Christian, Tom Lehman, and Scotland's Colin Montgomerie to win his second U.S. Open golf tournament in four years, and when Els was presented the trophy on national television, the South African said, "I thank the Lord. I prayed out there today."

JUNE 18, 1997: The *New York Times* opened its story on boxing's heavyweight champion with Evander Holyfield joining hands in a prayer circle and a simple invocation, "Thanks God for today. Help us make the best of it." Joe Drape wrote, "The prayer and gospel tunes hinted at his reputation as a Holy Puncher who is always eager to thank the Almighty after each bout."

JUNE 20, 1997: When Evander Holyfield appeared on "The Tonight Show," Jay Leno introduced him as a man who has "a Bible in one hand and a cross in the other."

JUNE 25, 1997: Four of the first thirteen selections in the 1997 NBA draft—Tony Battie, Tracy McGrady, Olivier Saint-Jean, and Derek Anderson—thanked God when they were interviewed live on TNT. Tracy McGrady, an unknown high school player until he transferred to Mount Zion Christian Academy, jumped directly to the pros as the league's ninth draft pick and said he would start a $300,000 endowment at the school that helped him turn his life and career around. TNT reported Mount Zion's coach said the team broke its huddle sometimes saying, "Jesus," and other times, "Defense," depending on what it needed more at the time. TNT host Ernie Johnson, Jr., joked that this was the night God would be drafted and if Atlanta drafted guard God Shammgod, the Hawks' lineup would feature God, a Priest (Lauderdale), and a Christian (Laettner). Alas, God was drafted in the second round by the newly renamed Washington Wizards.

JUNE 28, 1997: Christian Evander Holyfield won the heavyweight boxing title when the fight was stopped after Muslim Mike Tyson bit Holyfield on both ears, severing part of one.

JUNE 29, 1997: Holyfield told ESPN he could not have imagined such a bizarre finish, but "It was told to me by the prophets that it would be a short fight and there would be some distractions."

JUNE 30, 1997: In a four-minute public apology, Tyson twice mentioned his faith, saying he would seek help from Allah and the medical community to help him understand why he turned to such viciousness, and saying he sought forgiveness from numerous people, "most of all my God." Later in the week, Holyfield said he already had forgiven Tyson. When the referee was deciding what to do, a trainer told Holyfield to pray, and he did. "How can you pray and not forgive?" he asked. "If he had not told me to pray, I know I would have bit back. I'm glad he told me to pray, or this story would have just been two guys out there biting each other."

JUNE 30, 1997: *Sports Illustrated* featured three stories plus a photo that have to deal with faith in sports: It described how

Holyfield thinks televangelist Benny Hinn helped heal his heart and lead him to his future wife. It showed a photo of Tyson pumping gas into a car with the bumper sticker I ♡ ALLAH. It profiled Tampa Bay quarterback Trent Dilfer, who said, "People think I'm a nut. How many people pray before a big third down? I pray for poise and confidence because I believe that when I'm poised and confident, I can't be stopped." It told how the self-described party animal became a born-again Christian while in college and had been criticized by Buccaneers teammates for not going to bars and socializing with them and becoming more of a leader. And it told how Jerry Reinsdorf, owner of the Chicago Bulls and White Sox, is not particularly religious but carries the Serenity Prayer in his pocket.

And on and on they went, faith and sports interwoven constantly throughout 1996 and 1997. That doesn't figure to change any time soon.

4

True Faith

Mary Joe Fernandez was reared by parents who traveled the world and believed in God, which would prove to be invaluable training for a pro tennis star.

Her father was born in Spain, her mother in Cuba, and she in the Dominican Republic before the family moved to Miami when she was six months old. José Fernandez is a lawyer, Sylvia Fernandez a real estate broker.

José fashioned a tiny tennis racket for Mary Joe when she was just a toddler, hitting balls on the local court while Dad volleyed with big sis. By five, Mary Joe was taking lessons. By six, she was playing in tournaments. By her freshman year in high school, she was a pro.

At fourteen years, eight days, she became the youngest player in history to win a U.S. Open match. Jennifer Capriati was second youngest at fourteen years, five months. But unlike Capriati, who went through a celebrated rebellious period when she dropped out of tennis and turned to drugs, Mary Joe Fernandez stayed grounded because of faith and family.

"My faith was instilled by my parents," the twenty-six-year-old said during a break in yet another tennis tournament. "I was brought up in a Christian home, with good values and morals. Ever since I was little, that's pretty much how I saw my parents live their life.

"As a teenager, I said all the right things: God comes first, then my family, and then everyone else. But in reality, maybe I was putting a little more emphasis on my career instead of placing the importance on my faith. I compete in a world where people are out there telling you to think about yourself first. But I realized that if I really focused on God, everything else would fall into place.

"I was about seventeen when I realized I have to have my own faith, that not just because my parents believe in something, should I believe in it. I wanted to believe in something because I truly believed in it. I was maturing. My faith grew a little stronger. Now, I really realize that everything happens for a reason. There is a plan for everybody's lives. I get my whole strength in everything I do because of my faith. It has helped me get through the really tough times."

She passed up millions and played professionally only part time so she could stay in school. She maintained an A average in high school while earning a Top Ten Women's Tennis Association (WTA) ranking and avoiding trouble.

"I was fortunate," said Fernandez, who has won two gold medals in Olympics doubles, plus more than twenty titles in WTA singles or doubles, including two Grand Slam events. "I went to a private Catholic school. I was very sheltered. I wasn't really influenced by any negative stuff. My parents always traveled with me when I was growing up. But I can imagine for a young person, especially for a young girl, it has to be hard. If you don't have that base or that foundation to lean back on, you can easily be influenced by something else.

"My faith just helps me guard against all problems that come your way. When tough times do come, it helps me handle them better. During those tough times, you grow the most spiritually. I just think there is a reason for everything, and God is behind them. That makes it easier for me to take what comes my way."

And a lot of adversity has come her way. After a blazing start her first full year as a pro, when she ranked fourth in the world in 1990, she has been besieged by injury and illness. First, tendinitis in her shoulder and spasms in her back. Then an ankle sprain and a torn hamstring and torn knee cartilage. And then, after reaching the 1993 French Open final, doctors diagnosed a persistent pain in her side as endometriosis. They prescribed surgery and five weeks of bed rest. The operation and necessary medications have left her susceptible to illness, and she has endured a series of colds, viruses, asthma, and even pneumonia. Each illness derails her tennis stroke and stamina.

"I have had some tough times," Fernandez said. "The surgery in 1993 was a scary moment in my life. I didn't know if I was going to be able to play again. I got through it. I think I became stronger because of it. There were times I asked, 'Why me?' I had to stop and think, 'Maybe it's because I'm stronger and can handle it.'

"It's definitely hard. Just because you have faith and believe in God doesn't mean you're perfect. But I have that comfort. I know there is someone higher to protect me."

Athletes come to faith in many ways. Some are born into it and gradually grow in faith. Others are born into it, forget it, and come back to it. Some find it when they change religions. Others find it for the first time when they bottom out. Still others find it when they reach the top and wonder, "Is that all there is?"

Here, in their own words, unencumbered by anyone else's interpretation, a few of them give their testimony. Maybe they will strike a familiar chord with you:

TUNCH ILKIN, former Pro Bowl lineman for the Pittsburgh Steelers and now a businessman who speaks to groups frequently about faith:

"I was born in Istanbul, Turkey. In 1960, when I was two and a half, we moved to America. In retrospect I see God's hand in our move. I used to think it was my dad's foresight. My dad was a very successful businessman in Turkey. We had a nice house, a live-in maid. He gave up everything to go to Chicago and move into a one-bedroom apartment. I slept on a cot in the kitchen. I remember my mom saying, 'This is America, land of opportunity.'

"I grew up as a Muslim. When I was a kid, my parents shared their perception of God, and it was a God I could not believe in. The God of Islam is a fickle and I would say an unjust God, not like Jesus. You live a good [Muslim] life, you may or may not be rewarded. So I became an atheist or at least an agnostic.

"I lived my life with the philosophy, 'Live fast, die young, leave a good-looking corpse.' That fit my perception of manhood. I wanted to live a full life and experience everything. I was into drugs and alcohol and a lot of things I'm not very proud of. I only mention it because it proves when God gets hold of someone, he can do powerful things.

"I lived like a lot of college students did. I had a negative image of what Christ was all about. My image of Christ was of a weird, meek, goofy, nerdy guy. We'd walk across campus and the evangelists would go, 'You're going to burn in hell!' and we thought, 'If that's a Christian, I want nothing to do with them.'

"One of the first strong Christians I met was a football player who was a big, buffed guy. I wasn't very strong. I thought, 'Maybe I'll learn about lifting from him.' As we worked out together, he told me something I'd never heard before: God so loved the world, he gave his only begotten son. He started laying out God's plan. He said the wages of sin is death, but if you give yourself to God, you get the gift of eternal life. The words struck me: wages. What you work for is death. I heard it and thought, 'That's cool'—but then I wanted to ask, 'Okay, what about the bench press?'

"Two weeks later I was confronted by another Christian at spring break in Daytona Beach. I got back home and told Sharon [then his girlfriend and later his wife] about it. I said, 'This is the second time in two weeks. What's going on here? Do I look like a guy who needs to be saved?' She said, 'Well, Tunch . . .' She was Catholic and she didn't like that I just tuned out everything on religion. I didn't want to hear it.

Led by Reggie White (number 92, right foreground), the victorious Green Bay Packers and the fallen New England Patriots kneel together in prayer after Super Bowl XXXI (January 26, 1997). White is not only one of the greatest defensive ends in NFL history, "The Minister of Defense" is also an ordained Baptist preacher who fervently shares his faith. *(Courtesy AP/Wide World Photos/Elaine Thompson)*

When he was traded by one NFL team and released by another, Tony Dungy did not understand what God's purpose was. Now he says he realizes the moves helped him learn to coach from two Hall of Fame coaches, Pittsburgh's Chuck Noll and San Francisco's Bill Walsh. *(Courtesy the Tampa Bay Buccaneers)*

Gary Carter, an All-Star catcher for the Montreal Expos and New York Mets, believes God helped him get a key hit to spark the Mets to victory in the 1986 World Series. *(Courtesy the Florida Marlins)*

An entire nation watched as New York Yankees relief pitcher John Wetteland prayed on the mound after getting the final out to clinch the 1996 World Series. Two years earlier, Wetteland was pictured in *Sports Illustrated* holding the Holy Bible in one hand and a baseball in the other, and the story profiled his metamorphosis: "hellion, flake, Christian." *(Courtesy AP/Wide World Photos/ Roberto Borea)*

Mary Joe Fernandez, shown here preparing to serve in the French Open, is one of the world's top women's tennis players and remains a devout Catholic. *(Courtesy AP/Wide World Photos/Lionel Cironneau)*

Nancy Lieberman-Cline, one of the greatest players in women's basketball history, grew up in a Jewish family but says she didn't really find fulfillment until she became a Christian. *(Courtesy NBA Photos/©WNBA Enterprises, LLC/Barry Gossage)*

Tom Lehman, the PGA Tour's leading money winner in 1996, shared Bible verses with fellow Christian Steve Jones on the dramatic final holes of the 1996 U.S. Open. *(Copyright Sam Greenwood/PGA Tour)*

Loren Roberts, nicknamed "The Boss of the Moss" for his putting prowess, says he turned his life and career around when he fully committed himself to following Christ in 1983. *(Copyright Sam Greenwood/PGA Tour)*

Even his friends scoffed when Curtis Martin decided to enter pro football a year early. He admits it wasn't logical, but felt God calling him, and he wound up one of the NFL's best running backs. *(Courtesy the New England Patriots)*

Defensive cornerback Terrell Buckley (number 27, with ball) redirected his career when he joined the Miami Dolphins and became a born-again Christian. *(Courtesy the Miami Dolphins/Dave Cross)*

In 1996, Heisman Trophy winner Danny Wuerffel not only led the Florida Gators to a national championship in football, he also led them in prayer, clasping his hands in thanks after every touchdown he scored or threw. The All-American son of an Air Force preacher, he now plays in the NFL for the New Orleans franchise appropriately named the Saints. *(Courtesy AP/Wide World Photos/Dave Martin)*

United States wrestler Kurt Angle prayed on the mat before a worldwide audience after winning the freestyle wrestling gold medal in the 1996 Olympics in Atlanta. *(Courtesy AP/Wide World Photos/Michel Lipchitz)*

Eli Herring (number 76), seen here blocking for a Brigham Young University teammate, was a top offensive lineman with NFL potential. However, after being drafted by the Oakland Raiders, he turned down their seven-figure offer because he believed that playing professional football on Sundays went against his Mormon faith. *(Courtesy Brigham Young University)*

Karim Abdul-Jabbar's Muslim name is almost identical to that of another former UCLA star who wore number 33, basketball great Kareem Abdul-Jabbar. But this Karim was a star running back for UCLA before joining the Miami Dolphins. *(Courtesy the Miami Dolphins/Dave Cross)*

The faith of David Robinson, the 1995 NBA Most Valuable Player and a perennial All-Star, was the focus of a *Sports Illustrated* cover story. *(Courtesy AP/Wide World Photos/HO)*

Hakeem Olajuwon, who led the Houston Rockets to a pair of NBA championships in the 1990s, talks to reporters about Islam and the teachings of the Koran regarding the national anthem. Olajuwon said fellow Muslim and NBA player Mahmoud Abdul-Rauf misunderstood Muslim teachings when for a period of time he refused to stand for the anthem. *(Courtesy AP/Wide World Photos/Pat Sullivan)*

Dave Dravecky tips his hat to the crowd in response to an emotional tribute given on Dave Dravecky Day, the heartwarming occasion when the San Francisco Giants honored Dave, his wife Jan, and their children. *(Courtesy the San Francisco Giants/Garibaldi Studios)*

When Dave Dravecky was forced to retire from professional baseball after his valiant bout with cancer, some of the fans seconded the All-Star pitcher's devotion to his faith with their signs. JESUS LOVES YOU, DAVE, reads one, and another encourages him that WITH GOD'S HELP, DAVE & JAN WILL ALWAYS COME BACK. *(Courtesy the San Francisco Giants/Garibaldi Studios)*

"I was drafted by the Steelers, and my first day at training camp, eight thousand fans showed up. We didn't get eight thousand for homecoming at Indiana State. I'm seeing Jack Lambert and Terry Bradshaw and on and on and on. I'm small and slow and coming from little Indiana State and thinking, 'What am I doing here?' We get in the Oklahoma drill and I'm fifth in line and I start counting to see who I'd be going against. It's Mean Joe Greene! I turned to Craig Wolfley behind me and said, 'Craig, want to go first?' He was like, 'Are you kidding?' I lined up at center, with Bradshaw behind me calling snaps. I was 240 pounds. Joe Greene was 280 pounds and a future Hall of Famer. I hit him as hard as I could and all I felt was an explosion. I was laying on the ground saying, 'I can't see! I'm blind!' when Rocky Bleier helped me up and said, 'You're never going to make it in this league looking out your earhole.'

"I began to learn about football and life from [Steelers tackle] Jon Kolb and [safety] Donnie Shell. They were great, tough football players, but the biggest thing in their lives was not football. I thought Christians were not tough guys. I thought they were wimpy, Milquetoast. But Jon Kolb was the second strongest man in the World's Strongest Man Contest. He won the NFL Strong Man competition. I thought he was the best offensive tackle in the NFL. He was John Wayne, a man's man. Here was a man with spirit. He did not go around acting like a tough guy, but he was as tough as they come.

"They called Donnie Shell the Human Torpedo. He'd hit anything that moved. But he also had a tremendous passion for God. You talk about a guy who would walk the walk, and this guy was it. Then there was Mike Webster, maybe the greatest center in NFL history. I remember we played Oakland and I played well against John Matuszak and I was pretty pleased with myself. Webby asked me, 'If you died right now, where would you spend eternity?'

"I said, 'What?' He said, 'If you died and stood before God, what would you tell him?' I said, 'If God grades on a curve, I'm okay.' He said, 'You're going to spend eternity in one kingdom or another. The question he'll ask you is, "What did you think of my son?" ' I told him I thought Jesus got held up in a con and they put him on a cross.

"My roommate, Craig Wolfley, shared the same faith in God. His dad was dying of leukemia, he was trying to make the Super Bowl champions as a rookie, and yet he was the coolest cucumber. I asked him why and he said, 'My father loves Jesus. He'll be in the presence of God. He'll be the happiest he's ever been. As far as the Steelers, I've just got to do my job and the rest is up to him.'

"I started thinking about what good players these guys were, how tough they were, how at peace they were, and I wanted to be part of this club, I really did. I became a Christian in 1982, but it took a good three years before I was walking the walk. I'd like to tell you my life changed on the spot, but that's a lie. I had a savior, but the works part, I struggled with that. I felt funny about that. I was still drinking, doing drugs, doing things I knew I shouldn't have. I wanted the security of salvation but I wasn't prepared to give up on a life in sin. It was too much fun.

"I found you get chafed trying to ride that fence. As I read my Bible, God started preaching directly to me. Galatians 6:7–8: 'Do not be deceived; God cannot be mocked. A man reaps what he sows. The one who sows to please his sinful nature, from that nature will reap destruction; the one who sows to please the Spirit, from the Spirit will reap enternal life.'

"My parents did not approve of Christianity. They vote people dead in the Muslim faith if they go to Christianity. My dad didn't even want to come to the church when Sharon and I got married. I didn't know how to tell my dad. I thought I could tell my mom. She freaked. She said, 'I've failed as a Muslim.' I thought, 'If my mom feels this way, my dad is going to go ballistic.' So we decided not to tell him.

"They were living in San Francisco by then, and every year for five years, we'd spend two months with them. Every year I thought I'd tell my dad and I chickened out. I spent a lot of time praying about it. Finally, we were watching Dallas and Chicago and I said to myself, 'I'll tell him at halftime.' As we sat there, he said just matter-of-factly, 'How come you never told me you became a Christian?' I said, 'I was afraid.' He said, 'You know me. I'm a little guy. What would I say to you?' I was so relieved, I went upstairs and said, 'Thank you, Lord.' It was the first time I saw God act.

"It wasn't until a few years ago that I realized God's hand was in everything. My dad had to have heart bypass surgery, and I was afraid he might die without going to heaven. I started hammering him with Christianity. Now, both my parents have become saved.

"When I was a young football player, I didn't understand how to walk with God. Football was my god. I thought football would save me. One day I was reading about Norm Evans, who played for the Dolphins when they went 17–0. He was going to the Pro Bowl, one of the best tackles in the game, and he says, 'I stood in front of my locker and everyone was celebrating a championship. I had a flight to go to Hawaii for the Pro Bowl. I should have been so happy. But I felt a terrible emptiness.'

"There's a void that can't be filled with money, with cars, with houses. We live in an if-then country: 'If I get this, then I will be happy.' When Muhammad Ali explained his conversion to *Sports Illustrated,* he said, 'I had the whole world, but it ain't nothing.' In 1981 there was another *Sports Illustrated* story about a Heisman Trophy winner and a Hall of Famer. He said, 'I have everything every man could ask for, but I'm so lonely, I can't stand it.' It was O. J. Simpson.

"Solomon was the richest man in the world, but he said, 'It all leaves me empty,' that striving to possess everything was just chasing the wind. The Steelers had a playbook with one hundred fifty plays. If we mastered them, we could win. God has a playbook, too. It's called the Bible. Everything we need to know is in God's book."

TONY DUNGY, long respected as a brilliant defensive coordinator and one of the NFL's all-time good guys, was named the Tampa Bay Buccaneers' coach in 1996, just the fourth black coach in NFL history.

"My grandfather was a Baptist minister. My dad was a teacher but two of his brothers were Baptist ministers. My mom taught Sunday school and would practice her lessons on us. I can remember all the Bible stories from early, early on, from as young as I can remember. From the time I can remember, four or five years old, I accepted Christ as my savior. I didn't really have all the mental capacity to know what that meant, but I just assumed that's what everyone did because that's what everybody around my sphere did.

"As I got into elementary school and junior high, I was fortunate to be in a two-parent home, a good family, going to good schools. I gravitated toward sports. Faith and sports seemed to intertwine because I was doing well. I had success on the athletic field. I just assumed I was being blessed athletically because I was a Christian.

"I went to the University of Minnesota and for the first time I was out on my own, and now all of a sudden I didn't have to go to church, didn't have to read the Bible and do all the things my parents instilled. Also, football was becoming bigger and bigger for me. From the time I was seventeen to twenty-one, I became stagnant spiritually. I didn't revolt or hang with the wrong crowd or anything. I didn't get into drugs and alcohol. But I didn't continue to grow spiritually.

"I just assumed I'd been good in high school, good in college, and the next step would be the NFL and someone would draft me and I'd go on. When I didn't get drafted, I was really shocked and discouraged. That was my first real experience with athletic failure. I remember thinking about what I could do and praying about it.

"I had a chance to go to Pittsburgh or a couple of other NFL teams as a free agent, or a chance to go to Montreal, where Marv Levy was head coach and general manager. They were going to play me at quarterback and give me a signing bonus of maybe $30,000 or $40,000, huge money at that time. Tom Moore, one of my college coaches, had joined the Steelers and talked to Chuck Noll about me. They offered me a standard free agent deal, not a lot of money, no guarantee of making the team.

"I can remember praying about it. To this day, there was no logical reason to go there. They were going to move me to a different position for a lot less money. Everybody I talked to felt there was no way I was going to make the team because the Steelers were loaded at all the positions I could play. [Dungy was a record-setting college quarterback but his arm was marginal by pro standards, and Terry Bradshaw already had led the Steelers to two of their four Super Bowl victories in the 1970s.] They didn't need a quarterback or receivers. The four starting defensive backs had all been to the Pro Bowl the year before and Donnie Shell and Jimmy Allen were backups. They were loaded everywhere.

"Something I can't explain told me that was the best place to go. Maybe it was competitiveness; they were the best in the business and I wanted to go to the best. Maybe it was because I knew Tom and felt I'd get a fair chance, I don't know. I still can't explain it. I just know that's where I wanted to go.

"When I got there, they moved me to defensive back. I had never played defense at all in any part of my career. I got roomed with Donnie Shell and stayed with him through training camp and preseason. I got to be Donnie's shadow. That's what turned me around spiritually. Donnie was very serious about his faith, as were a lot of guys on the team. Donnie took me to Bible studies, took me to chapel. That's when I started growing again as a Christian. As I look back, I just know it wasn't just a coincidence I went there. My growth and maturity as a Christian really started there in Pittsburgh in 1977.

"In college, the football team had meetings on Sundays and I went to church very, very occasionally. You talk to some people and it's a tragedy or some event that brings them around, but I've never had anything happen so negative that I felt, 'There can't be a God or this wouldn't happen.' Not at all. But my identity was more as the quarterback and athlete than it was as a Christian. Now, even though I'm head coach of the Buccaneers, to people who know me, my identity is really as a Christian, as a parent, as a father and husband, and then as a football coach."

DAVID ROBINSON, the 1995 NBA Most Valuable Player and an All-Star all but once since joining the San Antonio Spurs in 1989:

"As children, we went to church because Mom said we had to. I had a kind of faith, but it was never an important issue for me. It was just there. Did it matter in my life? Not really. I knew the stories about Jesus, but they were just like fairy tales. To a lot of kids, they're just neat stories, the same kind of stories you read in the history books about George Washington or different battles. Do they matter or affect what you do tomorrow? No. That's the attitude I had for the longest time. Faith was never a big part of my life (until I was born again in 1991). When I went to the Naval Academy and didn't *have* to go to church, I stopped going. I'd go on occasion.

"Everyone has his own moment when he comes face to face with God. For me there was one dramatic episode. On June 8, 1991, a minister came from Austin to San Antonio. He was there with a group called Champions for Christ. He and I talked, and he asked me some questions. It was obvious the Lord had sent him to me because it was the first time I was really affected by what someone said about God. I started to think, 'Where am I going? What am I doing? Who am I as a man? What makes me any different than the next guy?' In all honesty, I knew nothing really makes me different than the next guy. That was the scary thing. That very day, I was saved. I committed myself to Him that day. The Lord showed me that without him, I had nothing. That was a scary thought. All the money, everything I had—without him, I had nothing.

"That very day I was saved. Now serving the Lord is the central point of everything I do."

GARY CARTER, a perennial All-Star and probably a future Hall of Fame catcher, now a broadcaster:

"I lost my mother at an early age. She died of leukemia when I was twelve. She was thirty-seven. We were a churchgoing family. I knew about Jesus, I knew about God, but I didn't know it to the extent of when I signed professionally. In my first big-league training camp, in Daytona Beach, my roommate was John Boccabella [then a veteran Montreal Expos catcher]. We talked about different things, about my mother's death, about life in general. He started sharing the gospel with me. I committed myself to God that same spring, March 22, 1973.

"I just felt that's what I needed to do: to make a commitment, to devote my life to God. My faith has always been there, but it just grew stronger, knowing God on a personal basis. I feel fortunate I got my start early, that I had a chance to be able to know Jesus on a personal basis.

"That's what I've given my heart to. That's what I have grown in my life. Not only to become a father, a better ballplayer, a better husband, everything about being a Christian is what I've learned. And each year I've learned something more. My faith has always been there. I knew that God had blessed me with the ability to play baseball, and then it was a matter of going out there and letting my abilities flow.

"To be able to play eighteen years, I look back with no regrets. I was able to accomplish everything that he wanted me to. I feel very blessed to have a wonderful family. Everything that happens, especially the glories that come with it, will go to him."

ANDRE DAWSON, another perennial All-Star and possible Hall of Fame outfielder, played twenty-one years before retiring in 1996.

"I've had faith from my early childhood, based on the early teachings from my grandmother, who was a churchgoer. She instilled in me how I should believe in myself, in my blessings, in my talent, in my ability, and let faith be my guide. To this day, I still pray, and I'm thankful for all I've accomplished.

"I've been through all types of adversity, with the injuries to my knees, with people predicting how long and how far I could go in the game. You have to really dig within, reach back, and block out all the negatives. Without faith, adversity can make you or break you. It's very easy to get off track. People have a tendency to pull at you from all different angles.

"It's very easy to make a lot of money and forget your purpose. There are people in this game who don't get caught up in their fame, in who they are, and how much money they make. Giving all the credit to God is a constant focus for them. And then there are players who are unable to make the adjustments—and it's ruined their careers."

LOREN ROBERTS, who endured qualifying school five times before finally making the PGA Tour for good and emerging as a perennial contender:

"I came from a very moral home, but it was not a born-again Christian home. I believed in God and when you look back at that period in history, at our society in general in the U.S., religion played a bigger part in family life. Americans lived a little more of a morally right life, whether they were Christians or not. Church was a part of family life. That's what's disappeared in society today.

"I went to church, I participated in after-school programs, in Sunday school, in activities of the church, in Bible studies, and I believed the stories. But it was like taking a course in college. I thought it was true, but I didn't know how to apply it to my life. In 1983, I went to Bible study a couple of times and liked some golfers who were there. It was a horrible year for my golf game.

"I missed the cut at the Milwaukee Open, and without question, that tournament was my lowest point professionally. Making golf my god was putting so much pressure on me. If you derive all your significance from playing, sometimes you're going to feel lousy. That's when I decided to ask Jesus Christ into my life, to have a personal relationship with him. I was nearing the end of my second year on tour. I was having no success. I was frustrated with golf and the way my life was going.

"I asked myself, 'What do I want out of life?' The real key question I asked myself was, 'If I were to die today, what would become of me?' Obviously, golf wouldn't do anything for me. Anything I owned wouldn't do anything for me. After being so focused on my sport, going through long periods of struggle, I realized, 'Gosh, there's got to be more to life than struggling at work and all these ups and downs.' The number one thing in my life then was golf. My number one thing now is love of God, then family, then golf. If you don't have things in perspective, you can get off track.

"What convinced me that my faith in Christ would be satisfying and fulfilling? Because I realized everything else is temporal—the money, the big cars, the fancy homes. You choose how you want your life to go. You look at it and say, 'I have a soul and I'm going to go to heaven or hell.' As a Christian, you'll have eternal life. Everything else this life offers is temporal. You can't take a big house with you. Those things only give temporary satisfaction anyway."

MICHAEL CHANG, the youngest male ever to win the French Open in 1989 and the world's second-ranked tennis player in 1996:

"I became a Christian in 1988. At fifteen years of age, I was doing a lot of searching. I think at that particular age, at least for me, you're wondering about things like the meaning of life and you're really trying to find yourself. I just had a lot of questions.

"My grandparents had given me a Bible and they wanted me to read it every day. On this one particular evening, I didn't have anything else to do so I decided to take a good look at my Bible and see what it had to say. I looked at the index in the back and found that it covered all these different subjects. So I looked up subjects like friendship and love and found the Bible to be very true, very pure, in a way in which I wanted to live my life. From then on, I began reading about the Lord's life and his love for all people. Eventually, I accepted him as my Lord and Savior.

"I've been fortunate in that I became a Christian the first year I was on the tour. Before all the fame and money, the Lord was there, teaching me his way first. The wonderful thing is that I look back at my life and I can see that even when I wasn't a Christian, he was looking out for me. Now I'm just constantly trying to surrender myself to the Lord, so the Holy Spirit can do his work through me.

"I do a Bible study first thing in the morning and also at night. Throughout the day, I'll pray, because the Lord is always there. He teaches me a lot through circumstances in my life, whether it's through a tennis match or some other thing that's going on. Life will have its ups and downs, but regardless of what's happening in our lives, if we're focusing on him, we'll have the joy that he gives us."

BRUCE SMITH, the 1996 NFL Defensive Player of the Year and second in NFL history in sacks:

"My father read the Bible each and every day. My mother was a God-fearing woman. I had a praying grandmother. Religion was always part of my life. It's the one rule we had: You could play ball all you wanted, but on Sundays you were going to make time for the Lord.

"I still pray each and every night. I've been a Christian for a lot of years. That doesn't mean you go without sin. We sin each day. But by the grace of God, we are cleansed. We try not to repeat the same sin all over.

"God is blessing me right now. It's amazing because there are a lot of times I feel I shouldn't be blessed, but he continues to bless us and make a way for us."

TERRELL BUCKLEY, a fine cornerback for the Miami Dolphins:

"When I was growing up, my family went to church on Sundays, and that's basically all we did. I went to college and started with the Fellowship of Christian Athletes and got a little more interested. Then I arrived in the pros and met Reggie White in Green Bay. He was an ordained minister, and I could see his ways. We talked a lot, but we didn't get into intimate conversations. He'd go home to his wife and kids. I stayed in a hotel my rookie year. I lived close by the stadium so I could get in and get out. I wasn't happy.

"People tell you when you've got all that money you should be happy. You go out and party, drive a nice car, have a nice house, do the things the world tells you should make you happy. I had the money, the cars, the house—and I was still empty. I felt that was not the way it's supposed to be.

"When I became a stronger Christian in 1996, it changed my life around. It gave me unbelievable courage. I already had confidence, but when you know you've got the Lord on your side and you're doing everything he wants you to do, that's the ultimate confidence.

"I remember my third year in Green Bay, when I was down, we were playing Detroit in the playoffs and the other players were pumping the crowd up, waving their hands to the crowd, and I just stood there with my arms folded. After I became a Christian I caught myself waving my arms to the crowd and I stopped and thought, 'Hold up! You haven't done that in years! Whatcha doing?' I just started feeling good. Then I broke up a pass at the end of the game to win it and I went crazy. That's what the Lord has done for me. He brings the enthusiasm out in me.

"Now, even when people talk bad about me, I'm happy inside. Now, it's like I'm in hog heaven. I walk around with a smile on my face all day."

The restaurant waitress giddily volunteered to play with Buckley's little girl while we talked over lunch about his enhanced faith. She gave eighteen-month-old Sherrell Buckley balloons and crayons, the manager picked up the check, and "T-Buck" just kept flashing that mega-watt smile of his. I spent a lot of time getting to know Buckley while writing a book on the Dolphins' 1996 season, and his attitude adjustment was no act. This was a genuinely happy, committed Christian.

He had taken a pay cut and yet felt more fulfilled than ever. He was so happy with his teammates, coaches, and team prospects, he spent the 1996 off season recruiting several former teammates to join him with the Dolphins. He wasn't perfect—as a player he did not win every match-up and as a person he worried too much about outsiders' criticism—but his play was excellent and his faith was true.

True faith does not pray to God only in times of crisis. It does not thank Jesus only in victory. True faith does not appear just for show when the media or teammates are around. True faith does not just talk the talk, it walks the walk. True faith puts God, family, and career in the proper priorities in everyday life. True faith knows how to handle success and adversity, celebrity and money, the challenges of life and sports. True faith does not connote perfection, but merely striving to be the best person you can be. The coming chapters will address these issues.

But just as athletes develop their faith for different reasons, just as they use faith to deal with different issues, so too do they develop different answers and strengths of conviction.

5

False Faith

While imprisoned for three years on a rape conviction, heavyweight champion Mike Tyson became a Muslim, and he has spent time praying and talking about his religious awakening ever since.

But he leaves skeptics wondering if he really found peace with Allah by committing himself to the five basic beliefs and practices of Islam—or if he turned to religion to protect himself from other inmates and uses it now as a publicity ploy.

He was charged with sexually assaulting a woman after hours in a nightclub. He spoke of giving up all his worldly possessions at the same time that he splurged on luxury homes and cars. He knew his faith discourages boasting, but he bragged about the money he could make and the damage his punches could inflict. One day he would talk about the calming influence of religion, and the next he would say he was "dealing with some situations" and would not be surprised to find himself back in prison. He said his faith gave him peace, and then he said, "In thirty years of life I have never been happy."

He denied the rape charges, showed no remorse toward his victim, and even allowed his handlers to say he would "rape" his next opponent, Evander Holyfield. That drew a scathing reply from *USA Today*'s John Saraceno: "Mike Tyson, who professes to be a pious Muslim, likes it when his bought-and-paid-for cronies do his dirty work. He walks like the champion of heavyweight hypocrisy." And that was *before* he savagely bit Evander Holyfield's ears and earned universal condemnation.

Similarly, people have questioned the conversion of Cassius Clay. When he became Muhammad Ali and joined the separatist Black Muslims in 1964, some say it was as much out of hate of whites as it was love of Islam. "He was a hateful guy," said Ferdie Pacheco, his former fight doctor.

"Ali's religion was a sham to me," Kareem Abdul-Jabbar wrote in *Giant Steps*. "The so-called Black Muslims weren't Muslims at all but had stolen a few cultural identifications, and the name, and tacked them onto a racist demagoguery. There was then, and continues to be, a great public confusion between Islam and the Black Muslim. . . . They are not to be confused. Muhammad Ali became a Black Muslim. I am a Muslim."

In that 1985 Bantam Books autobiography, Abdul-Jabbar admitted he was no saint either. He slept with many women, sometimes while married, drank alcohol, snorted cocaine and got into an auto accident, and spent his first thirty years angry at life, flashing a bad temper often and a smile rarely.

Please do not misconstrue. This is not meant to single out Muslims. The demands of their faith are rigid, beginning with prayer five times a day, and yet many Muslim athletes meet the demands daily.

Hypocrites exist in every faith and every profession, and Christian athletes are no different. "Some of the biggest hypocrites in the world are from the Christian community, but that's the way it is in all walks of life," said Loren Roberts, a professional golfer and Christian.

Bill McCartney, then Colorado's football coach, warned his

players he would peer into their bedrooms to make sure they were sleeping alone. If he caught anybody living with a woman, retribution would be quick. Parents would be called. Unless they consented, the player would be punished.

"Every time he said that, it just kind of shocked me," former Colorado linebacker Chad Brown told the *Pittsburgh Post-Gazette*. "He wanted so much control over us, but he didn't have control over his own family."

McCartney's team knew the coach's daughter, Kristyn, was intimate with certain Colorado players. She gave birth out of wedlock to two children fathered by Colorado players Sal Aunese and Shannon Clavelle. Both distanced themselves from Kristyn. Aunese died of stomach cancer in 1989.

Editors of the Denver papers chose not to print the explosive Aunese story until an alternative tabloid revealed the story with a cover headlined "That Sinning Season: CU Coach Bill McCartney Keeps the Faith—and Gets a Grandson Fathered by His Star Quarterback." The story so infuriated McCartney that in his autobiography, *From Ashes to Glory*, he told of wanting to kill the writer. And when a *Sports Illustrated* story detailed the arrest of twenty-four players in a three-year span, McCartney said he seethed for six weeks. But he called the writer and asked his forgiveness for the anger he had in his heart. And while he was incensed that Aunese had abandoned Kristyn, he led Aunese to become a Christian before he died, so that he might have eternal life.

McCartney abruptly quit coaching after the 1994 season to devote himself to his faith, his family, and his Christian men's movement called Promise Keepers. Perhaps Promise Keepers could help other men avoid the mistakes he had made with his family.

"My obsession with winning at football caused me to often neglect the important things in my life—my wife, my kids, and my relationship with God," he wrote. "I wasn't always there when my kids needed me. I've caused a lot of undue pain and suffering. When my daughter needed a father who would really invest himself in her life, I was off instead chasing another bowl game. While my sons were looking for a role model, I was busy playing father to a bunch of college ball players. While my wife sat at home reading books, wishing for a husband who would be there for her, I was at the stadium bragging to the press about our latest victory."

McCartney said it was time to acknowledge his errors and begin to correct them. And that could be a valuable lesson for us all. Isn't that the measure of a man: to admit his failings and strive to become the best person possible?

Since his angry days, Ali has done great things for civil rights. Even today, his mind and body slowed by debilitating illness, he still speaks out. He wrote a book called *Healing: A Journal of Tolerance and Understanding,* and he spread the message at high schools, emphasizing we must love all peoples, no matter their race or religion. One morning, he appeared at a high school in Harlem, the notorious black ghetto. That afternoon he appeared at another high school in Mamaroneck, a white suburb, where twice in the past two years anti-Semitic graffiti had been sprayed on the homes of Jewish families, the latter during Rosh Hashanah.

And Mike Tyson seems at least to be trying to change his evil ways. Hakeem Olajuwon, a Muslim and the star center for the Houston Rockets, was skeptical when he visited Tyson in prison. But he said he could see Tyson loved the religion. He said Tyson told him he realized he had done all the things that Islam prohibits, and was trying to change. He told Tyson to share his faith publicly and Tyson cried. Tyson told him his role model was Amza, a terrifying fighter for evil who converted to Islam and brought a horde of new believers with him. Olajuwon told him he could be a warrior in the ring but must understand that Allah gave him the victory, that he must learn to mix two sometimes contrasting qualities: toughness and humility.

But Olajuwon had no patience with three Rockets teammates who "wasted" their lives on drugs and "dishonored" themselves; with the Nation of Islam and what he too viewed as a policy of racial division and isolation; or with the many selfish Muslims he has found. He also is not afraid to admit he has made mistakes. Before recommitting to his faith, Olajuwon lived with his girlfriend for four years and got her pregnant. He considered her his wife, but when he wouldn't make it official, she left him in 1988.

"Morally we should not have been living together or had a child if we weren't married," he wrote in his 1996 autobiography.

When the NBA suspended Mahmoud Abdul-Rauf for refusing to stand for the national anthem, the American Civil Liberties Union and the NBA Players Association offered legal assistance. But Islamic experts and the league's most prominent Muslim said the Koran says nothing of the issue. Olajuwon observed that the Koran teaches respect for the customs and traditions of a Muslim's country. "It's tough for me to understand his position, but in general, the Muslim teaching is to obey and respect. To be a good Muslim is to be a good citizen," he said.

"Muslims are supposed to be proud of their country," seconded Karim Abdul-Jabbar of the Miami Dolphins. "They're supposed to be patriots. They're supposed to be the best patriots. For me to denounce my country is almost like double-crossing all those who fought for my country. Sixteen African-Americans won the Congressional Medal of Honor [fighting in the Civil War]. For me to say this is not my country is like turning my back on them, like walking on their grave. That's disrespectful.

"I don't know Abdul-Rauf's intentions, but when I stand for the national anthem, I imagine all those who fought, all those who slaved, and all the blood my descendants gave to build this country up. You love where the Creator puts you. Not only that, our prophet has told us to be patriots. It's my country. It's a beautiful country."

Abdul-Rauf said he could not worship any object but his God. The Bible also warns Christians not to worship false gods. But American society today tends to worship athletes, to make them into role models and false gods when in reality they are less than perfect, simply blessed with the ability to slug a baseball or another human being or dribble a basketball or run with a football or baton.

We hold them to a higher standard and are quick to label them as hypocrites when, inevitably, they fail.

"In the media and in society in general, when they hear the 'Christian' label, they think, 'Oh, that guy has to be perfect,' and that's not the way it is," Loren Roberts said. "We're not perfect.

It's easy to point the finger when a Christian stumbles. The hypocrites turn people off.

"I can understand some of their feelings. When you come out publicly with your faith, because we are imperfect, it's easy for someone else to say, 'That's great for him to say when he's winning, but what's he say when he loses?' That's why my faith is so important. I know I cannot do and say the right thing every minute. I need Jesus Christ, who paid the penalty for my sins, to cover me for those times.

"There's a certain maturity in your faith that comes through time. For me, consistency is the name of the game. Consistency is the key to my walk. Can you back up what you say? Your faith is growing, a continual progression. I don't think you get there until you die and meet your maker. It's like the game of golf. You never perfect it. You'll never shoot eighteen. You'll never be perfect.

"We all fall off the line sometimes. It's the old line: Christians aren't perfect. They're just forgiven."

Not by the general populace, however. Even the most devout Christian athletes are subject to ridicule. When *Sports Illustrated* lavished ten pages of praise upon David Robinson for his fight against the seven deadly sins, the magazine received tons of mail, and it was not all positive.

"I'm getting fed up with the 'born again' Christian athletes," wrote Colonel Francis R. Lewis, a retired U.S. Army chaplain from Glen Cove, New York. "David Robinson believes that God wants him to be the best basketball player he can be. Nonsense. It's possible that God wants him to take a vow of poverty and quit basketball. He says that money doesn't matter to him, and yet he didn't turn down the highest salary in the league. He uses Jesus and God to rubber-stamp ideas that are anathema to Christianity. His theology about AIDS and fires and floods is abominable. Give us a break, *SI*. Jesus would be aghast at how we use his name to bless our sports contests. That is sheer paganism."

And Peter Fogo of Pasadena, Texas, wrote in another letter that *Sports Illustrated* published: "Have you taken leave of your senses? You devote a cover and ten pages to a robotic dunce who not only displays the most distasteful form of human pretension—

self-righteousness in the guise of devotion—but also has the nerve to publicly state that he plays basketball to honor God, not for the fans who pay his enormous salary. Nothing even remotely resembling an intelligent comment on the nature of faith or spirituality came out of Robinson's mouth."

They ripped Robinson, even though, by all accounts, he has lived an exemplary life. It is not easy to be faithful to your religion when you're rich and famous and beautiful women and drugs and alcohol and all sorts of temptations are yours for the asking.

Many are the athletes who call themselves Christians but do not back it up in real life, who taint the image of the true Christian athletes. Some use faith as a lucky charm, to help them fit in the crowd. Others use religion for excuses and manipulation—saying "The Devil is making me do it" or "It is God's will that we lost"— when they do not really believe. Some profess to be Christians but do not live their words.

Cheating on spouses is an accepted part of the macho world of pro sports. So is fathering children outside of marriage. For instance, Evander Holyfield had three children with his first wife and three more with three separate women he did not marry. And many athletes use drugs that are against the law (such as cocaine) or against league rules (such as steroids and human growth hormone).

Former Redskins coach Joe Gibbs said he drank, cheated in a few classes, got in fights in college, and put his obsession with football ahead of faith and family. He said he believed in God but was not committed to Jesus Christ until 1972.

Another Super Bowl coach, the legendary Vince Lombardi, "was such an odd contradiction," Bill Curry and George Plimpton wrote in their book, *One More July*. "He was very profane, yet he went to church every day; he was a daily celebrant, Catholic, very devout. He considered the priesthood at one point. Bart Starr said, 'When I heard about this man taking over the team in 1959, I could hardly wait to meet a man that went to church every day.' Then he went on to say, 'I worked for him for two weeks and then I realized this man *needs* to go to church every day."

Former Olympic gold-medal winner Joe DeLoach said he called

himself a Christian but for years he was really a "Hollywood Christian . . . a celebrity who would make bold public statements about the Lord but have no foundation or commitment."

Dolphins cornerback Terrell Buckley said he believed he was a Christian most of his life but he did not really begin to live the life until he was born again in 1996.

"I was pretending," Buckley said. "I might not have been a hypocrite because, at that time, I had not been baptized [as an adult] or accepted the Lord and had not read the Word and tried to make the Word true. I wasn't a hypocrite as much as I put a mask on, acting like this but doing other things. I wasn't totally wild or out of control.

"I was not a bad person. Probably the worst thing I did involved women. I'd have three, four, five girlfriends at one time. If they didn't ask, I didn't tell about the others. I always told them I didn't want girlfriends. That gave me the right to go date other girls. I look back on that, hurting people, and I feel bad. A couple of those girls I've seen and I've apologized to. Now I see I was wrong, see how it affected their lives. I told them, 'I'm sorry, I thought I was being honest and wasn't doing anything wrong, but I really was.' "

Now, Buckley is married, with "a lovely wife and a lovely daughter," and a new commitment to life.

"I was watching a show on a Christian station the other day about Jesus of Nazareth," he said. "When they were about to stone the adulterous lady to death, they asked Jesus what they should do. He told them, 'He who is without sin, cast the first stone.' And they threw down their rocks. He was the only one without sin. He expected us to read his Word and make his Word truthful, to follow it, but he also understood we are human. We're trying to make ourselves not really from this world, to not follow in the footsteps of man but to try to be perfect. It's tough, but that's what I'm striving for."

Athletic figures such as McCartney, Robinson, baseball's Mark Dewey, and football's Reggie White are not very forgiving of same-sex relationships. "Homosexuality! The Bible says in Romans it's an abomination. God created Adam and Eve, not Adam and Steve," railed White, whose Southern Baptists voted to boycott Disney in 1997 because of its alleged bias in favor of gay lifestyles.

But Nancy Lieberman-Cline, a Christian with a husband and son and also a famed gay friend, former tennis star Martina Navratilova, does not think Christians should throw stones. "We can all point fingers; we're really good at that," said Lieberman-Cline, who helped Navratilova with her conditioning. "I see Christians who point at gay people, but they're sinning in another manner. I mean, who are we to be that self-righteous that we should tell people what to do? There are a multitude of sins. As God sees it, that [homosexuality] is one of them. But I see 'Convenient Christians' all the time. You can talk the talk, but you've got to walk the walk. It's not that difficult to put on a front and tell people, 'I'm a Christian.' I might be able to fool you, but I have to deal with God eventually. We all live in a glass house. God sees what we do."

Lesbianism has been less an issue in basketball than in tennis and golf. Like Lieberman-Cline, Chris Stevens does not berate gays in her sport. "I can't criticize because we all want to be loved," said Stevens, who does not exclude anyone interested in Jesus Christ from her LPGA Christian fellowship. "As people, no matter if we're gay or straight, we all long to be loved, to be significant. We all look for ways to meet that need. For me, that's where the gospel is important and freeing. God does not change us in order to love us, but loves us in order to bring the changes in our lives to make us healthy and whole. Those life choices are evident in all career paths; it's not just on the LPGA Tour."

It is obvious but probably bears repeating: athletes might be famous, and they might strive to be pious, but they still are human. They still have flaws.

6

Finding Fellowship

Three Rivers Stadium, home of the Pittsburgh Steelers and Pirates, is jammed with men. They are cheering. They are chanting. They are doing the Wave.

But they are not here for a game. Unless you call life a game. They are here for a conference of the Promise Keepers, the evangelical Christian men's group launched by former University of Colorado football coach Bill McCartney.

Promise Keepers is one of many outlets for athletes—and now, nonathletes alike—to find faith and fellowship. Sports figures have found support from many organizations, including the Fellowship of Christian Athletes, Champions for Christ, Sports Outreach America, Professional Athletes Outreach, Athletes in Action, plus their team- or sport-specific ministries or Bible studies. But none has spread from sports to the general public like McCartney's organization.

Promise Keepers was born in March 1990 when McCartney, a

few months after sweeping the national Coach of the Year awards, was driving to an FCA meeting with the state FCA director. McCartney asked Dave Wardell what he'd do if he could do anything in life. Wardell said he'd disciple men one on one.

Then Wardell asked McCartney the same question, and the coach's answer surprised him. "More than anything," McCartney said, "I want to see men come together in great numbers in the name of Jesus. I can see stadiums full of men. I see a vision of God moving men."

McCartney circled his finger in the air. Wardell asked what that meant. "We could turn this thing around," the coach replied. Wardell, puzzled, thought, "Turn the car around at eleven at night?" And McCartney said, "The United States of America."

They prayed about their shared vision, and soon they had seventy men involved. The next summer, 4,200 men gathered in Boulder, Colorado, for Promise Keepers' first conference. Folsom Stadium drew 22,500 men the next summer, a capacity crowd of 50,000 the year after. By 1994, 278,600 men came to seven conferences. Their numbers mushroomed to 727,342 in 1995 and 1.1 million in 1996. Their budget exceeds $100 million. Their political clout grows.

And so here we are in Pittsburgh, 44,309 men strong. It is mid-July, baseball season, except the Pirates do not draw this many men for two, sometimes three games. They have come by the carload and busload from Pennsylvania and every nearby state. They have come not for a game but for God.

It's Friday night, the beginning of a two-day convention. The male bonding begins slowly, hesitantly. Men are accustomed to sharing in the fraternity of sports here. They are not used to sharing feelings, especially feelings about God.

Just before 6 P.M., one section stands and begins a chant:

WE LOVE JESUS,
YES WE DO!
WE LOVE JESUS,
HOW 'BOUT YOU?

They turn and point to the next section, hoping to get the Wave started . . . and nothing happens. They try again, and finally the two adjoining sections halfheartedly join in. They try a third time, and three, then four sections of the stadium join in. Soon, men spanning the area from third base to first base are chanting, and the chant begins to gain momentum. It is sweeping the stadium, and yes, it is going in waves, clear around the stadium.

Now a guy in a red shirt and a baseball cap stands on top of the Pirates' dugout and leads the section in a spelling contest.

> J! E! S! U! S!
> What's that say?
> JESUS!
> Again?
> JESUS!
> One more time!
> JESUS!

At six-thirty, as men are still trickling into the stadium, the music begins, and at the prompting of the emcee, nearly 40,000 men stand and clap and sing, "How Great Thou Art." I leave the neutrality of the press box and walk through the stands and sit among the participants to glean more from their experiences. All around me, they stand and cheer as loudly as they do for any Steelers touchdown. Only now they scream for Jesus. Many wear Promise Keepers baseball hats, or Promise Keepers T-shirts with the 1996 theme, "Break Down the Walls." They carry paperback New Testaments. One man carries a cellular phone and wears a T-shirt that reads, "Christ is coming. Look busy."

A man leads his wheelchair-bound son to an aisle seat, helps the boy sip from a drink, unwraps a hot dog, sprinkles condiments on it, and holds it for the frail, crippled son to eat. The son's plight and the father's love move us all, and several men leave their seats and walk down the aisle, lean over, and tell father and son how happy they are to see them there, and offer help and encouragement.

Then Dr. Tony Evans, co-founder and senior pastor of the three thousand-member Oak Cliff Bible Fellowship and chaplain of the

NBA's Dallas Mavericks, bounds onto the stage and opens with the universal Guy bonding technique: he talks about sports. Only he is from Dallas, and we are in Pittsburgh, and he razzes us about Dallas beating Pittsburgh in the Super Bowl six months previous.

We boo good-naturedly. The sports site and sports theme relaxes the men, makes the listeners more receptive to his message. Evans tells the stories of Solomon, how Solomon owned houses and gardens and parks and gold and silver, and found riches did not fulfill him. Solomon had 700 wives and 300 concubines, but even they did not fulfill him. Solomon sought fulfillment in knowledge and became the wisest man who ever lived, only to realize the sage and the fool meet the same fate.

Evans tells us, "Solomon raised the question, 'Is this all there is? There's got to be more to my life than wealth and pleasure and knowledge.' His conclusion was, everything was vanity, like trying to grab the wind. We grab after fame or money or significance. Solomon raised the question: Why break your neck to live when you're only living to die? Some of you ask the same question: Is this all there is? These thoughts terrify you because you're a successful businessman, but vanity of vanities, what's it all about? He said you cannot find the meaning of life through life. He came to see only in a dynamic relationship with God would he understand what life is all about."

His message connects. I look around and see some men nodding, others looking to heaven, others with eyes closed, reflecting, giving real thought to their lives. Evans's voice grows more passionate and he says only Jesus Christ offers us fulfilling life and eternal life. "You're saying, 'I live a good life. I'm not a bad guy.' Listen, unless you're perfect, you're not good enough! You've got to be as good as God to be accepted by God. The problem is, nobody qualifies. Enter Jesus Christ. He says, 'I have come to give you life.' You can't work for it. You can't earn it. It's not by righteousness but by his mercy. If you stop trying to be your own savior, if you let Jesus save you, he will. Gentlemen, it's time to come home."

And Evans asks the men to pray with him, to ask the Lord to forgive them, to acknowledge Jesus Christ died for their sins, and to tell God they are coming home to him. Evans tells all who are committing themselves for the first time, or recommitting, to come down to the stage, and men by the hundreds rise from their seats, walk down the aisles and across the turf and toward the stage.

And they do. Fathers and sons, arms on each other's shoulders. Men in their sixties and young men in their teens. Men with crew cuts and shoulder-length hair. Men with gray hair and no hair. Men with baseball hats and cowboy hats. Men, supposedly so gruff and tough, let the tears run down their faces, and for once they are not afraid to share their emotions. A sea of 985 men, stretching nearly from one baseball foul line to the other, and probably twenty yards deep, fill the area in front of the stage. They receive orange stickers from volunteers and a standing ovation from their new brethren.

The moment is electric. The speech, the scene, and a closing prayer tug at every heart. Emotionally drained, 44,309 men need to exhale. They take a break, and after Christian music, after a review of the seven promises of a Promise Keeper, they stand as one when McCartney is introduced.

The ex-coach says his dad grew up here, and in provincial Pittsburgh that's one way to connect with his audience. He gives them a little sports challenge, to stay on the edge of their seats, and they do. And then he launches into a sports story, an even better way to connect.

"In 1908," McCartney says, "the football rulebook was limited, to say the least. As a matter of fact, history records a game played between Carlisle and Syracuse. The game was in Carlisle. The Carlisle Indians came out in game jerseys with a patch right down where they carried the football. The patch was the exact size and color of a football. Their offense had some deception to it, where they would fake the ball to a couple of guys, and Syracuse did not know who to tackle. Syracuse thought *everybody* had the ball. So sure enough, Carlisle ran up and down the field against Syracuse and scored a lopsided victory when the game was predicted to be very close.

"Well, the next week, Carlisle went on the road to play the Crimson Red of Harvard. Now, at that time, there was one other rule: the home team would provide the game ball. So the night before the game, the two coaches met, exchanged pleasantries, and the coach of Harvard asked the Carlisle coach, 'Are you going to wear the same jerseys you wore last week?' The Carlisle coach got defensive and said, 'Why not? It's within the rules. We didn't do anything wrong. Sure, we're gonna wear them again.' Well, the next day, Harvard came out in crimson red—and the footballs were all crimson red."

The men roar with laughter.

"Harvard had a little deception in its offense. When Harvard faked the ball, you could not tell who had the ball. They just went up and down the field and beat Carlisle, taking advantage of the rules," McCartney continues. "Well, if you will, the rule of thumb for 1996 in America, in the big cities we live in, can be found in Psalms 12:8. It says, 'The wicked freely strut about when what is vile is honored among men.' "

McCartney screams: " 'The wicked are freely strutting about because what is vile is honored among men!' " And he says the most popular Internet sites belong to *Penthouse* and *Playboy* and pornography.

"Now there's also a verse in Scriptures that details for us the way it is supposed to be. It's Proverbs 28:1. 'The wicked man flees though no one pursues, but the righteous are as bold as a lion.' The wicked are supposed to be running! The righteous are supposed to be bold as lions! What's wrong with this picture? I suggest you can find the answer in John 12:42–43. 'Yet at the same time, many even among the leaders believed in him.' They believed in Jesus, 'but because of the Pharisees, they would not confess their fate for fear they would be put out of the synagogue, for they loved praise from men more than praise from God.' You see, the synagogue was the center of social life back then. It was also the power center. Men believed in Jesus Christ, but they would not stand up and say so for fear of other men."

McCartney tells them the wicked strut now because today's righteous men have proven fearful. He says the righteous must fall deeper in love with God and their neighbors through repentance and prayer. He explains while quoting Scriptures, then launches into another story, citing sports.

"The University of Illinois was getting ready to play a very important game in November one particular year. If they won this game in Champaign-Urbana, Illinois, they qualified as Big Ten champion to go to the Rose Bowl, and they hadn't been to the Rose Bowl in twenty years.

"The team was put up in a local hotel. John Long went to his coach's room on Friday night before the game and banged on the door. Coach came to the door and John greeted him and said, 'Coach, you've just *got* to start me tomorrow.' The coach stepped back and said, 'John, you've done everything I've ever asked you to do the entire time you've been here. You're a senior and you're a tremendous kid, but you're second team. You've always been second team. Furthermore, you play behind the captain of the team at linebacker. With the stakes like they are in tomorrow's game, how can you ask me that?'

"Big tears started down John Long's face and he said, 'Coach, I know all that's true, but you've just *got* to start me.' Under that kind of pressure, the coach said, 'Come back and see me in the morning and I'll give you the answer.' Early the next morning, John Long is banging on the coach's door. The coach says, 'I'll tell you what I'll do. I'll put you in on the opening kickoff and that way you'll be starting the game. It's the only thing I can promise you.'

"As fate would have it, Illinois kicked off and John Long ran faster than anybody had ever seen him run. And I mean, he made a resounding tackle on the eighteen-yard line and he jumped up, his fists clenched, and the captain started on the field and the coach grabbed him and said, 'Hey, after a hit like that, let's give him one more play.'

"Well, as fate would have it, the opposition ran a trick play. The quarterback handed the ball off to the halfback and he started to the wide side of the field and stopped and threw back to the short side, where the quarterback was slipping out. Somehow, John Long diagnosed the play. He runs, he steps in front of the pass, picks it off, there's nobody in the way and he runs eighteen yards into the end zone. Illinois misses the extra point but they're ahead 6–0 and they can't take him out now—he just scored a touchdown!"

Thousands laugh.

"Do you know," McCartney continues, "John Long dominated that game? He was all over the field, made plays no one had ever seen him make before. Somehow, that 6–0 lead holds up until the waning seconds of the game. The opposition tries a desperation pass down the far sideline, and so help me, Long retreats from his linebacker position, leaps, deflects the ball, it falls harmlessly to the ground, and Champaign-Urbana just erupts! The celebration spills onto the field, they carry the coach off the field, there's pandemonium, they finally make it to the locker room, and off in the corner, all by himself, is John Long, crying like a baby.

"The coach freed himself and went over and said, 'John, what's the matter? You played better than anybody thought you could. You dominated the game. Why are you crying?'

"And John Long got control of himself finally and said, 'Coach, you know my father's blind.' The coach said, 'Of course I do. Many times your fraternity brothers wheeled him onto the practice field so he could listen to us.'

"John Long said, 'Coach, my dad died Wednesday night—and I figured this was the first time he had a chance to see me play.' "

Forty-four thousand men, their eyes misty, applaud.

McCartney pauses, then drives home his point. "The relationship between a father and son is special," he says. "There's a bond that's truly extraordinary. Almighty God ordained that relationship first for his relationship with us. It's that bond he has with us. It's entering into that relationship that tells us everything about what life is all about. Almighty God is not blind. He sees us. He watches us everywhere we go. He knows everything we do. He loves us with a love that no man can ever know for his son. A repentant heart understands we would *never* grieve this God who loves us.

"The second thing is prayer. Almighty God wants us to court him. He wants us to call on him all day long. He wants us to be thirsty and hungry for a relationship with him. We have a choice.

Each one of us can say, 'Lord, I want you, I'm after your heart, I want to fall deeply in love with you.' Or we can continue to keep God at a distance and only call on him irregularly. It's impossible to live life as rich and full if you're not in that relationship."

He suggests everyone join him in a national day of fasting and prayer. He says fasting allows men to say no to the physical and yes to the spiritual.

"How do we love our neighbor more? The deepest craving of the human spirit is for significance," McCartney says. "I suggest every single guy needs to feel loved every day of his life. If I ever coach again, I would find a way every day to let every single player know that I affirm that I love him and I care about him and I'm involved in his life. What Jesus was saying when he told his disciples, 'Now go wash each other's feet as I have washed your feet,' was you've got to get involved in each other's lives. You've go to get past surface relationships. You've got to have a sensitivity to each other. That's how you love each other more. You get involved. You give up your own comfort for them.

"Now, I'm going to show you how this comes together. Last October I was in Dallas at a Promise Keepers gathering and the speaker was talking about our marriage relationships. He said, 'I want every guy to take out a piece of paper to grade your marriage. A bad marriage is a one and a great one is a ten.' I wrote down a seven. Then he said, 'Now write down the number your wife would give your marriage.' I wrote down a six.

"He said, 'Okay, now get with three other guys and discuss your numbers.' The guy right across from me was Howard Hendricks, the former president of the Dallas [Theological] Seminary. He looked right at me and said, 'My marriage is a ten, and my wife would say it's a ten.' When he said that, I felt exposed. I felt humiliated. My eyes welled up with tears and I said to myself, 'I'm going to do better.'

"Well, four weeks ago, I brought my wife Lyndi to a prayer group and asked her to compare numbers. I wrote down an eight. Lyndi thought and pondered and deliberated and finally she wrote down a number and she turned around and showed me what that number was."

Dramatic pause.

"She wrote down an *eight!*" McCartney shouts. "I jumped out of my chair and went over and slapped five and grabbed her and hugged her and I said, 'Yes!'

"You see, Howard Hendricks explained, to have a ten, you must have unreserved passion for Jesus Christ and you must have unreserved passion for your wife. And I knew my relationship with Almight God and my relationship with Lyndi weren't what they needed to be. But I worked at them. And I'm going to tell you what I'm after now.

"I'm after an eight and a half.

"Then I'm going for a nine.

"Then I'm going for a nine and a half."

The applause sounds as if a jet were taking off.

"Now, my first waking thought in the morning is, 'Holy Spirit, what is my grade? What would you give me today? Will I ever be a ten with you?'

"We need to have high numbers with God, with our wives, and with our children. If we ask our children to grade us, what will they give us? What about our grades with our friends? How many of us can put up tens? How many of us can put up high numbers with men of other colors? You want to know what a real man is? I suggest to you that's a *real* man."

McCartney's voice is rising again, and so is the applause.

"He's a man who can put up high numbers with his God. High numbers with his wife. High numbers with his kids. High numbers with his friends. And he can cross colors. That's a man of God. That's a *real* man."

The applause thunders down from the top of the stadium and all around it. McCartney pauses and lets the emotion sink in. Knute Rockne never gave this good a speech. Bill McCartney won a national championship and national coaching honors, but only when he gave up coaching did he find his calling.

His calling is here and now, ministering to millions.

He waves his arm back and forth.

"Look around this stadium," he commands. "Where are the men of color? Why are there not more men of color here? I think I can tell you the answer. But are you ready to hear it? There is a spirit of white racial superiority that exists in our land.

"For the last year, I have been in forty-three cities meeting with men of color. I have listened to their hearts. I have heard their pain. It doesn't surprise me the O. J. Simpson case has polarized our nation. It doesn't surprise me that a million [black] men marched in Washington, D.C.

"White racial superiority can be defined as insensitivity to pain of people of color. We do not know their pain. We have not washed their feet. Jesus did it, privately and publicly. We have not been willing to do that. You know what the results are? Deadly souls. Unresolved pain.

"How would you like it if you had to come into the company of somebody every day who thought they were better than you? How many of you know what it's like to work in that environment? We as white guys, if we found ourselves in that predicament, would get another job. We could go somewhere else. Men and women of color are trapped. They *can't* go anywhere else. There's *nowhere* else to go. They can't escape it. It's everywhere!"

He tells his listeners "God's heart is ravaged" over racism in America. He tells them we must realize no one is better than anyone else. He asks them to join him in Washington, D.C., when they will ask "Almighty God to forgive us because we have dropped the ball." He tells them to stand up if they want to put up high numbers with their God, their spouse, their children, their friends, and men of color.

The men stand as one. They cheer. They clap. He asks them if they are willing to go to Washington with a man of another color, and almost all remain standing.

And then McCartney slips off the stage and is gone.

Will his message stick? Or will it vanish like his body, here one moment, gone the next?

The message is not always ministered to millions.

A month earlier, also in Pittsburgh, Dr. Don Mercer began the South Hills Christian Fellowship Group for Young Adults. When he explained his concept—how he wanted to draw young adults toward faith with the help of an athlete's name—Tunch Ilkin readily agreed to talk. A longtime Steelers lineman who had made the Pro Bowl, Ilkin remained well known in the community because of his broadcasting for NBC-TV and its local affiliate.

"There's no ministry for young adults. There are groups for youth and college students but not young adults," said Ilkin, who had done youth ministry with his wife for three years. "There's a real need, so when he asked if I'd speak to this program, I said yes."

Except when he began to talk, his audience consisted of two ministers, two volunteer youth counselors, Dr. Mercer and his wife, and a reporter and his wife. A few others straggled in later, but the group's size showed it would take a lot of work to reach the target audience.

"I guess this is what they mean about preaching to the choir," Ilkin said, laughing.

Dr. Mercer was undeterred. He said when he introduced a scientific breakthrough his first audience consisted of six or seven people. Now it is considered the gold standard for heart disease diagnosis, and he addresses groups of five hundred. He hopes this idea can show similar growth. Maybe it will die. Maybe it will grow like Promise Keepers. Who knows? But if it helps one person, Mercer and Ilkin figure their efforts will have been worthwhile.

Most athletes' introduction to the sports/religion mixture begins with the Fellowship of Christian Athletes, which has about 6,000 "huddles" for junior high, high school, and college student athletes, and another 450 adult "chapters."

The huddles, which are not limited to athletes, are led by students, though guided and sponsored by coaches or parents. Agendas vary, but most feature weekly meetings on and off campus, with activities including devotionals, games, community projects, and speeches by coaches, athletes, and pastors. The emphasis is on growth in their Christian walk. The adult chapters read devotionals and offer financial and emotional support to the local huddles.

The camps, for people twelve or older, include sports camps for boys and girls, leadership camps for college-age student athletes, and camps for the coaches themselves. In 1997, for instance, youths could get sports pointers and hear testimonials from figures such as Tampa Bay Buccaneers coach Tony Dungy, Nebraska football coach Tom Osborne, Liberty University football coach Sam Rutigliano, New York Knicks guard (and former Heisman Trophy quarterback) Charlie Ward, and former major-league pitcher Frank Tanana.

The FCA's biannual convention is mostly for the 375-member FCA staff, but some coaches and athletes attend, and the FCA has a presence at almost all the big national sporting events and most national conferences for college or high school coaches. The FCA's magazine, *Sharing the Faith,* has a circulation of about 70,000, and the FCA has its own Web site, as does Athletes in Action.

If athletes reach the professional level, they can find fellowship in many ways. Only the athletes' gods can gauge just how devout they are, but the faithful are everywhere in every major sport.

Every NFL team has a chaplain, provided by Athletes in Action under the umbrella of Campus Crusade for Christ. Because players would have a hard time preparing for their games if they attended normal Sunday services, the chaplains usually lead a team service about four and a half hours before the games. Those typically draw anywhere from a quarter to half the team—and even more "right before the final cut," Ilkin said, only partly joking. Every chaplain's involvement is different, but Miami Dolphins coach Jimmy Johnson relies upon his team priest, Father Leo Armbrust, not only for Sunday services but for one-on-one meetings with players who are having problems, and in 1996, Johnson even canceled one of his key X's and O's meetings so that Father Leo could deliver a motivational speech to the Dolphins, who were depressed after two consecutive losses.

Each Major League Baseball team has a chapel representative, and Baseball Chapel director Vince Nauss also is trying to organize reps for all 173 minor-league teams and maintain partnerships with ministries such as Pro Athletes Outreach and Unlimited Potential.

Every NBA team also has a chaplain. Some serve more than one team in their city; for instance, Miami Heat chaplain Steve

DeBardelaben also holds chapel and Bible study services for the Florida Panthers hockey team and the University of Miami football and basketball teams.

Fellowship leaders accompany the men's and women's pro golf and tennis tours. NASCAR also has a chaplain, Motor Racing Outreach president Max Helton. Not every NHL team does, but Hockey Ministries hosts annual retreats. Champions for Christ, Professional Athletes Outreach, Athletes in Action, and Sports Outreach America also hold sessions at least once a year.

How do all these organizations interact?

Let us take NFL cornerback Terrell Buckley as an example.

He joined the local FCA huddle along with his college roommate, fellow future pro Lawrence Dawsey, when he went to Florida State. He talked often with Reggie White when he went to Green Bay. But his greatest commitment came when he joined the Miami Dolphins in 1995 and started playing golf on his days off with safety Michael Stewart.

"I found out about his religious beliefs and how he overcame some situations that would normally crush people. I saw where he got his inner strength from—and I wanted it. That led to Bible studies on Friday nights. Three of us players attended every week, and sometimes other players and wives and girlfriends would trickle in. We'd take notes and discuss things about the Lord and athletes. I'd never realized how much the Bible addressed your daily routines. If you follow these guidelines, you find out how much your life will be enhanced. I was blown out of my mind. Bible study was supposed to be an hour, but we'd go two and a half, three hours. That was wonderful. Then I'd go to Bible study on Tuesday night in Miami at a church called New Birth Baptist Church, trying to learn all that I could. That was very exciting to me, and it still is."

Dawsey had encouraged him to attend the Champions for Christ gatherings for years, but Buckley did not find the time until he quit playing minor-league baseball and started getting into the Bible. In February 1996 dozens of players from the NBA and NFL gathered in San Antonio for three days of fellowship during NBA

All-Star weekend. Alongside NBA All-Stars were NFL stars such as Darrell Green, Henry Ellard, and Hardy Nickerson.

"Champions for Christ gives athletes from different sports a chance to get together to discuss their concerns and gives the wives a chance to sit down and discuss what they're going through," Buckley said. "All these players had been in the limelight, had families and kids, had achieved what you want to do. To see them praising the same God you're praising and thanking him for it, it was uplifting.

"We talked the last day that it was time to make a stand, to make a commitment one way or another, because the Lord doesn't like lukewarm people. Either be very good or very bad. The last evening, I was praying and talking to the Lord, asking forgiveness for my sins, just doing the things I should have been doing all along. Something just came over me. Once I got all that garbage off me, I felt like a different person. I thought, 'If I'm going to do all this and really make an effort to read the Word and live the Word, why don't I just go ahead and do it now, instead of prolonging it?'

"Three of us got baptized that night, around eleven o'clock in the pool. It was exciting. I just felt so good. I felt like a big monkey came off my back. I could really be real and be honest because the Lord spoke the truth."

Women's golf is not a team sport, its fellowship director is not a minister, and so the LPGA Christian fellowship follows a slightly different path. Cris Stevens has a bachelor's degree in human services and a master's in counseling. She had worked at a federal agency in human resource management for nearly ten years when she met some LPGA players who asked her to do some speaking while their fellowship director was on maternity leave. When the director resigned, Stevens was offered the job.

"I did not know that much about the LPGA then," said Stevens, now in her sixteenth year. "It was God's timing and design that crossed our paths. As I came out, I started building friendships with the players, and the transition came. It was not my intended direction for my life, but now, I wouldn't trade it at all. My background in counseling has been helpful on the tour, not that I do any major therapy, but it helps to listen and know when to talk and not talk. The philosophy of our ministry is discipleship and evangelism. I see my role as coming alongside players. The players get people all the time asking for their autographs and time and energy, so to build a relationship with them takes time. They have to know you're not someone who wants something from them. My philosophy is to hang loose and be there. As players get to know me, they can know the Christ who lives within me. That's my desire, that they get to know him. It's a very low-key friendship evangelism."

Stevens, who is affiliated with Alternative Ministries and based in Knoxville, Tennessee, travels to thirty-five to thirty-seven events a year, usually arriving Tuesday and organizing fellowship meetings Tuesday nights for players, caddies, and LPGA staff. Those meetings typically draw seventeen to thirty attendees, but can range from as little as a dozen to as many as sixty-five. Stevens usually speaks at these meetings, but special speakers and Christian singers (such as Dick and Mel Tunney) are sprinkled throughout the year and attract some of the biggest crowds. Because the tournaments conclude on Sundays, golfers cannot attend the traditional Christian sermons unless they miss the cut. And if they missed the cut every week to attend church they would not make any money and would not be allowed to stay on the tour. Besides, when you are at a different event every week, it is hard to know which church suits your faith, and there is no continuity from week to week.

"Our Sabbath is on a Tuesday," Stevens said. "It's kind of like their church on the road. Sometimes we have a time of singing and worship, sometimes special activities, but usually, it's a nondenominational Bible study. It's very informal. For instance, right now, we're studying the book of Exodus. Each week we cover a couple of chapters. We try to look at when it was written historically, then try to see what kind of principles are in them and apply them to our life today. We always try to make Bible study applicable to our own life."

That is something you do not see in every church, but Stevens thinks it is important to keep Christians interested in learning the Scriptures. "Have you heard of Bill Hybels? He has a megachurch in Chicago. He says the reason the church has exploded is he presents the Bible as an effective way to manage your life, a practical way to help."

The LPGA fellowship also arranges small-group studies, usually led by the players themselves. About twenty-four players normally attend, including Betsy King, Chris Johnson, Barb (Thomas) Whitehead, Nancy Ramsbottom, Alison Nicholas, Suzanne Strudwick of England, and Chela Quintana of Venezuela. They meet weekly at various times. Similar to discipleship groups or accountability groups, these groups are smaller and restricted to players only so that they might feel more comfortable discussing their lives and special prayer requests. "The small group is a more intimate setting, a chance for players to have support and encouragement of each other," Stevens said.

Their male counterparts are just as involved. Fifty-four of the 125 PGA Tour regulars have caught at least one session of the traveling Bible study that chaplain Larry Moody has led since 1981. Wednesday is their Sabbath.

The seven promises of a Promise Keeper have as much to do with men's relationships with their wives, families, friends, and men of other colors and denominations as they do with faith. Even non-Christian men could leave the Pittsburgh conference with good practical advice on secular matters. The speakers can make the Bible come alive for men no matter their faith.

Dr. Bruce Fong of Multnomah Biblical Seminary spoke on "Going All Out for Your Wife." He quoted 1 Peter 2:1, "So put away all malice and all guile and insincerity and envy and all slander," and showed his listeners how the Scriptures applied to their everyday lives with their wives.

"Malice is filth in the eyes of God," he said. "Hitting is not an option for a man of God. Hit no more! But malice is more than physical harm. It also means active ill will. Even if we think ill, that is malice. A Promise Keeper should be the greatest cheerleader a wife ever had."

And he gave a wonderful example of how some new wives were sitting around, complaining about their husbands' idiosyncrasies, each trying to top the other, until they came to his bride, who gave an example of how good he was. Which caused the wives to switch to a game of can-you-top-this? bragging about their husbands. That, he said, is a godly way of living.

Next came Joe White, a former college football player and assistant coach who now runs a Christian children's sports camp, Kanakuk-Kanakomo Kamps in Branson, Missouri. He joked about the Steelers and with his son did a wonderful impersonation of the famed Abbott and Costello "Who's on First" baseball skit. And then he turned serious toward his topic: "Turning Your Heart Toward Your Children."

He told of one survey that found only 3.7 percent of children would go to their fathers first to help them solve a problem. He told of a survey in which teens said their fathers spent only one to three minutes a day in serious conversation with them. He told how he thought his world was over when his first wife left him, how he cried for three months.

"Then I saw a savior, pinned to the same cross I was nailed to, pulling for me, feeling my sorrow," White said. "I never forget the night I was on my knees and I felt this big old hand reach out and take this Olympic barbell with about nine 45-pound plates on each end off my shoulders."

He pointed to his son. "That boy and his mom are living proof there is life after failure," White said.

He told the men to end the transgenerational curse building in their families for decades because their grandfathers did not know how to show their love. He told them to bury any bitterness they had toward their fathers. He told them to forgive, to break down the walls separating them from their fathers and children. He told how he spent half an hour with his seven-year-old daughter after she was cut from the gymnastics team, rocking her in his chair, comforting her, telling her that God did not care who fell off the balance beam and who did not.

"When I put her to bed that night, she said, 'Daddy, thanks for tying my heart back together tonight. My heart was broken but you tied it back together.' "

He told how his dad had written his mom a love letter every day for fifty-eight years. He told how his son dreamed of being a basketball player, and how he must have rebounded a quarter million of his boy's shots. He told how he helped his children memorize one Bible verse a day. He told how, when his daughter began dating, he asked a friend who was six feet nine inches and 250 pounds and as fearsome as all get out to come over and greet the boy and tell him, "You know that girl is like a sister to me. You're not going to touch her, are you?"

"Dads are the ones who are there when the healing heart of God is needed," he told them. "One time a day, catch your kid doing something good and tell him. One time a day, catch his mom doing something right and tell her."

He told of his friend Gene Stallings, a longtime pro and college football coach. Stallings has a mentally retarded son, but the handicap has only strengthened their love. Every day the son asks, "Who's your favorite boy in the whole world?" and the father replies, "You are, Johnny." And the son says, "You know who my favorite father is? You are, Dad."

The crowd stood to applaud White, and he asked all the children eighteen and under to remain standing. He asked the dads to applaud them, and they did, long and loud. He asked the dads and sons to pray together, and they did, teary-eyed.

"This," he said, "is the future of our country."

This is the beauty of Promise Keepers.

"Ten years ago, if you said you were going to bring men to fill stadiums to sing songs and talk about God, we wouldn't have thought you'd be in business long. Boy, were we wrong!" said Dr. Bruce Wilkinson, who closed the conference with his "Walking with God" speech.

"You sense a lot of deep decisions being made this weekend. So many men who come to Promise Keepers have been Christians for a number of years but have slid. Maybe church wasn't challenging them. Maybe they slipped. Maybe they thought it wasn't manly. You'll see many men weeping openly because their hearts are so in need of what God can give them. Promise Keepers gives all of us permission to walk with God."

Promise Keepers was founded by a college football coach and a director of an organization devoted to Christian athletes. It uses sports analogies and sports stadiums to help attract men.

But today it transcends sports.

"Sports probably did attract men initially in the early years in Colorado, but not to the same degree nationally and not as much now," said Pete Richardson, PK's vice-president of communications. "The movement does not feature the man Bill McCartney. We've done conferences where he's not even there, and we still drew great crowds, and we think that's good.

"You won't find the focus on football. The focus will clearly be on Jesus Christ. We call this setting in the stadium a male-context setting because of sports. Many men who would not walk into a church building feel safe to come to Three Rivers Stadium. We've been at motor speedways, too. But the focus is not on sports."

That prompted a small, totally unscientific poll. Fritz Rushlow of Frederick, Maryland, said McCartney's name recognition had nothing to do with his attendance. He said he went to the 1995 Indianapolis conference when a good friend invited him to go.

"Good friends and people I respect had enjoyed one before and said they got a lot out of it," said Rushlow, who helps restore historic sites for the National Park Service. "I was somewhat skeptical. You hear about these religious things on TV and bringing all these guys together and changing them, and I thought it was some sort of scam. I learned it was very well run and the people running it are very sincere, really trying to do something. It was an incredible thing, to see a stadium filled with guys, all there for one reason. It brought back a lot of faith in our country."

And it brought him back in 1996. This time, he had come to Pittsburgh after convincing his brother, Dr. David Rushlow of Shawano, Wisconsin, and his cousin, Mark Tonn of Pittsburgh, to join him. Dr. Rushlow had heard of Promise Keepers when the Wisconsin Badgers played the Colorado Buffaloes and he read how McCartney had given up coaching Colorado after the 1994 season to devote himself to his family and Promise Keepers.

"For someone that popular and famous to give it all up to do this, when he had no idea how big it would become, added some legitimacy to it for me," said Dr. Rushlow, a family practitioner who had played football for 1985 NAIA champion Wisconsin-LaCrosse. "A few people from our church went and Fritz went and thought it was good, and that pushed me to go the next time. We tried to get tickets for the Twin Cities, Detroit, Chicago, and Indianapolis, and all were sold out. You call around and hear the stadiums are full and you can't get a ticket and you think, 'This really must be something special.' "

He said he hoped to leave Pittsburgh with a stronger faith.

"It's supposed to be the most important thing in your life, but as the speakers said, sometimes you're so busy making money, you lose track of your priorities. I hope to come closer to the church, make it become the most important thing in my life and stop paying lip service. I have a long way to go. There's so much you can do that you don't, if you think about it."

And that's a big part of Promise Keepers: to get men thinking. Thinking about their relationships with their god, their wives, their children, their friends. Thinking about things they might take for granted. Thinking about making things better.

"This is just a beginning, a catalyst," Richardson said. "The real ministry goes on year round as men go back to their families and churches and their lives."

Dr. Crawford Loritts, one of the last speakers, reminded the men of that. "One of my concerns is you'll put everything into neutral until the next rah-rah meeting. Christianity that is real is down in the trenches. Joshua said you can't just talk about it, you have to live it. Practice it! Practice it! Practice it! There's too much of a gap between what we say and how we actually live. If we are to be men of integrity, we must work on erasing that line between what we say and how we live."

Many athletes have found they need a regular dose of fellowship—whether it be from Promise Keepers or the Fellowship of Christian Athletes or Athletes in Action or Champions for Christ or whatever organization—to not only find faith but to live it.

When together the men explore verses from their holy books,

they begin to see how ancient teachings can apply to their modern lives. They remember true faith is not about going to church for an hour on Sunday. It is about how you live your life all 168 hours a week. The Bible, the Koran, and the Talmud are not books with archaic, useless stories. They are instruction manuals for how to live your life.

7

Faith and Life

Nancy Lieberman's family was Jewish, but her parents divorced when she was young, and although they celebrated the high holidays, Judaism was not part of their everyday life. She knew next to nothing about religion until she played on the Pan American and Olympic teams. Teammate Nancy Dunkle read the Bible a lot, and Lieberman asked why she seemed so calm and relaxed.

"She'd talk about Jesus and God and I would be like, 'Who's Jesus?' I was fifteen, sixteen, seventeen, and I really didn't know a whole lot about faith," recalled Lierberman-Cline, then a teenage prodigy and now a married mom who has cemented her place as one of the greatest players in women's basketball history. "She was very patient and she answered my questions."

They won the silver medal at the 1976 Olympics in Montreal.

"You always see people win championships and it's supposed to be such a great feeling," Lieberman-Cline said. "I went back to my room at the Olympic Village and I sat on the edge of my bed and cried. I was so empty. I was happy we won, but it really wasn't fulfilling like I thought it would be. I remember thinking, 'This is supposed to be so much better.'

"There was something missing in my life, and I think it was some sort of faith. I didn't have strong faith as a Jew or a Christian or anything. When I got to Old Dominion my freshman year that fall, the men were doing an exhibition game against Athletes in Action, and one of their players, Ralph Drollinger, who had played at UCLA with Bill Walton, came over and talked with me and shared his testimony. He was casual about it, or I would have felt uncomfortable and walked away. We sat on the bench, and a lot of things he said made sense to me. He said, 'If you want Christ in your life and you want to accept it, all you have to do is sit here and say a prayer.' I was pretty ignorant about even how to pray. I didn't know. He was very patient, sat down, and we prayed, and I asked Christ to come into my life and guide my life. That was October of 1976.

"I just felt a peace. I felt more relaxed. That was when I accepted Christ, but I really didn't know anything about Christianity. Every day is a learning process, even now. I've always felt to be a Christian and to be born Jewish is the greatest combination you can have, because of God protecting the Jews. God obviously has taken care of Jews throughout history. The Jews are God's chosen people. It's not like I denounced Judaism. I didn't know that much about it. We observed the high holidays, but it wasn't a day-to-day thing in my family. All I did was accept faith in the Lord Jesus Christ as well."

But she did not tell her parents or the sports world about her conversion for four years, when she became a pro for the Dallas Diamonds of the short-lived Women's Basketball League.

"I was a little afraid," Lieberman-Cline said. "I was embarrassed. I didn't want to be ridiculed. I didn't have enough information to say, 'This is why I accepted Christ.' I was a baby Christian. So I never really said anything to anybody. Finally, when I went to Dallas in 1980, a columnist was doing a story on me and I thought, 'I'm gonna just say it and deal with it.' He does this whole long story on me and there's like one blurb, 'born-again

Christian'—and I got thousands of hate letters from Jewish people all over the country. How could I denounce Judaism? How could I do this to them? I was supposed to be one of them.

"It was just unbelievable. People have no understanding of what you're taught, but people have an opinion. If I'm not taught mathematics or English, I'm not going to know much about mathematics or English. If I'm not taught very much about Judaism, how am I supposed to know about it? Send those letters to my parents, not to me. Even my mom and dad and relatives said, 'How could you do that?' I just told them, 'I feel comfortable. I feel good about my decision. I can't live my life for everybody else. I've got to live it for me.' I'm a public figure, and people think they can control your destiny.

"The thing I've learned as I've matured as a professional athlete is you have to be happy with who and what you are and what you do. You can't fit your life into everybody else's expectations. Being a Christian helped me be a better person. I'm a little kinder, a little more understanding. Every day, I'm working to be a little better in how I deal with people. I mean, I want to be a competitor and I want to win, and when I'm on the basketball court I play hard, but I hope people can see a difference in how I conduct my life. I don't tell anybody, 'You have to be a Christian.' But whether you're Jewish or Buddhist or Catholic or whatever, I think it's important to have a strong faith in God."

Her faith does not appear just on religious holidays or on Sundays. Now it's part of everyday life. "It's not a diet," Lieberman-Cline said. "This is how I want to conduct myself for the rest of my life. I want to be a good role model for my son, for young people, for people who see me playing at thirty-nine. It means a lot to me and my husband and that has got to be the foundation of our family."

Husband Tim works in sports marketing for Host Communications in Dallas. Son T.J. was two when Nancy launched her comeback for Athletes in Action in the fall of 1996 and he turned three in July 1997, while she was playing several hundred miles away, for the WNBA's Phoenix Mercury. How does a Christian mom in the competitive sports world juggle priorities in a two-income, two-city family? It helps to have a husband whose company gives him flexibility, and to earn enough money to pay for commuter airline tickets and a devoted nanny.

"If my faith is number one, everything else falls in place," Lieberman-Cline said. "I made sacrifices to get back to play at this level. Tim made sacrifices to enable me to come back and concentrate and dedicate myself. We worked very hard to figure out the summer. My little boy will be in Phoenix ninety percent of the time I'm here. Our nanny will come here with us, and then when she goes home, Tim comes on the weekends."

Even so, she admits she is not as dedicated to basketball as she once was. "It's not the most important thing in my life, but it is important to me, and I think I'm better at handling situations. I'm better at sharing than I was in my early twenties, when everything was about me. Not everything is about me. It's about coming home from practice, and sometimes I want to lie down and my boy wants to go to the park. After three hours of practice and an hour of weights, everybody wants to relax and chill out and here I am, doing the mom thing. But I don't have a problem with it because he's my boy. I'm very organized. I'm good at juggling."

TONY FOSSAS, a left-hander who has pitched for several Major League Baseball teams, changed faiths in a different manner. Raised in Cuba until he was ten and then in Boston until he began college and professional baseball, he was a Southern Baptist most of his life until 1989, when he began attending his mother's Spanish-speaking church. But the minister had a spiritual conversion, and while still believing in Jesus Christ as the Messiah, chose to incorporate the Jewish rituals and beliefs that Jesus had practiced.

Fossas listened to the advice of his new rabbi and signed with the Milwaukee Brewers, even though they offered the smallest guarantee, and was rewarded with a job in the big leagues. Fossas went on to pitch for the Boston Red Sox and St. Louis Cardinals before he and his wife joined their congregation on a 1995 trip to Israel. They discovered they had Jewish roots through a genealogy computer at Tel Aviv's Museum of the Diaspora. He was stunned to learn his grandmothers' maiden names traced back to the Old

Testament. He knew his ancestors had migrated all over Europe, then to Mexico and Cuba, and now he thought he knew why: Jews fled Spain during the Inquisition. He decided his ancestors were Jewish, and suddenly, "All the teachings came alive," he said.

CURTIS MARTIN played just one full game for the University of Pittsburgh in 1994. Common sense and college coaches, friends and family, pro coaches and scouts—all told him to return to Pitt for his red-shirt senior season. They said he was loony to turn pro after the injury-marred season. They said he was way too brittle and a little too slow. They said he ran upright or ducked his head. They said a lot of nasty things.

"I was called knucklehead, bonehead, no-brain, crazy, stupid," Martin remembered, smiling. "I was called everything. And if it weren't for my faith in God, I would have felt that way too. Because it made actually no sense at all. No logical reason pointed me to leave college."

Except God told him to go pro.

God won.

Martin won, in both life and career.

"It was my faith in God," said Martin, who has quickly emerged as one of pro football's best backs. "It wasn't like I prayed, 'God, I want to go to the NFL. Please make me a big star. Please make me Rookie of the Year.' It was simply, 'God, it doesn't matter to me. I want to do what you want me to do.' That was my prayer. I actually didn't feel it was my decision. I feel it was something God put in my heart, a confirmation in my heart. To most people, that might sound crazy, way off the wall, like I'm some crazy religious guy. But I've grown into a relationship with God where I understand different ways of living. I was positive in my heart."

Positively wrong, even his friends and family said.

"The Pitt coaching staff and many NFL scouts—everyone, really—disagreed. My mother was one of the few who said, 'Go ahead.' I could probably count them on one hand."

He watched his hometown Steelers play and said he could make a go as a pro. "You're good," his stepfather said, "but that's a whole 'nother level. You can't be out there with them."

"I see the way the hole opened," Martin replied, "and I bet you I could get through there and get some yards. Maybe one day I'll show you."

His next visit to Three Rivers Stadium, Curtis showed him. The New England Patriots had made him a third-round pick despite fears about his history of injuries, and by the time he returned to Pittsburgh on December 16, 1995, he had dispelled those fears and turned into a rookie sensation. He wangled thirty tickets for his family. At least another forty scrounged up seats for the perennially sold-out Steelers to see if the American Football Conference rushing leader were for real.

It did not take long. The league-leading Blitzburgh defense was allowing just eighty-one rushing yards a game. Martin had fifty-four his first two series.

He ripped twenty-three yards off the left side and NBC's Bob Trumpy exclaimed, "He makes Darren Perry miss! He makes the inside linebacker miss! He has that shiftiness you need in a running back. You'd like to teach it to a kid, but they're either born with it or they never have it."

All-Pro linebacker Greg Lloyd met him at the line and Martin spun and left him grasping for air. "Very few players make Greg Lloyd look foolish," Trumpy said.

He dodged and darted twenty-two yards for the tying touchdown. "Watch this move!" Trumpy triumphed. "Levon Kirkland is an excellent tackler, and Martin just freezes him. Then he runs by Perry for the end zone! Man, he got there quickly, didn't he?"

Martin finished with a hundred and twenty yards rushing and sixty-two receiving. Nobody gained more or made the vaunted Steelers look worse all year.

"He's the best pure runner that I've played against," said defensive end Brentson Buckner—and Buckner had played against Emmitt Smith, Marshall Faulk, Chris Warren, Rodney Hampton, Thurman Thomas, Harvey Williams, Natrone Means, and Barry Sanders.

"I just felt I was in a whole different dimension that day. My senses just felt extra aware," said the runner touched by God.

The next week, Martin capped 1995 with his ninth hundred-yard game. No rookie ever had more. He scored fifteen touchdowns. Only one rookie ever had more. He ran for 1,487 yards. Only three rookies ever had more. He set single-season Patriots records for rushing yards, rushing touchdowns, total touchdowns, and hundred-yard games. Not bad for a guy whose own stepfather said he should not turn pro.

"When he said I couldn't, I'm the type who takes everything as a challenge," Martin said. "I'm never discouraged. They're saying I can't do it. I'm saying I can."

He was the only rookie selected to the Pro Bowl. He was named Rookie of the Year by just about everyone save *Ladies' Home Journal*. Not bad for the seventy-fourth player and tenth running back drafted.

"A lot of people have told me, 'Curtis, when you were saying that God stuff—that's the way they all say it—that God was leading you to leave, we all thought you were trying to hype yourself up, to find an excuse to leave, but nobody but God could have done what's happened to you.'

"It's even made a lot of people believe in God who didn't believe in God. Or it's made a lot of people have more trust and faith who previously didn't. That means more than anything to me, because I feel it's very important for people to have a relationship with God. I don't preach to people, but I know what I believe. I don't try to push it or press it on anyone, but they know from the way I live my life."

He says God must have given him his elusiveness, because it's been there "all my life, back to my childhood days, when I was five, six, seven, eight, playing 'it' tag."

He says his mom, a single parent who worked two and three jobs at a time to support him, helped keep him safe despite growing up in three Pittsburgh neighborhoods infested with crime, drugs, and gangs. His best friend was shot and killed in a case of mistaken identity.

Martin turned to Christianity in 1993, to help him deal with the rough neighborhood and the injuries he endured in college. He had never been to church before, but he felt something in his heart start to pull him there every week, and his developing faith helped him cope when he was injured in the second quarter of his second game in 1994 and was unable to come back.

He now sees the injury as a blessing, because in the "greatest, most crucial time" of his life he had nothing to do but study the Bible and become closer to God. Now God is part of everything he does on and off the field. He is one of the most community-minded Patriots, going into the community, encouraging children, spreading joy and the Word.

"If I didn't have football, I wouldn't be able to reach them," he said. "God has given me football to touch other people."

KERRY CASH's prayer was not answered like Curtis Martin's was. Released by the Oakland Raiders in 1996, the veteran tight end had several contract offers. He chose the Miami Dolphins.

Why? "I prayed about it," he replied. "I called my mom and we both prayed about it. I prayed to him and he gave me the answer. Guys get caught up in money sometimes. I could have gone somewhere else for more money, but God put me here for a reason."

Did the reason have anything to do with Dan Marino, the great quarterback, and Jimmy Johnson, the great coach who believes in throwing to his tight end? "Those are all in the back of your mind," Cash said. "With Jimmy here, you knew players won jobs on the field. Any time you get the opportunity to play with a great quarterback, you take that into consideration. But the final word came from God."

And just how did he supply his answer?

"It wasn't a thunderbolt. It wasn't the face of Jimmy, although around here, some people think he's God," Cash said, grinning. "The Dolphins called and I prayed about it and something kept telling me Dolphins."

So he signed with them even though just the day before they had signed young and talented Johnny Mitchell. Within two weeks, Mitchell had quit, and Cash's decision looked providential. But after a strong start in training camp, Cash faded, lost his starting job and then his job, period. Later, he spent a few weeks with the Chicago Bears but was released after the season.

"If it's God's will, I'll do well," Cash said.

SHAREEF ABDUR-RAHIM's father is an imam, or prayer leader, at an Atlanta mosque. Still, his parents never hit him over the head with religion "as a sledgehammer," said Abdur-Rahim, the Pacific-10 Conference's leading scorer as a freshman in 1996 and one of the NBA's top rookies in 1997.

"They instilled my faith in God, told me what was wrong from right, then at the same time left it to me when I got older to make my own decisions."

He decided to attend the University of California partly because of its world-renowned Islamic studies department, partly because of the sensitivity toward the Muslim faith he found from the coach and the campus.

"I call on my religion a lot more now because I'm on my own," said the six-foot-ten forward, who was chosen third in the 1996 draft by the Vancouver Grizzlies. "It's like what I would call on my mother for, or my sisters, or call on somebody else, or ask somebody else a question, now I'll just pray on it. Or when I'm going through something hard, instead of trying to talk to somebody about it, I'll just pray on it."

Islamic rituals such as praying five times a day and fasting during the holy month of Ramadan have instilled structure and discipline into his life.

"If I have that kind of discipline to get up and pray [at dawn] and to fast all day [until sunset], then getting up for practice, lifting weights, being on time for this, being on time for that, you know, nothing's that hard. I feel all my confidence comes from my religion, because I feel God is with me, and if God is with me, I can't be stopped."

HAKEEM OLAJUWON, the two-time NBA champion and one-time MVP, grew up in Lagos, Nigeria, the son of devout Muslims. His mom always prayed five times a day. But his parents never pushed their faith on him, and though he would answer the Call and pray in the mosque every Friday, he lived more by Nigerian custom than Islamic custom.

When he received a hard-to-get visa to come to the United States to play college basketball, his mom cried and prayed and said, "This is from Allah! This is from God!" and his dad said, "This is God's will." But Islam became an afterthought during his early years at the University of Houston and then with the NBA's Houston Rockets.

Then one day in 1988 a man asked if he would like to pray at the mosque just two minutes away from the Rockets' practice site. Olajuwon had never even known it was there. When he learned it was a traditional Muslim mosque, and not part of the black separatist Nation of Islam, he decided to attend Friday prayer, or Jumma. He was pleased to find people of all different colors and nationalities, all so friendly. They performed the Muslim ritual of ablutions, cleansing themselves before entering the mosque to pray, purifying themselves in the presence of Allah.

"The room hummed from about three hundred men reciting the Call in unison, each in his own state of communion with Allah," Olajuwon recalled in his autobiography, *Living the Dream: My Life and Basketball.* "I felt goosebumps all over my body. Everything I had known growing up came back to me in that instant. . . . This was what had been missing. Missing for years. I was so comfortable, so excited. The Call usually goes on for three or four minutes, but I got lost in it and to me it seemed endless. Sitting on the floor listening to that Call, these were the happiest moments of my life.

"Islam had not been my major concern. Before Islam is called 'the dark ages.' I didn't understand my responsibilities. I was living according to my own understanding, but Islam isn't just a religion; it is a way of life. I asked, 'What are my responsibilities as a Muslim?' There are books of the lawful and the prohibited. For example, Muslims are prohibited from drinking alcohol; we can neither earn nor receive interest on our money, we eat no pork, we fast during the month of Ramadan. I used to drink beer, my diet was healthy but not restricted, and I was not at all observant of the holidays. That's where my changes began. I made a commitment and I kept to it. I made that commitment with joy, and I began to grow.

"I would arrive at the mosque after practice each day and I would pray and study, and before I knew it, it was eight at night. Then I would go to the home of one of my fellow Muslims where his wife would put out tea and plenty of food and we would study some more. . . . There weren't enough hours in the day to read [the Koran]. I had found a community, and I felt completely at home."

He became even more devout after he made the hajj, or pilgrimage to Mecca, in both 1991 and 1992. Determined to make his faith part of his everyday life, he became more patient and tolerant. When people upset him, he no longer fought. He felt sorry for them and prayed for them. He no longer cursed. He tried to be more honest and tell people exactly what he thought, even if they did not always want to hear it. He tried to live a righteous life so he could be a true role model for children.

LOREN ROBERTS believed his marriage improved when he became a born-again Christian.

"It meant a great deal to my marriage," said Roberts, who has progressed from a struggling pro in 1983 to one of the PGA's best in 1997. "It did nothing but strengthen my marriage. She became born again about the same time I did. Sharing our faith together really helped me get through the tough times. It taught me how to love my children and honor my family, how I should love my wife and protect her and give myself up for her, as Christ did for us. It taught me how to discipline my children, how to love my children.

"That is the greatest commission God gives us: how to raise and train our children. We need to share our faith with everyone around the world, but the greatest thing we can do is raise our children well and teach them about God."

How can you be a great parent and a great professional? Can you do both? When JOE GIBBS was winning 140 games and three Super Bowls in a dozen years (1981–92) as coach of the Washington Redskins, he was famed for being a workaholic who spent many a night sleeping on his office cot, never going home to his family. Is that the mark of a good Christian husband and father?

In his book, *Fourth and One,* which dealt much more with faith than football, Gibbs explained how he became born again in 1972, when he was an assistant coach. "I was still pretty naive about what it meant to be the right kind of a father," he wrote. "If I had it to do over, I would have been home more, even when the kids were real little. I know now how important that is. But back then I was still chasing dreams, trying to get ahead. My motives had been purified, but my priorities were still not where they needed to be."

He was obsessed not only with football but with winning the national seniors title in racketball. He did so in 1976. It was "one of the greatest and most fulfilling experiences of my life," but it also was "selfish," he wrote. "It simply cost me something I can never go back and replace: time with my kids when they were little. What a fool I was. What a price I paid for the national championship in 1976!"

Gibbs was trying to repeat as champion when he realized he was spending too much time away from his sons. He instantly vowed to change. He made sure to spend as much time as possible with his boys in football's off season, often skiing or racing bikes, motorbikes, and jet skis with them. Even during the season, he brought his boys around the team, so they could get to meet the players and coaches and spend at least a few minutes with Dad.

He often put his sons to bed, sharing Bible stories before they went to sleep. "I cherished that time with the boys and always tried to find something good to share with them. I'd read and then we'd talk before they went to sleep. That was my time with them, and it was great for me," wrote Gibbs, who credited God again and again during his 1996 Pro Football Hall of Fame induction speech.

He said it is important to learn from your failures, to do the best you can, and face difficult decisions by asking God for wisdom. But ultimately, he decided, you must relax and leave your future in God's hands.

"The lessons in my life have come from failures, my own shortcomings, naiveté, and buying into some of the biggest myths society has to sell. See, I bought into conventional wisdom hook, line, and sinker. I mean, I believed I needed to make money, gain position and power and prestige (in my case that meant landing a head coaching job and winning) and accumulate things. If I accumulated enough, I would be happy. That was the picture," Gibbs wrote.

"It was the nagging knowledge that this life is *not* all there is that kept working on me, even during my frantic, frenzied years trying to embrace the other myths, that eventually made it possible for me to see my mistakes and get back on track. . . . Even if I had become the greatest coach in the history of professional football and had seen my teams win Super Bowl after Super Bowl, I'd have missed out on those few things that really are important in this life. That would have been a tragedy."

Those whose religion is sincere and not a facade find their faith affects their careers, lives, personal relationships, and daily habits in a variety of ways, almost all of them good. Their faith does not guarantee they will always succeed, but it guides them on matters big and small.

8

Faith and Adversity

It was July 31, 1996. The toughest wrestler in the world—200-plus pounds of muscle and heart—fell to his knees, lifted his hands in prayer formation, and while the tears streamed onto wailing lips, gave thanks to a higher power. Television beamed the scene to nearly three billion viewers around the world, and newspapers around the globe preserved it in photographs. He cried on the medals stand. He cried when he gave the medal to his mom. He cried when he hugged two hundred friends and family. He cried in his news conference. But even that dramatic footage could not fully convey how Kurt Angle's Catholicism inspired him to surmount mountains of adversity.

Kurt Angle began wrestling when he was eight years old. He won two matches, lost sixteen, and was pinned nine times that first season. After nearly two decades of grueling work, after the death of his father, after the murder of his coach, after the threat of paralysis, he overcame the odds and won the 220-pound free-style gold medal in Atlanta's Olympics.

"My whole family wrestled, and they were always good, from the first year they wrestled to their last match," Angle recalled. "Me, on the other hand, I was bad, and it took me a long time to improve, and my brothers laugh now because I'm the one with the gold medal and they're the ones who sat in the stands and watched. My first year wrestling, there was no way in heck I ever thought I'd win a gold medal. But I never gave up."

He never gave up when his father died when he was a junior in high school and a good but not great wrestler and lineman. "I dedicated my athletic career to my dad, and my focus became a lot more clear. I started to really motivate myself. When there were times I didn't feel like doing something, I'd say, 'If you can't do it for yourself, do it for Dad,' and I'd make it through. That's when I started realizing success. It's amazing how you can let yourself down, but it's a lot harder to let down people you love."

He went to Clarion University and won the 1992 NCAA heavy-weight championship, but when he found little success on the Olympic level, he did give up. "I quit the sport for about six months. I thought I was doing the right thing because I didn't think I'd ever make the Olympic team. But something brought me back, and I know it was God and my dad looking over me and telling me not to give up on myself so easily."

He came back only to see Dave Schultz, his freestyle coach since 1989, shot to death five months before the Olympic Games by a benefactor gone mad, John du Pont. "Not having Dave around really hurt bad. I needed him more then than I ever did, and when Dave was killed, I started to panic. I wasn't sure what I would do. For about a week, I didn't do any training. It was hard to get a focus. Then one night I was praying that God would take Dave and bless his family, and I started thinking about what Dave would want me to do, because Dave was probably the smartest man I have ever known and the wisest and the best wrestler in United States history. I basically pretended I was Dave Schultz and did whatever he would do. Dave would have wanted me to find someone else who could help me as soon as possible. And that's what I did. I started to freelance train all over the United States. I found different college coaches to give me input on what to do, and I found the best one."

And then Angle, the 1995 world champion, was thrown on his head during the first round of the U.S. Open, and the neck pain was so severe, he did not think he could wrestle again. His brothers convinced him to try. "I did my normal routine before the match," Angle said. "I said a prayer, 'Just give me enough strength to make it through the match.' I was able to win, which seeded me first in the Olympic trials, but when I got home, I couldn't train. My neck was so bad that for three and a half weeks I couldn't do anything. The trials were coming up in another week and a half. I tried everything I could. I was going to rehab every day and nothing was working. So I started to really panic."

And then came real cause to panic. An MRI of the neck found a disk sticking into his spinal cord. If it were jarred any more, he could become paralyzed from the neck down. Angle cried when the doctor gave him the news, "because the only thing I wanted to do was wrestle in the Olympic Games and I might not be able to go to the trials to make it." He called the U.S. wrestling coach and asked if his trial could be postponed. Because he was seeded first, he was an automatic entrant into the final, where he would wrestle the winner of the mini-tournament best out of three matches. The coach said no.

Angle had worked most of his life for Olympic gold, and work is an understatement. No sport demands more exhaustive sacrifice for so little financial reward. A medal is everything to wrestlers, and most only get one chance, and now it looked like Angle had lost his. He called his doctor and told him he could not delay his match.

"What do you want to do?" the doctor said.

"I *have* to wrestle," Angle said.

"I don't advise you to wrestle," the doctor said, "because you're really chancing paralysis. If you hit your neck again, you're in trouble."

Angle did not want to be a paraplegic. He asked for God's guidance. "I prayed that day and God said to do it. I had that feeling inside me. It was the only thing I could do to fulfill my athletic career and pay tribute to my dad and Dave."

The doctor injected his neck with Novocaine every third day just so Angle could practice twice a week and not lose all his conditioning. The neck was still in bad shape when he reached the trials. "Before every match, I just said a quick prayer that I could make it through the match. We brought the doctor with us and he would Novocaine my neck up before each match. The funny thing is, I wrestled the best two matches of my life. I won, 7–0 and 3–0, and I found myself in the Olympic Games.

"I was ranked first not only in the United States but the world, so I knew I had a shot at winning the Olympic gold. Obviously, you're going to have more world champions from previous years there, but I felt I was peaking at the right time. So when I made the team, I had nine weeks to prepare for the games. I went through a really good rehab program, and after a month I was strong enough to go on my own without Novocaine. My neck was still hurt, but it was good enough to go to the Olympics. I knew it would be my last tournament. The doctor said my neck would be okay as long as I didn't do anything crucial with it.

"With all the things I had endured—losing matches, the death of my loved ones, my neck injury—I found out when I got to the Olympic Games that I was a much stronger person. A lot of times, I had whined and moped about my losses and not really thought ahead about how to beat the person. I felt sorry for myself. After a while, I realized those losses could turn into wins if I just used the right motivation, and that's what I did. It enabled me to work harder and gave me more focus and motivation. A lot of people tend to put their tail between their legs and walk away. That's the problem. You have to find motivation in everything, good and bad."

He has always found motivation in his conversations with God.

"I've been close to God all my life. I pray on a daily basis. I hear him, and he hears me. I'm a big believer in praying for other people. I think so many people knew my story and were praying for me that God was going to hear me and hear them. It was an amazing thing. My senior year in college, I wrestled a guy named

Sylvester Terkay for the NCAA title. He was a giant. He weighed about 270 and he was six foot seven. I was a very small heavyweight; I weighed 204 and I'm only five foot eleven. I remember it was tied and there were only about twenty seconds left in the third period. Something inside me said, 'You've got to score now,' and I hit my move and I scored. Same thing happened in the Olympic Games. There were about twenty seconds left, and something inside me said, 'You have to attack and score now,' and I did that.

"Both times, I was so tired, I wanted to quit. But something inside me kept me going. I knew what that was. That was my dad; that was Dave Schultz. That was the people in my life telling me, 'You've come too far. You can't give up now. You're both tired, and it's who wants it more.' I know they called on me. It's amazing, because those were the two most important matches of my life, and if I didn't score then, I would have lost the matches. I wouldn't be Kurt Angle, the Olympic champion. I'd just be somebody who wrestled in the Olympics, remembered the way people remember thousands of other people: as a lost memory."

And so when the referee raised his hand and proclaimed Kurt Angle the Olympic champion, it seemed only natural to thank God.

"Winning an Olympic gold medal was something I wanted to do all my life, and when I finally realized it, I was thanking God for giving me the strength and courage to do. Actually, I was thanking God for all the good *and* bad times I had, because all the failures and frustrations and adversities brought me to that point.

"I knew when my neck was hurt, God was there, watching over me. I knew when I was wrestling in the Olympic Games that he was watching over me. I knew when I won the gold medal that he intended me to win. He wanted someone like me to spread the Word and be a role model for kids. I knew that from the beginning. I believe in spreading my word and showing kids they can make their dreams come true and they have to be big believers in God. I feel he's called on me to do that. He made me the best in the world so a lot of people would respect me and I could tell them, 'Hey, God's the way to go.' "

DAVE DRAVECKY showed the nation what courage is all about. Ernest Hemingway defined courage as grace under pressure. Webster's Dictionary defines courage as facing up to any dangerous, difficult, or painful obstacle rather than running from it.

Neither definition does the word justice. True courage, wrote John F. Kennedy in his Pulitzer Prize-winning *Profiles in Courage,* is "that most admirable of human virtues." It is sacrificing, despite possibly dreadful consequences, to do what is right for others.

Courage is a politician taking a stand that could cost him his office but is good for the country. Courage is a soldier leading his battalion through an enemy minefield.

Courage is DAVE DRAVECKY.

Not just because Dravecky battled cancer. To save oneself is not the apex of courage; the will to survive is inherent and not in itself exceptionally valiant. No, what makes Dravecky so courageous is the way he fought the deadly disease and inspired thousands in the process.

He never quit, never complained, never cursed his fate. His baseball career is over, but his message lives on. He found strength and serenity in his religious faith, and he preaches fervently so that we might learn from his lesson and make his savior ours too.

We are accustomed to seeing athletes in victory. But anyone can revel in glory. The real measure of a man is how he copes with adversity. What trials have Christian athletes faced, and how did they persevere? What lessons can they share about handling the tough times in our lives and careers?

Dave Dravecky is a good place to start.

"I don't think I ever met a guy with more courage," said Roger Craig, his former manager with the San Francisco Giants.

"When they talk about what defines a champion, it's heart," said Boom Boom Mancini, a former boxing champion who, like Dravecky, was a Youngstown, Ohio, native known for his heart. "If you look in the dictionary under 'heart,' you see Dave's picture."

"Dave is truly a living inspiration," said Ozzie Newsome, a Hall of Fame-bound tight end. "I would like my young son to grow up like Dave Dravecky."

Dravecky, who pitched eight years with the San Diego Padres and Giants, lost half his deltoid—the muscle that surrounds the shoulder and controls the pitching motion—when doctors removed a desmoid tumor on October 7, 1988. Rare is the man who can strike out major leaguers with a strong, healthy deltoid. None ever had done it with half a deltoid. When Dr. George F. Muschler removed Dravecky's, his "greatest hope" was that Dravecky might someday toss a baseball in the backyard with his children.

But Dravecky would not surrender. His comeback took place on August 10, 1989, in the middle of a pennant race. He drove to the game with fellow pitcher Scott Garrelts, who expected Dravecky to be nervous and did not know what to say to soothe him. No worry. Dravecky was as calm and focused as could be. His cassette deck cranked to full volume, Dravecky sang along to a Christian song, "Give Thanks with a Grateful Heart."

In warmups, he received the first of six standing ovations from a crowd two or three times the size of a normal midweek game. "The first and last standing ovation anybody will ever receive in the bullpen," Dravecky said. "What a feeling! Then I walked out on the mound to start the game and stood there among the cheers and all I could do was give thanks to God for what he did."

Win or lose, Craig and Dravecky had called it "a miracle" he just made it out there.

How do you top a miracle?

Dravecky gave up just one hit the first seven innings.

"Nobody could believe it," Garrelts said. "My jaw dropped on the ground. He's got half an arm missing and he's throwing a one-hitter. I mean, this game isn't supposed to be that easy."

Turns out it was not. Dravecky gave up a three-run homer in the eighth and settled for a 4–3 victory. Five days later he pitched again. He was leading 3–0 and working on a two-hitter in the sixth inning when he gave up a home run and a single. Then, on a pitch to Tim Raines, even fans a hundred feet away could hear the loud *crack* as his arm broke in two. He lurched forward, crumpled face down on the ground, and held his arm in distress, wailing, "It's broken! It's broken!" He was wheeled off on a stretcher.

About a dozen teammates participated in an emotional prayer

session with him in the dressing room. And still he was at peace. Before he left for the hospital, he told them, "Just win the game!"

"It inspired the whole ballclub," Craig said. "Just being around Dave Dravecky makes us all better people."

Four or five teammates went to his hotel room at eleven that night. Garrelts stayed until 5 A.M. and was amazed at Dravecky's serenity. "Not once did Dave say, 'Why me? Why did this happen again?' " Garrelts recalled.

"Believe it or not," Dravecky said, "I was excited about what God was doing. What I saw through the broken arm was an opportunity to give something back. God was taking me from one stage of my career to another where I felt I could be used by him."

That did not mean his pain was over. He broke the arm again during the Giants' National League pennant celebration in October. The cancer had returned. Two months later doctors removed the other half of his deltoid, ten percent of his tricep, and another malignant tumor the size of a lemon.

"Even after the second surgery," Garrelts said, "he never asked, 'Why me?' So many people wanted to question his faith: 'Well, what do you think now? Who do you believe in now?' Yet he stayed firm. He's been such an example for me—and I would think for anyone—to watch conduct his life."

Doctors said there was a fifty-fifty chance the cancer would return. It did. Seventeen months and twelve thousand rads of radiation later, they had to amputate his arm and shoulder to save his life.

Imagine that. From the time he was a boy, his arm had defined him. "What an arm!" fans and friends and family yelled. "A major-league arm!" the scouts drooled. Everything Dave Dravecky was, everything he wanted to be, was wrapped in that left arm.

It was his identity, his fame, his fortune, his self-worth. He was a pitcher, and a pitcher is measured by his arm and its accomplishments. More than we should, all of us, to one extent or another, measure our lives—and are measured by others—by tangible results, be they career or car or home or family. Did you close the sale? Did you make six figures? Did you drive a Mercedes or

Lexus? Did you win in the classroom or boardroom? Did your children get straight A's and get voted homecoming king or queen?

Magnify the norm ten times, maybe a hundred times, and you get an idea of the fishbowl that is professional sports. A pitcher and his arm become one.

And they cut off Dave Dravecky's arm.

Forget the physical pain. Can you imagine the psychological trauma? You take away an athlete's arm, you take away a huge part of his life.

And yet while cancer could rob him of his career, his arm, his shoulder, it could not take away his heart, his soul, his faith. When his baseball career ended in tragedy, Dravecky did not sulk. He turned to helping others. He and his wife have written six books, produced a video, and started Dave Dravecky's Outreach of Hope, a nonprofit organization offering encouragement through Jesus Christ to those suffering from cancer or amputation. He has preached his inspirational message in hundreds of interviews and speeches.

"I was at Sloan-Kettering [Institute for Cancer Research] when he had his second operation," said Atlee Hammaker, another pitcher, friend, and Christian. "People there were dying with brain tumors, with stomach cancer. These guys were really a lot worse off than Dave, but they saw a strength in Dave that they wanted to be a part of and wanted to know what it was all about. All these other things (the many awards Dravecky has received) are temporary. Inspiration is for all time. He has been an inspiration and touched a lot of people's lives."

A large part of that message, whether people want to listen or not, involves his Christian faith. "The miracle wasn't the fact Dave Dravecky came back to pitch," Dravecky said. "The real miracle was when I committed my life to Jesus Christ. I don't want to offend anybody. I've had people tell me they don't like it when I talk about Jesus. But it's like a child on Christmas who receives a special gift, and that gift is so important to him, he's got to run around the house, call Grandma and Grandpa and tell them about that gift, it's so special. I received that gift when I committed my life to Jesus Christ in August of '81. That is the greatest gift in my

life. For me, telling about that gift is more important than anything else.

"Faith is so important, but you don't know what faith is until
it's been tested by the fire. My faith has been tested. The last
impression I would want to give is I'm some kind of superhuman
who didn't go through frustration, who didn't hit walls, who
didn't go through any down moments. That's obviously not what
happened. But my driving force was the strength and peace and
comfort I received through Christ.

"My heart's desire is to serve the Lord. I want to reach out to
young kids and hopefully give them something they can hold on to
forever. I hope to give people hope in the midst of their adversity.
Baseball was a great part of my life. But it's over now—and
greater things lie ahead."

That's inspiring. That's courage. That's Dave Dravecky.

BRETT BUTLER was the Giants' leadoff hitter the day Dave
Dravecky came back. "It's the most memorable thing that's ever
happened to me, standing in center field teary-eyed, watching
Dave Dravecky pitch when everybody in the country thought he'd
never pitch again," Butler said then.

Little did Butler realize it, but Dravecky would prove to be a
powerful role model for Butler's bout with cancer seven years
later.

Butler grew up in a Christian home. He got down on his knees
and asked Christ into his life in 1973. When he felt he was letting
baseball become his god in 1981 and then 1986, he recommitted
to his faith both times. He was a skinny little runt with a weak bat
and a weak arm, who barely played on his high school baseball
team, who walked on at Arizona State and could not make it, who
went through four minor-league clubs just to get out of Class A
ball. That he had emerged as one of baseball's top leadoff men
"was only by the grace of God," he was convinced.

But in May 1996, what was supposed to be a routine tonsillectomy revealed a plum-sized lump of cancer. Squamous cell carci-
noma is a rare cancer of the tonsils with an average survival rate
after five years of 70 percent.

Butler believed things happened for a reason, that God has a purpose for everything. But he did not know what cancer's purpose could be. "I didn't understand. I was asking myself, 'Why?' " said Butler, by then the Los Angeles Dodgers' star center fielder.

Nine months before, his mother had died of cancer. Now he feared he might die too. He was thirty-eight. God, what did he do to deserve this? At least one doctor told him a comeback would be impossible. He was shaken. He said he would retire from baseball.

Doctors removed fifty lymph nodes, one with cancer, and he began six weeks of radiation treatments that left him a withered 142 pounds. Manager Bill Russell said he looked like "a raw piece of meat." General manager Fred Claire said his neck looked "like someone had put it in a microwave." When he visited Dodger Stadium July 30, it took him fifteen minutes to swallow a single strand of spaghetti.

"For nine days, I was in excruciating pain. I couldn't sleep. I couldn't eat. I couldn't swallow," said Butler, who had to numb the back of his throat by swabbing it with an anesthetic just to eat anything. "The first thing you think about is death: 'Well, I'm going to die, I'm going to die.' From there you get the fear factor."

Then his faith kicked in. He vowed to beat cancer not only at life but at his career.

"For me, being a born-again Christian, it was, 'Okay, Lord, what the heck's going on?' " Butler said. "I was only thirty-eight years old, and I really had to get my thoughts and my wits about me. Once I was able to do that, we were able to deal with it. I've faced adversity before. When I had an eye injury in '86, the doctors told me there was a 70 percent chance I wouldn't get my sight back. I was five feet and eighty-nine pounds as a freshman in high school, and everyone thought I was too small to play.

"I've met a lot of people with more ability than I have, but I've never met anyone with more drive and desire. God instilled that in me. I'm going to attack this same cancer with the same vigor as I have everything else. It is etched in my soul. I'm determined to play because they told me I couldn't do it. I've been told that my whole life. That's the fiber of my being. If you're told you can't do it, prove them wrong."

He worked out for three and a half weeks with fitness guru Mackie Shilstone and the minor-league New Orleans Zephyrs, regaining most of his weight and strength. "I know other athletes who would have quit," Shilstone said. "His will is his strongest attribute."

"I really do think it's a miracle that he's coming back," Russell said. "To see him the way he was [after radiation treatments], you had to think, 'There's no way.' But here he is."

And look what he did: just four months after his cancer was diagnosed, just thirty-eight days after the last of thirty-two radiation treatments, still fueled by fifty-nine pills a day plus regular injections of an experimental cancer-fighting drug called laetrile, Butler got on base twice and scored the winning run to lift the Dodgers back into first place. "Another miracle," said his wife, Eveline. "Miracles happen around us, you know."

The returning hero played the conquering hero, just like in the movies they used to make, a few miles down Sunset Boulevard in Hollywood. "A fairy tale?" Butler said. "Yeah, they do come true."

When he was weak, God gave him strength. "When you hear cancer, you think, 'Hey, I could die,' " Butler said. "But after gathering my thoughts, I realized God was using me, but he was using me in a positive way. And now my purpose is to give people hope and help them to see that if they have a disease, they can beat it and return to a normal life. I think there's something bigger than this. Maybe it's about the hope that people see. That somebody with cancer can do this. It's the answered prayer for all those people who prayed for me all the time.

"God continually gives us signs. Things happen in life that we can't explain. A friend said that when she heard the news about my cancer, she opened the daily prayer book and the topic was strength. An illumination came over her and all she could see was my face. She told me, 'Brett, you had this peace in your body. You aren't going to die.' What causes these phenomena? It's got to be divine intervention."

Whatever inspiration he gave to others, he got in return. He said he has received more than 150 books, thousands of cards, and numerous phone calls from all across the country. One of the most moving cards came from teammate Todd Hollandsworth. "He wrote that he cried when he heard the news," Butler said. "And he said that Satan was trying to take one of God's angels and that the world would be a scary place without me."

But the best gift was the gift of prayer. He said people across the country, including competitors such as Mets outfielder Lance Johnson, told him they were praying for him.

"And I felt those prayers," Butler said. "It's stuff like that that has made a difference. There's no question about that."

Dodgers first baseman Eric Karros was convinced it was fate: "He is an example of how one can battle the worst of circumstances, no matter how grave. You feel sorry for yourself or want to make excuses? Go ahead and look at Brett, and then see if you still feel sorry for yourself."

But, like Dravecky, Butler's torment was not over. In the fifth game of his comeback he broke a bone in his left hand, and his season was over. He came back again to play for the Dodgers in 1997 in what will probably be his final season.

Only five players in this century—four Hall of Famers and one active player with that Cooperstown potential—have exceeded the combination of batting average and stolen bases that Butler has put together. He is a hero for all the little guys who supposedly cannot play, an inspiration for anyone facing adversity.

LOREN ROBERTS made the PGA Tour at age twenty-six.

But he really had not made it. He won just $8,935 the whole year, and lost his card. He sat out all but two events the next year, passing qualifying school in the fall so he could return to the tour in 1983. That year was no better. With his wife of one year in tow, he made just $7,724 and lost his card again.

But his life, and his game, began to change that year. After an awful outing at the Milwaukee Open, he committed himself to God. This did not create some miraculous change in his golf game, but he did begin to improve. He made between $53,655 and $92,761 each of the next four years. Subtract traveling expenses and many years he made so little money, he did not have to pay any taxes.

"I was a net loss," said Roberts, whose sponsors kept him afloat, albeit barely. "Almost everything we owned was in the trunk of an old Oldsmobile. We rented an apartment and had to sublet it while we were gone on the road. I probably would have quit playing if not for being saved."

When golf was his god, he realized, he was putting incredible pressure on himself. When he placed God first, family second, and golf third, he began to relax—essential for a sport that is as much mental as physical.

"My faith didn't make me a better golfer physically," he said. "I would hate for people to get the idea because I'm a Christian and I believe in Jesus Christ that things just got great in my life. That's not the way it happens. I still have weeks where I struggle. God does not make the ball go in the hole. I didn't start believing in God and my golf swing suddenly became great. Sometimes people feel a Christian has that attitude, and that's not the way it is. We don't feel that way.

"I haven't improved physically. I've improved mentally. Golf is a game you have to learn."

And learn it he did. It took five qualifying schools and seven struggling years, but Roberts made the PGA Tour for good in 1988. He has made six figures every year since, topping $1 million in 1994 and $2.4 million from 1994 through 1996. He has been good enough that he finished second in the 1994 U.S. Open and won three of four matches while representing the United States in the 1995 Ryder Cup.

Part of his improvement came because he learned the game's technical side, courses' intricacies, and the correct shot for each situation. Part came because his faith allowed him to better control his emotions. You see it time and again on the golf course: Even the seemingly strongest men can melt under the pressure, especially in the big events.

"The pressure at the Ryder Cup was three times as much as the U.S. Open," Roberts said. "I think your faith can help you calm down, but it still turns to making shots under pressure. The pressure affects you mentally and physically. When you're under pressure, you don't breathe as deeply and so you don't get as much blood flowing to your muscles. You have to be mentally and physically ready for the pressure.

"Before I became a Christian, I was not as positive as I am now. I was below middle of the road. I was lukewarm negativism. If I hit a bad shot, I'd tell myself, 'Here you go, another bad shot! You might as well pack it up and go home.' I have a temper. I don't have a violent temper where I snap and break things, I don't get mad at other people, but I get upset with myself when I feel I don't perform up to my best. My faith helped temper that down, but I still get upset. A little bit of fire in your belly is good to spur you on, but when it takes control of your emotions, then you have problems.

"That's what's unique about golf. Golf cannot be played on a high level on an emotional roller coaster. Golf has to be played on an even keel. So it was a combination of faith and maturity that helped me get my game together. The Bible is an instructional manual that God gave us. Anything you struggle with, you can find some answers in the Bible. Having the right perspective on life allows you to become much calmer mentally."

In times of trouble, Roberts turns to his favorite verse. "Philippians 4:13," he said. " 'I can do all things through him who enables me.' " He turned to the Bible to try to resolve his most dire personal moment, a breakup with a golfing mentor.

"I lost the friendship of a real close, dear person, and my faith really helped get me through this, helped me understand it," said Roberts, the sorrow still evident in his eyes, voice, and mannerisms four years after the split. He clasped his hands and lowered his head as he spoke.

"It was probably my lowest point as a Christian. He was very close to me. I have done all I humanly can, did what the Scriptures told me to do—to confront the problem and try to work it out—and I was rebuffed at every turn. I've left it at that. My faith has allowed me to deal with it and accept it, knowing I did my part to try to rectify the situation.

"It helped me to know God has a plan. We wonder why it happens. We look back later and understand why. We have great hindsight; God has the foresight. This was 1992 and I had not won a tournament."

He has won plenty since the split. And yet . . . "I still love this person and it hurts me to think he doesn't feel that way about me anymore. But I look at the way my career has gone and I guess God had the right thing in mind."

TONY DUNGY, the Tampa Bay Buccaneers' bright young coach, grew up believing in God and doing the right thing. He always studied and played sports. He never used alcohol, tobacco, or drugs. He never even cursed. He never lost close friends or family to death or tragedy.

"It's easy to say, 'I have faith,' as long as you have a good job and a refrigerator full of food and a good family and great wife and kids," he said. "I've often wondered if I did meet failure, would I still respond the same way?"

But just because his personal life has been blissful does not mean he has not met career failures. The first came when he set records as a University of Minnesota quarterback and yet was not drafted by a single team in 1977—and that was back when the NFL had a twelve-round draft.

"I was only depressed for a day or two. The day after the draft, teams started calling and trying to sign me as a free agent. I felt wanted again," said Dungy, who chose the Pittsburgh Steelers over guaranteed money from the CFL's Montreal Alouettes. "We won the Super Bowl in '78 and then the next year I was traded. That's traumatic. I felt like, 'The Steelers don't think I'm good enough.' I went from a Super Bowl team to San Francisco, the worst team or the second-worst team in football, and I didn't understand why. My pride was hurt. But at least someone wanted me, even though it wasn't what I wanted.

"We know that in all things, God works for the good of those who love him, who have been called according to his purpose. What good could come out of being traded two thousand miles away, from the best team in football to the worst? I didn't know then. All I could think was, 'Something good is coming out of it.' Then I got traded again to the Giants in 1980 and I was able to withstand that because it had happened before. Then Coach [Ray] Perkins cut me and I was waiting for someone to pick me up, certain someone would—and no one did.

"Now, that's where my faith had to really kick in. By that time, I was ready spiritually to handle it. I don't know what I would have done if I'd gotten cut immediately by the Steelers, before I matured as a Christian. I'm sure I wouldn't have had the same response, because I had grown a lot in those four years. I was down a day or two, but I knew I was in a different era now. My playing career was over and God had something else for me to do. I didn't know what it was at the time, but I was ready for it."

Dungy had planned to play nine or ten years in the NFL, build up a nest egg, then coach high school basketball. Suddenly, he was twenty-four, his playing days were over, and his nest egg had not hatched. God, he is convinced now, had a different—and better— plan for him. He went back to his alma mater, helping out as a volunteer coach and staying in shape in case an NFL team called upon him to play. Instead, two NFL teams called upon him to coach.

"Coach Perkins told me when he cut me, 'I think you're going to be a good coach and if I get an opening I'd like to hire you.' I thought he was making conversation as a way to let me down easy. I didn't think much about it," Dungy said. "But he tracked me down at UM and said, 'I've got a quality control position open. I'd like to talk to you about it.' "

When Giants owner Wellington Mara told good friend and Steelers owner Art Rooney that New York was about to hire one of his ex-players, Rooney told Dungy's old coach, Chuck Noll, who quickly called Dungy and asked if he were serious about coaching. Dungy said he'd like to try, and next thing he knew, Noll had created an extra position for him. By age twenty-eight, Dungy was the league's youngest coordinator, and he quickly built stellar defenses. He earned further experience coaching under two other perennial playoff coaches, Kansas City's Marty Schottenheimer and Minnesota's Denny Green, before getting a chance to turn around Tampa Bay. He learned how to coach from two Hall of Famers, Noll and Bill Walsh.

"Getting traded and released turned out to be great experience for me in the long run," Dungy said. "I'd been prepared by little adversities and I was ready to deal with adversity later in life. If I had known at that point that someday I was going to be a coach and all these lessons were going to be important for me, I would have felt better about the trades. But all I felt then was rejection.

"Looking back now, I can see God was preparing me to be a coach. I went to San Francisco and saw a different way of doing things, a different style with Coach Walsh, a team not at the top but at the very bottom, and watched him start it on the way up. Denny Green was the special teams coach and fifteen years later he hires me as defensive coordinator. Then the next year they traded me to the Giants and I learned different offensive and defensive styles under Coach Perkins. All these things made me a better coach."

And now, instead of coaching high school ball, Dungy is one of thirty men at the pinnacle of his profession, with a multiyear, multimillion-dollar contract. He is convinced this is God's plan, not his own, that it is divine intervention, not just coincidence.

"It's so illogical, I couldn't have planned it," Dungy said. "I grew up in Jackson, Michigan, halfway between Michigan and Michigan State. My mom went to Michigan State. My dad went to Michigan. Everybody in that area dreams of playing for one of those two teams. I end up six hundred miles away, Tom Moore recruits me, he ends up going to Pittsburgh, and now, rather than go to Montreal for guaranteed money, I go to Pittsburgh and all these other things happen. If you wanted to plot it all out, there's no way. It would have been a million-to-one chance of all that happening. And so I know it wasn't a coincidence.

"Part of it, too, is you do your job to the best of your ability. You don't just float through and all these good things happen to you. You do as well as you can and you let the Lord take it from there."

GARY CARTER's mother died when he was only twelve, too young to cope with the death emotionally or spiritually.

Probably the biggest test of his adult faith came in 1991, when nobody in baseball offered him a guaranteed contract. He was an eleven-time All-Star, a two-time All-Star MVP, a record-setting catcher accustomed to big paychecks, but here he was at thirty-six, scrounging for a job, wondering if his career were over. He made the Los Angeles Dodgers as a nonroster invitee, but it was a miserable year.

"I was confused, disillusioned, disappointed, a number of things," Carter said. "I sat on the bench a great deal. I would say my faith was tested then. A lot of things crossed my mind, just as far as not really understanding how some players are treated differently than others and good fortunes come their way. We all go through letdowns. I wondered where I was headed. Baseball had been my life since I was five years old. When I saw it coming to an end, there was a bit of disappointment, a bit of unsureness. A lot of things raced through my mind. But God is constant. He never teeters one way or the other.

"After the Dodgers, I went back to the Expos and had one more fabulous year with the club I started with. I was able to end up my career on a winning note. My last at-bat was a game-winning double at Olympic Stadium, in front of a Fan Appreciation Day crowd."

Carter stood on second base, raised his arms in victory, and felt his skin tingle as the fans gave him an incredible standing ovation that lasted five minutes. Just three weeks later a brand-new team, the Florida Marlins, named Carter their color commentator. He would continue to earn paychecks from the game he had loved since boyhood.

"I couldn't have written a script better than that," he said.

PAUL AZINGER's Christian faith was tested when he learned the pain in his shoulder could end not only his golf career but his life.

He was thirty-three years old.

He had cancer. He did not have enough faith.

Two mornings after he learned the awful news, a false fire alarm roused him and his wife from their hotel bed. While they waited in the lobby, Toni Azinger noticed a sign announcing church services in one of the ballrooms. A few hours later they slipped into the ballroom.

"That false alarm had not been so false after all," Azinger wrote in a *Guideposts* magazine excerpt from *Zinger,* his autobiography with Ken Abraham. "There was a fire in the air, a spiritual charge I could feel throughout me. I felt I was face to face with God, and an excitement I hadn't felt in years came over me. I knew that Christ wanted not just my cancer, or my golf, or my fears about my family, but all of it—my whole life, if only I would give it to him and recommit myself to faith. 'I need you now more than ever, Lord,' I whispered silently."

Two days later Dr. Lorne Feldman told Azinger he did not believe the cancer had spread beyond his scapula.

Azinger began chemotherapy that day, and the first treatment left him so nauseous and dehydrated, he had to be rushed back to the hospital for emergency care. Still, the initial sense of nightmare turned into a sense of peace. Azinger spent hours in his backyard, just staring at the flowers and trees and birds. The emotional guy had turned mellow.

"Then one morning while I was getting ready for the day, something happened," he wrote. "I was standing in my bedroom praying, wondering in the back of my mind what would happen if I didn't get better. The sun was forcing its way through the blinds when suddenly a powerful feeling swelled over me like a huge, gently rolling wave lifting my feet off the sandy bottom of the sea. I stopped everything I was doing and experienced an incredible, peace-giving sensation. I knew that God was with me; I felt absolutely assured that I would be okay."

Today, Azinger is cancer-free, and "what keeps me going most these days is the chance to be an example for others who are struck by disease, to help them see that God is there for them no matter what. That's all you need to know to get through anything in life."

KAREEM ABDUL-JABBAR scored more points, blocked more shots, and played more games than anyone in NBA history.

But the path from a Catholic boy named Lew Alcindor to a Muslim man named Kareem Abdul-Jabbar had many a roadblock.

He received hate mail when he boycotted the 1968 Olympics and again feared for his life when Black Muslims massacred seven members of his mentor's family in a townhouse Abdul-Jabbar owned. He anguished over separations from his mentor, his parents, and his first wife. When his house and all his possessions—including elaborate oriental rugs, Korans from the Middle Ages, three thousand jazz albums, basketball trophies, and thousands of irreplaceable photographs dating back to childhood—were destroyed by fire, he despaired for a time.

But, he wrote in his autobiography, "Islam had taught me how to face the world, and once again, I turned to it for strength."

Abdul-Jabbar turned to the Koran, 29:1–3: "Do men imagine that they will be left at ease because they say, 'We believe' and will not be tested with affliction? Truly! we tested those who were before you. Thus Allah knoweth those who are sincere and those who feign." And 2:155–56: "In the name of Allah the Compassionate and the Merciful. And surely we shall try you with something of fear and hunger and loss of wealth and lives and crops; but give glad tidings to the steadfast who say when the misfortune striketh them: Truly! we are Allah's and truly! unto him we are returning."

When he severely sprained his ankle in game five of the 1980 NBA finals, and every step throbbed, he played through the pain "after asking Allah for some special strength"—and led the Los Angeles Lakers to victory with a remarkable forty-point performance.

EVANDER HOLYFIELD knocked out Buster Douglas to win his first heavyweight championship and lost it to Riddick Bowe in a bruising battle when he tried to prove his punching power. As part of his prefight ritual, he closed his eyes, an open Bible on his legs, and prayed. "The Real Deal" says boxing is 10 percent physical and 90 percent spiritual. A Las Vegas pastor told him to say, "Here I am, Lord. Thy will be done," when he entered the ring, and "It is done," every time he hit Bowe.

He repeated the prayer twice in the ring. And with each punch, he said, "It is done!" And soon Bowe *was* done. Holyfield, a 5–1 underdog, won a unanimous decision and became just the fourth fighter to regain the heavyweight title.

But when his left shoulder gave out, he lost the title again in a split decision against Michael Moorer. He was taken to a hospital, where doctors diagnosed shoulder and kidney problems and two heart problems. His left ventricle was not pumping enough blood. And he had a tiny hole in his heart. Dr. Ron Stephens said it was a miracle he fought twelve rounds in heart failure. Doctors unanimously recommended he retire, and his boxing license was revoked.

Holyfield asked the Lord to heal him and repeated Scripture. He prayed for God's guidance. His pastor told him God was calling him and someone with spiritual insight would enter his life so he could achieve God's will. He went home and read a letter from a woman he did not know. She told him she had been healed at a Benny Hinn crusade, and suggested the Christian evangelist could heal Holyfield too. Holyfield went onstage at Hinn's Philadelphia crusade and told Hinn he felt he already was healed, but Hinn said he and the audience would pray anyway. People prayed, sang, and called out to the Lord, and Hinn asked those who wanted to rededicate themselves to come forward.

"With Evander standing up front, Hinn walked across the stage," Bernard Holyfield wrote in his biography of his brother, *Holyfield: The Humble Warrior.* "He turned in Evander's direction and shouted out in his 'prayer language.' Hinn was standing about six feet away from the former champ, and with his right arm made a large, sweeping motion in Evander's direction. Evander felt himself falling and tried to resist, but his legs didn't respond. His fall was different from anything he had ever felt. Instead of having his knees buckle, as you would expect, Evander dropped directly back, as if somebody had pushed him and he was too unconscious even to move his legs. It was the first time in his life that he had been 'slain in the spirit.'

"Two men standing next to Evander caught him and laid him out on the stage. Evander felt his heart racing, and a warm feeling spread through his chest. . . . When he heard Hinn say, 'His heart is being healed,' he rejoiced at the news, receiving it as a confirmation of something that he believed had already happened."

The following week his doctor told him he was getting better. By his third visit his doctor was shocked. Two more doctors were consulted and had to be convinced the "before" and "after" results were of the same heart. They pronounced the heart healed, and after a battery of tests, a Mayo Clinic doctor told Holyfield, "Your heart is not only healthy, but you are more healthy than anyone I have ever examined."

Sports Illustrated reported that the Mayo Clinic doctors decided the defect had never existed. But Holyfield believed God healed him so that he could fight again and spread the Word, and he did, all the way to his third heavyweight championship and the 1997 rematch victory against Mike Tyson.

Whatever their denomination, athletes tend to turn to faith to face adversity. Whatever the obstacles—whether they are life- or career-threatening illnesses or setbacks, the loss of loved ones or loved possessions—religious athletes find themselves comforted and steeled by religion.

9

The Challenge of Sports

"Blessed are the meek, for they shall inherit the earth."
—Matthew 5:5
"Thugs win football games."—Joe Walton, longtime NFL coach

Reggie White was not quite sure he believed in God until one day when he decided to test God. The little ten-year-old was playing baseball, terrified he would get hit by a pitcher who threw hard and fast and all over the place.

"The pitcher threw two strikes behind me, and I was scared," Reggie recalled. "There were two or three men on base, and I prayed, 'Please let me hit a home run.' On the third pitch, I closed my eyes and swung—and hit a home run. From then on, I believed. I was saved at thirteen and made a real commitment at the age of fifteen."

The other kids snickered at the kid who toted a Bible everywhere he went and recited the gospel. They laughed, too, when he impersonated everyone from Elvis Presley to Muhammad Ali to Rodney Dangerfield, everything from the U.S. Army to the Incredible Hulk to Lassie. He was "a nice Sunday school boy who wouldn't harm a feather," said Robert Pulliam, his high school football coach, who thought that was fine for the person but not the player.

"We knew if we ever got him to be intense, he'd be a holy terror," Pulliam recalled. "He played pickup basketball with me and some older guys. They'd victimize him and he wouldn't fight back. I got annoyed. I challenged him. Every time he played a pickup game, I made sure I was on the opposite team. I'd use roughhouse tactics to get him upset and frustrated, get him to stand up and bang inside with me."

Pulliam was six feet two and 250 pounds, a former Tennessee football player who was as strong and tough as they come. When he elbowed and shoved, it hurt. Reggie, already six-four and 225 pounds as a sophomore, ran inside the locker room and broke down crying.

"We took a water break," Pulliam said. "Reggie was the last guy to the fountain. I called him over and he was still wiping tears away. I told him, 'I don't care about you crying. I want to see you *fight*. If you think I'm going to apologize, we might as well go back and I'll beat you again.'

"Two weeks later, in a student-faculty game, there was a crucial battle for a rebound. Next thing I knew, I was *sailing over his head*. By the end of the year, I had to back off. It got too rough. He had gotten the point."

A Christian *can* be both faithful and ferocious.

"Coach Pulliam helped instill that meanness in me the first time he made me cry and didn't apologize. He gave me a tougher attitude toward sports," said White, now the NFL's career sack leader and one of the greatest, toughest players that football has ever known. He is doing his best to erase the perception that Christian athletes are soft and meek.

"A lot of people perceive meekness the wrong way," said White, who became a licensed Baptist minister when he was seventeen and is an associate pastor in Knoxville, Tennessee. "Jesus was meek but stern in everything he did. That's the attitude I've taken also. It's helped me to gain stern meekness.

"My junior year at Tennessee, I was injured and wasn't playing well and people said, 'It's because he's a Christian and he's not tough enough.' My senior year, I was great and they said, 'You're not supposed to do this; you're a Christian.' What do people want me to do? Be a chump? My purpose is not to hurt anybody but to get the job done.

"In Israel, God told them to wipe people out. Reggie White's not doing that. He's not wiping people out. He's playing a game that's fun. True, sometimes people get hurt. It can happen in any sport. I don't want to put anybody out of a game or hurt somebody, but if I do, it's part of the game and sometimes it does benefit my team. If I have a chance to hit him, I'm going to hit him. I'm not going to lay back and say, 'I'm a good Christian, I won't hit him hard.' That's my job."

His job—and even his duty. White feels he has been called by God to spread his Word, and the more glory he earns on the football field, the more he can spread his message off it.

"I don't play like a demon," the Minister of Defense said. "I play like the Holy Spirit lives within me. If I played like a chump, nobody would have anything to say or do with me.

"I'm six feet five, 290 pounds. I've got a God who can wipe Reggie White out at any time. He created man himself and he can destroy this world with the snap of his fingers. How can I be a sissy when I'm serving a God like that? It takes a *man* to walk for Jesus. The man or woman who walks for Jesus is going to be ridiculed. I got harassed, I got spitballs thrown at me, got joked about, called preacher boy because I carried a Bible. But I stood fast in my beliefs because I had a God that was real. As I got older, kids respected me for it. He's put me in this position so I can be his mouthpiece."

The Bible preaches about turning the other cheek and loving those who hate you. Football coaches preach about being tough and physical and intimidating and violent. Yet White sees no contradiction in being a punishing preacher.

"What makes you think football is violence?" he said, his voice rising. "I've been asked this question for years. Football is not violent. When a kid puts a gun up to another guy's head and blows it off, that's violence. Our game is aggression. We don't go out to kill each other. We go out to win. I get personally offended by people who label our game as violent because it's not. Some things happen, you get hurt, you may break your leg, but we're not out there to murder each other.

"I can't take this notion that Christian football players are weak. I've seen where the reason the Rams traded Sean Gilbert is because he became a Christian, so that supposedly made him soft. I played against guys who were not Christians who were some of the scariest guys you ever met in your life because they didn't have any heart. Why is it that when Christian players give our all, when we go out and terrorize, we're not supposed to be doing that, and yet when we don't go out there and terrorize, then we have no heart because we're Christians? Stuff like that, I don't understand."

St. Louis traded Gilbert, a Pro Bowl defensive tackle, for a 1996 first-round draft choice the Rams used to select Lawrence Phillips, a Nebraska running back. The Rams preferred a girlfriend-abusing rookie to a born-again Christian.

"Reports in St. Louis indicated some in the Rams' organization wondered in 1994 whether Gilbert lost intensity after he was born again," the *Washington Post* wrote. "It's part of the strange conflict inherent in the NFL: It wants violence and mayhem in well-defined amounts and at specific moments so it can be packaged for family consumption. Then, when the games are over, it wants its players to be model citizens."

Gilbert told the newspaper: "The one stereotype that's been placed on Christians is that they are soft. When you see Reggie White, you don't think soft. Or Mike Singletary or Darrell Green or Tim Johnson or Charles Mann or Fred Stokes or Aeneas Williams or Cris Carter or Curtis Martin. When you see those guys, do you say, 'Wow, he's soft'?"

The Redskins certainly did not. A bunch of Christians, including future Hall of Fame cornerback Green, had starred for them. And so did Gilbert. "Anyone who thinks Sean Gilbert is soft," defensive coordinator Ron Lynn said, "hasn't tried to block him."

On the field, "I'm still mean," Gilbert said. "When it's time to destroy and conquer, that's my main goal, to leave nothing standing. That's what's in my heart. If you know God like I know him, revenge is his."

In fact, the Bible speaks directly to competition, and it does not suggest turning the other cheek. "My favorite Scripture is Colossians 3:23," White said. "That says whatsoever you do, do it heartily, as to God, not to man."

"I don't see how people can say Christian athletes are soft, because it's surely not true," Dolphins cornerback Terrell Buckley said. "They're not reading the Word. Reggie White is one of the toughest guys I've ever seen."

Buckley said he has become tougher and more focused since he became a Christian.

"It's one thing to go in and watch five hours of videotape and you're sitting there like this, nodding your head, half asleep," he said, and leaned back with a blank look on his face. "Now I've cut down on the time, but I'm going in there with a pencil, pad, taking notes, watching this guy, watching that guy, and always reminding myself. I'm challenging myself now. I want to grade out 100 percent.

"Part of that is maturity, but I also have to give the Lord credit. Even with maturity, sometimes you get tired. You don't want to do it. Your body, your mind, something tells you, 'I'm tired today.' That happened in training camp and then I reminded myself that the Lord was in the desert. The Devil was tempting Jesus. He had him on the cliff. Jesus didn't give up. He didn't say, 'Ah, just this one time.' I'm like, 'Hey, you're not doing this for you. You're trying to show what having the Lord on your side will do for you.'

"When Jimmy Johnson became coach, you had to prove yourself every day in training camp. You know how tough that is, mentally, physically, in that South Florida heat? The Lord got me through two-a-day practices. I never would have gotten through every second of two-a-days in pads before. Wheewwwwwwwww! I didn't think I could make it through. But not only did I make it through, I competed every practice, every drill. I cannot take the credit for that, because if it were up to me I'd want to take a day or two off. But it's not up to me."

Both Christian and Muslim athletes say their faith motivates them to be competitive, not complacent. They say they must give their very best so they can give their glory to God or to Allah.

The notion of "soft" religious athletes drew particular attention in the late 1970s when the San Francisco Giants were denounced by manager Dave Bristol, teammate Bill Madlock, and the local media.

"When I got traded to the San Francisco 49ers in 1979, there was a perception those Christian guys had ruined the San Francisco Giants baseball team, that it didn't matter to them if they won or lost, that they just played their best and winning wasn't important," said Tony Dungy, a former NFL defensive back turned coach.

"They were called the God Squad. That can be the perception to a lot of non-Christians. Those people don't understand what it's all about, don't understand that as a Christian, you're called to excel. While we may respond differently to finishing second or third than a non-Christian would, that doesn't mean we accept it or feel it's okay."

But what about Christian athletes who easily dismiss losses as God's will? "You could take it to the extreme," Dungy said, "and say, 'I really don't have to do anything. If God wants me to succeed, if he wants me to have a good season, there's nothing I have to do. And if he doesn't, we're going to struggle and fail no matter how hard I work.' But that is just not the position you can take. You have to say, 'God has given me opportunities, given me skills, and my job is to do the best I can with those skills and let the results fall where God allows.'

"As a Christian, you're going into competition to excel. It's not the most important thing, but that's why you're there. Now, when you meet with failure, how do you respond? Do you go in the tank? Or do you grow from it, get better, and say, 'We didn't win this one, but what can I take out of it?' A lot of the world—the media and fans—want you to visibly show how shaken you are

when you don't win. I don't think you have to do that. It's important to win and excel. There are many places in the Bible that talk
about competition, that we are to run to win and to excel, to do
everything as well as we can. It's a hard concept to explain; I can
see where people can take an explanation like that the wrong way.
But it's more a misconception than anything."

Maybe they had a point, maybe they did not. But surely few
athletes ever showed more guts than Dave Dravecky, who came
back from cancer to pitch for the Giants a decade later. "A lot of
people think Christian athletes are wimpy, don't put forth the
effort, they give in too easily, but Dave Dravecky is a Christian
athlete I admire," Giants pitcher Scott Garrelts said.

All of America admired the 1996 comeback from throat cancer
of another Christian baseball player, Brett Butler. And who is going to challenge the courage or the heart of heavyweight boxing
champions Muhammad Ali, Evander Holyfield, and Mike Tyson?
None felt that hitting another person in the boxing ring contra-
dicted his faith.

Two of basketball's best centers, David Robinson and Hakeem
Olajuwon, are deeply religious, and a third member of the NBA's
elite centers, Shaquille O'Neal, says he believes in God, too. These
big men wage fierce battles, shoving, elbowing, muscling each
other to establish or deny position for rebounds and shots down
low. If they do not dish out some abuse, they get abused.

"All the big men wanted to know what kind of player I was and
whether they could dominate me," Olajuwon wrote in his autobiography. "It was a constant physical power struggle. If a player
can establish his superiority the first few times he plays, that relationship gets set in stone. If someone thinks he can take you, he
will; he gains confidence and will push you and push you, and if
you back down the first time and then the second, he will push you
your entire career. . . . I never play the game to hurt people. I try
to intimidate players with my game. . . . As long as they keep it
clean and they're playing basketball, we will not get into a fight.
But once you start hitting me, you will know the result, and you'll
get the same result every time—I will attack. Always."

And yet, while he is willing to use his fists, he will not use his mouth. Olajuwon denounced guys who make a nice play and scream in their competitors' faces, who use street language that is not professional, not sportsmanlike. "Trash talking is a combination of arrogance and ignorance and insecurity. It shows no class," he wrote in *Living the Dream*. "How you play your game on the court is a reflection of your character in life. If you are selfish and arrogant on the court, you are very likely selfish and arrogant off the court. . . . You can tell a true winner by how he handles adversity. When someone does something spectacular against him, he is not afraid to give that man a compliment. . . . Being sportsmanlike does not make you less competitive."

Becoming a born-again Christian in 1991 "changed my basketball life because it's given me more of a purpose and determination," Robinson said. "When I used to play for myself and my own glory, sometimes it was so much harder to be motivated. Because at what point do you have enough money? At what point do you have enough fame? How do you get over the little aches and pains? How do you find the motivation to get up and work out and push yourself harder and harder and harder?

"Some people have that drive in them. But I never really had that drive. If I could do things well enough for everybody's satisfaction, that was enough. Until people pushed me, I never went past that. God gave me a whole 'nother reason to excel. He gave me something beyond what anyone on earth has ever given me.

"God saw in me a perfection, a place to go I could never envision. I don't know what God has in store for me, but if I don't go get it, if I don't push myself toward that, then I have cheated God. There's no way, when I come before him, that I want him to ask me, 'What did you do with what I gave you?' and I have to say, 'I buried it in the ground.' There's no way I want to say that to him."

Different faith, same philosophy:

"It is up to me to maximize my talent," wrote Olajuwon, a devout Muslim since 1988. "I take responsibility and I guarantee I will be accountable. In the court of Allah I will be asked: 'This talent was given to you, what did you do with it and how did you use it?' I have been given something by Allah that may be used to benefit people. They enjoy watching me play. How can I destroy that talent by not working hard or by abusing drugs or by letting my success turn me into an arrogant person? . . . The real value of your talent is how you use it to do good and to encourage others, for the pleasure of Allah. With that I feel rich, not in material things but for what I have inside myself. The richness of the soul . . . You prepare yourself for victory. You think and plan and train and sweat and work as hard as you can to reach your goal."

The same philosophy holds true in golf, even if participants are hitting little white balls, not each other.

"An aggressive sport like football, it's tough to keep that aggression and still walk the line with your faith," said Loren Roberts, a PGA star nicknamed "The Boss of the Moss" for his putting prowess. "Golf is a little easier line to walk. Sometimes when I talk at FCA meetings, kids say, 'Christians are meek and mild. How are you going to be competitive if you're a nice guy all the time?' But God wants you to try your best. He wants you to give glory for your achievements to him. So obviously, he wants you to win. It's still my job. I still want to be the best I can be."

But if you're a good Christian and a good sportsman, will you win as much as if you were cold and ruthless?

Consider Father's Day 1996, when Steve Jones won the U.S. Open by one stroke over good friend and fellow Christian Tom Lehman.

"About the sixteenth hole," Rick Reilly wrote in *Sports Illustrated,* "Jones is just as nervous as a priest with a Sunday tee time, and guess who talks him off the ledge? Lehman!

"Yes, sir. Lehman lays a little Joshua 1:9 on Jones. They're walking down the fairway, supposedly trying to beat each other's brains in, and Lehman says to Jones: 'God wants us to be strong and courageous,' real nice-like. 'That's God's law.' And Jones looks at him and says, 'Right. Amen.' This calms Jones down enough that he is able to beat Lehman and Love by that one shot.

"Now, my question [to Ben Hogan] is, You never said anything like that to Snead or Demaret or Nelson, did you? . . . I mean, the only Scripture I could see you giving a guy during the middle of the last round of the Open would be something like 'Turn thy other cheek so I might smite that also.' "

Instead of being steeled by his faith, Lehman wilted under the pressure of a major championship with three bogeys on the back nine and lost by one stroke in 1996. The next year, he had three bogeys on the final five holes and lost by two strokes. This time, Reilly wrote, Lehman was "the answer to an ugly trivia question: Who is the only man to lead three consecutive U.S. Opens with eighteen holes to play and blow them all?"

LPGA fellowship director Cris Stevens said she was aware of that criticism and had spoken with both golfers about it and, as a Christian, she did not think it was valid, but as someone trained in counseling, she could see the argument. "The sports world would look at it as head-to-head competition, but they're still playing the course," she said. "They're playing different shots. I know both those guys really wanted to win."

But when they are tied for the lead, and Lehman says something to help Jones, doesn't Lehman lessen his chances of winning? On this dilemma, Stevens is a bit torn between her Christian faith and her academic training.

"I know some psychologists would say yes," she replied. "Psychologists say one championship trait is paranoia, that you've always got to be looking back so you can keep ahead. I agree that happens psychologically, but from a believer's perspective, you're transcended about that. I don't want to sound mystic, but there is another way. In fact, the Bible says there's a way that seems right to man, but it's not the right way. It makes sense from the world's perspective to say, 'I'm going to keep looking over my shoulder to see who's moving up.' But as a Christian, I am not to live my life from the world's perspective but from God's perspective. I believe if I honor him and follow him, I can be caring to someone else, even if I'm playing a match with him. God will recognize that and won't harm me. It's living life from God's perspective and not the world's."

Roberts said non-Christians did not understand. But many new Christians—sometimes called baby Christians—do not understand either. Athletes who once fueled their performances with anger or an us-against-the-world mentality become confused about how to be fierce yet Christian. For instance, when Robinson became a born-again Christian, he was constantly knocked for being soft, and even though teammates said the knocks were wrong after a year or so, even though he was the NBA's MVP in 1995, the knocks persist.

"As you grow and read the Bible more and you understand what you're called to do, you do get a different feel," Dungy said. "We've had a lot of discussions on the different clubs I've been with. Is it wrong to have a great deal of material success? Is it wrong to want to succeed? Is it wrong to have a goal of winning the Super Bowl or should our goal just be to do the best we can? As you grow, you realize no, it's not wrong to have those goals. It's not wrong to be tough within the rules, to be as physical as you can be and play as well as you can play. It's not wrong to want to go to the Pro Bowl.

"But the proper perspective is: why do I want to do these things? Because I'm commanded to use my gifts and not settle for underachieving. Not because I want to go to the Super Bowl for personal gratification, but because I've been gifted to play this game and I'm going to play it to the best of my abilities unto the Lord."

Dungy said most coaches prefer devout athletes, even if they do not admit it.

"Chuck Noll [the Steelers coach who won four Super Bowls and made the Hall of Fame] would talk about the type of guys we had success with—self-motivated, diligent, hard-working, determined, good character, good family people, guys who'd be a credit to the team—and without saying it, that's a Christian athlete. But if you specifically ask, 'Do you want Christian athletes?' many coaches would say, 'Oh, no.' Because we have a stigma that's something you shouldn't talk about. But all the characteristics most coaches talk about in the people they want, the Christian athlete meets that standard.

"There's a false impression in some places that guys won't be tough enough as football players. But we had a group of guys in

Pittsburgh who really dispelled that. Jon Kolb, Donnie Shell, Larry Brown—those were guys you wanted to go to war with."

Dungy made a devout Christian, Florida State halfback Warrick Dunn, his first pick in 1997 even though some teams thought he was too small to be a full-time back. Dunn's big plays and toughness quickly made believers of the skeptics.

"As a head coach now," Dungy said, "I consciously say to myself, 'I can't play favorites. I have to pick the best players.' But by the same token, part of what goes into your evaluation is dependability and teamwork and guys who are good parts of a team, so invariably, you're going to keep guys who, based on pure ability, wouldn't be on the team or you wouldn't feel as good about them having a prominent role, but their intangibles help you win.

"I've always tried to coach people the way I would like to be coached: positively and encouragingly rather than with criticism and fear. Maybe I'd do that if I weren't a Christian. Because of my faith, I've tried to be as fair as possible. I've been less stressed. I realize it's my profession, but even if I lose enough to get fired, I have a sense of serenity that the Lord will provide."

So can a man of God compete to win? Muslims and Christians alike say they not only can, they are called to do so. They can point to 1 Corinthians 9:24–27, where St. Paul challenges the Christians at Corinth: "Do you not know that in a race all the runners run, but only one gets the prize? Run in such a way as to get the prize. Everyone who competes in the games goes into strict training. They do it to get a crown that will not last; but we do it to get a crown that will last forever. Therefore I do not run like a man running aimlessly; I do not fight like a man beating the air. No, I beat my body and make it my slave so that after I have preached to others, I myself will not be disqualified for the prize."

Evander Holyfield not only adds Philippians 4:13 to each autograph he signs, he considers the verse the motto for his life. The sign on the wall where he trains reads:

> I Can Do All Things Through Christ
> Who Gives Me Strength
> Phil. 4:13

10

The Challenge of Faith

The helmet of the Brigham Young University defender speared Karim Abdul-Jabbar in the small of his back. UCLA's star running back was carried off the field and later lifted off the team plane in a wheelchair. "I just knew he was out for the year," his position coach said.

But Abdul-Jabbar turned to the Muslim ritual of five daily prayers. He visualized new blood flowing to his injured back and healing it. He employed ancient Chinese medicine: acupuncture, acupressure, and an herbal antispasmodic and anti-inflammatory called Shao Yao Gan Cao Tang.

The next week he started and ran for 127 yards.

"I did as much as I could, and then it was all faith," Abdul-Jabbar said. "You know the Creator is going to work through somebody, something, some medicine, some acupuncture. You just don't know where. So you have to keep on pushing and do as much as you can until it works. Some people get sick and say, 'I'm just going to pray. I'm not taking any medicine.' No! It's important to take the medicine and then let the Creator make the medicine work. I can't just sit and pray all day and expect to get well."

The next year an eerily reminiscent scene occurred. Abdul-Jabbar and fellow rookie Zach Thomas collided head on, the sound reverberating around the Miami Dolphins' practice field as if it were a demolition derby crash. And then everything grew silent and still for Karim Abdul-Jabbar.

He could not move his legs, his hands, his head. Nothing worked. He lay there realizing he had ducked his head, exposing his spinal column to damage, an often paralyzing error in the ferocious world of football. Immediately, fears flooded his mind. Paralyzed. A lifetime in a wheelchair. And just as quickly, the nightmare vision was replaced by a sense of serenity.

"My mind went to Allah," Abdul-Jabbar recalled. "Instantly I fastened my mind and got ready to deal with what was ahead of me. I didn't curse the Lord, didn't cry, didn't say, 'Why did you do this to me? Why hast thou forsaken me?'

"There was almost a smile inside me, like, 'I've got a new struggle. This is my new test. I'm blessed with this test to show the Creator how strong my faith is. I'm not going to curse him. I'm going to stay steadfast and be strong and do the best I can with what he's given me.' I was instantly ready to prepare for it. I automatically had a love for the test he was about to give me."

All this flashed through his mind in what seemed like minutes. In reality, it was probably only fifteen seconds. And then he moved his hand and told the trainers and coaches, "I'm okay."

And then he kept on practicing, like nothing ever happened. No! "Yeah," Abdul-Jabbar said, and laughed.

So strong is his faith that he can face fear and find harmony and even laughter within seconds. It was similar to training camp, when coach Jimmy Johnson questioned the rookie's courage and willingness to play through pain. Abdul-Jabbar thought it was possible he might be waived before he ever played a regular-season game for the Dolphins. And yet the twenty-two-year-old displayed a sense of serenity that is rare in one so young.

"It was my faith," Abdul-Jabbar said. "In my heart, I knew I was doing everything I could. I was trying to come back and work. My faith was in the Lord. You can't worry. Whatever happens, happens. I would feel bad if I shortchanged myself by not giving my all, by not working as hard as I could and doing everything I can. It'd hurt me to know that I didn't push through this injury when I have such a great opportunity.

"This opportunity to play in the NFL doesn't come by all the time. I'm living a lot of dreams here by way of my family. Both my brothers were NFL-bound and had injuries."

One tore up a knee and another injured his neck. Their brother's NFL career almost was short-circuited by two sprained ankles that frustrated his coach no end. But Abdul-Jabbar got healthy using a mixture of faith and medicine, blending ancient and modern remedies with futuristic healing techniques, including yoga and visualization.

Then he ran for a hundred yards in two of his first three games and finished with 1,116 yards, the Dolphins' first thousand-yard runner since 1978. Johnson admitted he had been wrong about Abdul-Jabbar and said he did not even mind his rookie's unconventional ways. "You never can tell," the coach said. "Jabbar could be smarter than all of us."

He grew up in Los Angeles as one of seven children of Naim and Ava Shah, who viewed their Islamic faith not as just a part of life but as "a way of life," Ava said. Their son was not as faithful to his faith. His girlfriend bore a child when they were high school seniors.

One of the prime tenets of Islam is that struggle is important, a blessing to bring out the best in an individual. This did. A lot of young black men run away from their responsibilities. Sharmon Shah embraced his obligation and his faith. He stayed in Los Angeles, starred at UCLA, and made his family's faith his own. His imam, or spiritual leader, gave him his new name during the commitment ceremony of shahadah in 1995. It means most generous (Karim) servant of God (Abdul) who changes hearts (Jabbar). The birth of his son, Ibrahim Abdullah, had changed his heart.

"I knew I was a Muslim, but I didn't know anything about my faith. It's hard to be righteous, to live right, by Islamic law when you don't have any knowledge," he explained. "I'm still growing. I was blessed because my girlfriend, who's now my wife, plus my mother-in-law and my parents really took care of my son when I was in high school and my early years of college. I couldn't do as much as I wanted because when you're on athletic scholarship you can't work [and earn extra money].

"But my third and fourth years in college, I took in my son and he lived with me during the week. This was after I got into my faith. All the time I had devoted to the desires of this world turned around and I just made time for him. It's hard for a college student, but he lived with me and a couple of my roommates. It was like *Three Men and a Baby*."

Remember that comedic movie? How helpless Ted Danson and his buddies were when they first took in the baby? "We were just barely better," Abdul-Jabbar said, giggling. "It was wild, it was really wild. I'm blessed to have my son sane right now."

But the experience drew him closer to his son, his wife, his faith. It helped him get his priorities and day-to-day life in order. He does not smoke or drink. He married his girlfriend. He has fasted during Ramadan. He wants to visit Mecca soon. When his school or football obligations do not allow him to pray at the prescribed five times a day, he finds a way to make up as many as possible. Now Islam *is* his way of life.

"It's all-encompassing," Abdul-Jabbar said. "I greet people and my family in the name of the Lord. I eat in the name of the Lord. When I sleep, when I play football, I'm remembering the Lord. When I wake up, the first thing I do is pray. If I'm not practicing, I can make all five at home. If I'm practicing, I'll have extra morning and evening prayers to make up the ones in between. You do what you can. You don't make your prayers a burden because they're not a burden.

"Sometimes I have a roommate in the room and I don't want to disturb him, so I'll go into the shower, or I'll say my prayer laying down or on my side, as opposed to going through the entire act [of cleansing himself before Allah, then kneeling on the prayer rug]. The remembrance is the most important thing. Taking the time out to remember. But it's in everything I do."

Christian athletes say they put God first, family second, and career third. Karim Abdul-Jabbar said his priorities are similar.

"Life is a bunch of decisions about what you're going to do and how you're going to do it. You think of your Creator and others before you remember yourself."

But when you're in a career as competitive as pro sports, how do you keep those priorities and still excel against those who put career ahead of all else? How do you please coaches who want you to think of nothing but your career? How can you excel in all phases? These are the questions that adults of all ages, races, religions, and professions must wrestle with.

"There's room for it all," the running back insisted. "To be a Muslim, I have to be the best football player, best doctor, best lawyer, or whatever occupation I have, best father and husband, best worshiper. It's a balance. I can't sit at home and pray all day and not support my family, because that's not Muslim.

"We don't hope. We have faith. Faith is based on work first. It's based on a concept we call 'tying our camel.' It's the story of a man asking our prophet for advice. His camel was outside and somebody could steal it. He asked, 'Should I go inside and put my trust in Allah and the Creator, or should I tie the camel first, then put my trust in Allah?' The prophet told him to tie his camel first, then put his trust in Allah.

"It's a saying that shows it's important to put in the work. You do everything you can possibly do, and once you've done all the work as well as you can do it, you put your trust in the Creator because you know he's the one who makes things go. So I have to work as hard as I can, and after the work is done and I don't do as well as I think I should, then I'm not worried about it, because my faith is in the Creator. By the same token, if I haven't put in the work, then I shouldn't have any faith. I can't just sit around and hope I run for a thousand yards without putting in the work. That's not how my faith works."

That makes sense, and NFL players do have time for other priorities, especially in the off season. But when NFL coaches typically work anywhere from sixty to ninety hours a week with no more than a handful of days off from July until January, how can they put faith and family first if they're devoting that much time to their profession? A group of seven head coaches, including Super Bowl champion Mike Holmgren, discussed that issue at a March 1997 meeting of the NFL Coaches Outreach.

"It's a mental priority," Tampa Bay Buccaneers coach Tony Dungy explained. "If God is your first priority and you're playing or coaching to glorify God, then you *are* serving God first. Even though I spend more time on the field than in church, I feel I'm putting church first. In my priority system, it *is* God first. You say that and a player says, 'I need to go to a funeral,' and you are tested. If you say, 'No, you can't go,' then you find out you're not living it. I have been able to say, 'Go.'

"You have to block out time every day, whether it's fifteen or twenty or thirty minutes or an hour, and say, 'At this time, I'm going to read or listen to a tape or do something to get stimulated spiritually.' You have to consciously make that decision. You have to block out time for your family. For instance, Tuesday is our longest day. We work from 8 A.M. until midnight. I'm going to get up early and spend seven to seven-thirty with my family. During the off season, we have a month off, and those are our four weeks together for a family vacation. My kids know that. They know Friday afternoon during the season is their day. They get home from school, I'm going to be there and we're going to do something. You have to schedule it in and stick to it.

"Some of my assistants are used to being workaholics and I had to tell them, 'There's a bomb threat at seven o'clock and you had better not be in here.' They're starting to get the idea."

Greed is one of the seven deadly sins. 1 Corinthians 6:10 lists the greedy among the sinners who will not inherit the kingdom of God, and Luke 16:19–31 tells of the rich man who went to hell and the beggar who went to heaven. Mark 10:17–31 tells the story of a rich man who comes to Jesus, asking how he can find eternal salvation. The man's face falls when Jesus tells him to sell everything. "It is easier for a camel to pass through the eye of a needle than for a rich man to enter the kingdom of God," Jesus says.

Even two thousand years ago, the world was materialistic. It is an important parable for today's professional athletes, many of whom are lavished with riches beyond imagination. Sometimes wealth is a blessing, sometimes a curse. Many cave in to temptations and turmoil. But those who are true to their faith feel their wealth comes with a responsibility: to share their wealth and the Word with the world.

"You have to read the whole passage to understand it," said cornerback Terrell Buckley, who became an instant millionaire when he turned pro in 1992. "The rich man had read the Word, had done everything fashionable to do, but Jesus felt he was just doing it to gain favor, that God wasn't in the rich man's heart. Coming from the heart is most important to the Lord. That's why he told the guy to go sell all his possessions.

"Jesus didn't want him to make money his god—like I used to do. In college, I was like, 'Oh yeahhhh! I'm gonna make millions!' I used to be all about money and material things because that's what the world teaches you. If you don't have two cars, one of them a Mercedes, and a big house, a cat, a dog, two kids, about $100,000 in the bank, then you're useless, you're not achieving anything.

"By studying and getting into the Word more and more, I've changed. I've learned you can be rich and still be a great steward of your money, not let money be your god, if you're gracious, you're caring, you're giving, it's not driving you, and you spend time with your family and don't let it control your life. Every now and then I catch myself saying, 'If I do this, I can earn this'—and then I remember what's important.

"Because money doesn't buy happiness. The way I feel right now, I'd rather be happy than the richest man in the world. Because when you're happy, you're happy. It's hard to explain. You walk around with a smile on your face all day. You're feeling good. You're speaking to everybody and you don't even know them. I catch myself at the red light sometimes, smiling and waving to people I don't know, and they look at me like, 'Hey, what is he doing?' "

Jesus explained to his disciples that Christians cannot enter heaven based on money or merit or achievement. Salvation is the work of God, not man. Christianity is a faith of grace, not works. There's nothing wrong with being rich as long as you use it the right way.

Golfer Loren Roberts, basketball star David Robinson, football stars Reggie White and Barry Sanders, and many other Christian athletes believe in the concept of tithing, or giving 10 percent of their earnings to the Church or charity. Some give more than 10 percent. Some give less. Some ignore the idea altogether.

Likewise, giving alms to the poor is one of the five pillars of Islam, and Karim Abdul-Jabbar said doing the right thing with his money is the biggest struggle he faces.

"We grow up with a desire for what we see on TV," the football star said. "This society makes us desire certain clothes, cars, music videos, and audiotapes. I want my desires to be in accord with my faith. I want to work on what I desire. I know my intentions are correct. I want to go to Paradise.

"There's nothing wrong with some desire. Poverty is not piety. Righteousness has nothing to do with making money. But it's what you want to do with the money. I'm giving money. I want to help my family. I want to help empower my community. I'm not getting the money just for a nice car.

"Giving alms, or paying zakat, is 2 percent of your extra earnings. A lot of people are not even eligible to give zakat because they don't have the money to take care of their families. We also have a concept called sadaka and that's just charity at any time. When you don't have money to give, you can give a hug, you can give encouragement, you can give a doughnut to your neighbor. Many people can't give zakat, but they can give charity. It doesn't count if your intentions are wrong. If you want to give charity just so your name can be 'Karim Abdul-Jabbar, Man of the Year' that's not right. Really, the best charity is only between you and your Creator."

Abdul-Jabbar said there is nothing wrong with Muslims having nice things, and Reggie White said it is unfair to call a Christian a greedy hypocrite when he holds out for the biggest contract. White heard that criticism in 1993, when he was a free agent shopping for a new team. He said he wanted to work in inner-city ministries where God wanted him, wanted to go where he could win a championship, only to take the biggest offer and end up in lily-white Green Bay, which was the league's smallest city and an average team. But he wound up helping religious and racial matters in nearby Milwaukee and throughout Wisconsin and the country, and the Packers wound up winning Super Bowl XXXI.

"Why can the wicked people have all the money? Why can't a Christian ask for what he's worth?" White asked. "I'm not trying to be greedy. I'm going to help other people with my money. Players are out there busting their butts, jeopardizing their careers. We could get our knees torn up and be gone tomorrow. We have to get what we can, while we can."

Similarly, Evander Holyfield did not see anything wrong with building a $15 million home that contains 54,000 square feet, seventeen bathrooms, three kitchens, a bowling alley, an Olympic-size swimming pool, matching five-car garages, and a 135-seat movie theater. He sees it as a reward for his devotion—and wants poor children to tour it for inspiration. Holyfield, White, Robinson, Sanders, and Hakeem Olajuwon are among the athletes who have set up charitable foundations and donated millions.

Andre Dawson, who ended what could be a Hall of Fame baseball career in 1996, said his toughest times came when he listened to management bad-mouth him during contract negotiations.

"Those things eat you up inside because you tend to search for a source of loyalty when there really isn't any," said Dawson, a longtime Christian slugger. "I looked at these people as being the evils, the devils, you were confronted with.

"There is greed on both sides, players and management. Everybody is out to get whatever they can. The fulfillment of the sport is overlooked. The enjoyment part is overlooked. I think that's one of the downfalls of the game today. It's turned entirely into a business, and the concept of winning, having fun, enjoying the game, trying to get the most out of your ability is not something that comes totally into play. It's making as much money as you can for as long as you can, and then trying to get out of the game while you're still ahead.

"It's very easy to make a lot of money in this game and forget your purpose, why you're here, to get caught up in the glamor. There are players who are unable to make the adjustments, and it's ruined their careers. But there are people in this game who don't get caught up in their fame, or who they are and how much money they make. Giving all the credit to God is a constant focus for them."

Giving back to the church and community is a focus for them. As with the front page of the paper, the sports page is more devoted to the bad news than the good, but the average athlete probably gives more time and money to charity than the average nonathlete.

The athletes with true faith take the admonitions "To whom much is given, much is required" and "faith without works" very seriously.

Groups of six and nine LPGA golfers went to Romania in 1993 and 1994 to share their faith and help orphanages. Fifty-two golfers and caddies built a Habitat for Humanity home from the ground up in Guadalupe, Arizona, just one of eight Habitat projects the LPGA has helped. The fellowship has donated efforts and dollars to disaster relief after hurricanes Hugo and Andrew.

"Habitat is an opportunity for the players to put away their golf clubs and come together in a way that is fun and helps people," said Cris Stevens, the LPGA fellowship director. "That organization is a real good match for our ministry outreach. We try to have an international evangelistic outreach every other year."

The Romanian orphanages were the most memorable. Maybe you have seen the stories on television. The conditions are horrid. Children living on scraps of food, dressed in rags, crowded into tiny rooms, amid rodents, parasites, and fecal matter.

"The churches in Romania had undergone tremendous persecution," Stevens said. "We wanted to come alongside them and encourage the believers. Romania has a tremendous problem with orphans, homeless kids, street kids, and we provided them with food, clothing, and care. They were overfilled with children but had very few workers, so we tried to assist the workers in any way we could. There's been a lot of abuse in the system over there. Part of it is the transition from a Communist country to a free capitalistic society. When things are tight economically, the orphanages suffer. It's not that the workers don't care, but when their own families are hungry and life is tough, it's hard to put someone else's kids first."

The golfers worked with Seattle's Extended Hand Ministry to help a couple adopt a boy named Daniel.

"We picked him up at an orphanage, and he stayed with a couple of players for a day or two while the paperwork was being done for his adoption. He now lives north of Seattle, and we see him every year when we go out for the Seattle tournament. We get together with him and his adoptive family, and he's doing great. When he first came over, the doctor said he probably wouldn't have lived much longer in the orphanage because of the abuse and the parasites he had. Now he's doing great. He speaks perfect English. He's a happy kid with brothers and sisters.

"There are many stories like that. I'm thankful we got to see first hand the rescue of a young man. It's neat to see. When people have been in an orphanage for a long time, they don't necessarily connect real well. He didn't know us, and we spoke a strange language. But his adoptive parents said it was amazing that within that first year, every time he saw golf on TV, he looked for players he knew and could point them out. He didn't connect with anything else. It was like we were an important part of that transition for him. He still goes right to the television and can point out the golfers he met in Romania.

"Giving back is important for any believer, whether they're on the golf tour or not. It's following the heart of Christ. There's a verse that says don't love in word and speech but in deed and truth. We can do a lot of talking about our love of Christ, but it also involves doing something tangible in a way that communicates Christ's love. Each player could have easily just sent some money to Romania. But it's one thing to send the money and another to take it there and be involved, and that's what they did. The financial part of tithing is important for any ministry or church, but when the Scriptures talk about tithing, we can tithe our time, our talents, our creativity. There are so many ways to give to the Lord."

* * *

All the coaches and athletes interviewed for this book said they felt God has blessed them with their skills and they must return the favor by spreading his Word with zeal. All said they want to use their sports celebrity as a platform for spreading their faith.

"If I make it to the Hall of Fame someday, believe me, I will be standing up in front of that podium and giving a lot of praise to God for what he gave to me in my career and my life," former catcher Gary Carter said. "A lot of people don't have this opportunity to live this kind of abundant life. I feel very fortunate, very blessed. I was able to produce on the field and off the field. But more importantly, I was able to take a stance for him."

"I have always felt that there are two languages for young people in the world—music and athletics," said Jerry Falwell, who emphasizes sports success at his Liberty University. "Athletics is a way we have of getting an audience that no preacher is going to gather. To us, sports is a platform."

Is it proper to use that platform? "That's a good question and I don't know the answer," Stevens said. "Because so many people do know their names and look up to them because of their platform, it can become a very good platform. So yes, sometimes they do use that platform. We link up with the Fellowship of Christian Athletes, and six or eight times a year, FCA will sponsor a breakfast at a tournament site, and the players will go and sit at tables with the kids, and one will stand up and tell their story of faith. So they're using golf as a platform to reach out to high school and junior golfers. We also have a number of players who take off tournaments to participate in junior golf camps with FCA.

"A number of players will use golf as a platform to speak at churches or organizations during tournament week. But in Romania, golf wasn't the platform. In Romania, the word for golfer is 'joker.' In Romania, there was one golf course before the war. During the war, it was changed to a cemetery and it was not rebuilt, so Romania didn't even have a golf course. Nobody knew anything about these players. I mean, they had television, but we didn't use golf as any part of our outreach."

Stevens said the LPGA members have not been criticized for

using their fame to spread their faith, but she would not be surprised if they are. "Our philosophy is not to beat someone over the head with the gospel, but we believe the good news is really good news, and it's something that people can welcome. So hopefully, when they speak, they speak not from the arrogance of a professional athlete but the humility of someone who's experienced God's love. I would hope the presentation would be one with gentleness and passion and yet not one that would make someone be critical. But the gospel is divisive. Some people will not like to hear the message. So that's why I say I would never be surprised if criticism came."

Nancy Lieberman-Cline, who got thousands of critical letters when she revealed she had changed from Judaism to Christianity, said she does not "try to suffocate people" with her faith, but she shares it when asked. She has spoken at Fellowship of Christian Athletes events, and when she played for the Athletes in Action team in the fall of 1996, two players gave their testimony at half-time of each game.

"We hope we showed people some good things about Christian athletes. We wanted to beat everybody but we weren't mean. We didn't curse. We tried to set the right example because we were representing Christ," Lieberman-Cline said. "Morality seems to be in the minority these days. Dennis [Rodman] has turned his image into $20 million a year, but then an athlete like Timmy Brown— you know the All-Pro wide receiver for the Oakland Raiders?— doesn't get the endorsements because he's squeaky clean. He's a Christian. That kind of guy has become boring to America. Isn't that kind of ironic?"

Muslim athletes try to dispel myths about Black Muslims or Mideast terrorists. "There are so many misconceptions about Islam and many faiths, period," Karim Abdul-Jabbar said. "I don't know what the Creator has in store for me. I've never been a preacher, but maybe I can set an example when the media talk to me about it, and by my actions."

Black leaders say Reggie White could become the most important spokesman for his faith and race since Martin Luther King, Jr. David Robinson's father thinks he could become as big as Billy

Graham once he leaves basketball for the ministry. That would be quite a feat: Graham preached to more than 200 million people in live audiences, and more than 3 million stepped forward during his sermons to commit themselves to Christ. His parents are convinced God saved David from death when he was six months old so that he might minister to millions.

Robinson said he knows he is going into some sort of ministry; he is just not sure how. "We have a [charitable] foundation here in San Antonio and I could spend the next few years working with the foundation. I love to teach. I love to speak. I don't know what the Lord wants me to do, but wherever he takes me, I'm going."

In the meantime, Robinson is not shy about trying to convert coaches and teammates. When Larry Brown was his coach, he corrected him when he cursed, and Brown tried to watch his tongue. When teammates used bad language, looked at girlie magazines, or went to strip joints, his scoldings were not always appreciated, especially when he was teamed with NBA wild thing Dennis Rodman.

When a teammate took Christ's name in vain, former Pirates All-Star Andy Van Slyke playfully added "came to save" or "died for you and me." He received angry looks and replies on more than one occasion.

When teammates cursed in Arizona's defensive huddle, Pro Bowl cornerback Aeneas Williams, who rises at 5 A.M. every day to pray and study the Bible, has refused to talk to them until they clean up their language. When opponents have used foul language around White, he has made them pay. "It makes me go crazy," he said.

White has preached to his own congregation and others. He has held weekly Bible studies in his home and on the streets of Philadelphia for athletes and nonathletes alike. Many teammates, opponents, and fans credit him with their decisions to become born-again Christians. But athletes have to be careful.

"I don't think people like fanatics," tennis star Mary Joe Fernandez said. "That's why I think it's better to just set an example. Because if you start talking, 'God this, God that,' people get a little scared."

So Fernandez does not volunteer thoughts on her faith unless she is asked about it. She prefers to let her example show through. "It's good for people to know where you get your strength from, what motivates you to do things. It's good for people to say, 'Wow, she does things for a reason. She believes in God, and that has helped her with her successes.' You forget how many people are watching, and how many people you are affecting. Little children look up to TV celebrities, movie stars, and athletes. They're so excited to get your autograph, it means so much to them, that I think I should sign as many as I can."

Like Fernandez, wrestler Kurt Angle is a devout Catholic who enjoys spreading his faith but does so cautiously. In both his media interviews and motivational talks he says "very, very little" about religion because "it's a very touchy subject."

"The hardest part when I talk to kids is not talking about God," Angle said. "A lot of kids get uncomfortable. It's something I would very much like to do, but if you talk too much about it, it's really weird how people respond: 'He's a Jesus freak.' Or 'He's a religious-crazed guy.' People are uncomfortable talking about religion, and it's a shame. I was president of the campus Fellowship of Christian Athletes as a senior and a member for three years. So I feel comfortable talking about it, but I won't push God on people I don't know. When I went on NBC with Bob Costas, I thanked God and then got into the subject of my matches. I fell to my knees and thanked God in front of almost three billion people that night. So I don't preach it, but I let people know."

By contrast, it is hard to talk with Reggie White for more than a minute without God entering the conversation. White said he works feverishly to become not only the best Christian he can be but also the best player, because the more famous he is, the more people will look up to him and listen to him.

"The most overrated people in the world are celebrities," he said. "We put them on a pedestal where they don't belong. The only one who belongs on a pedestal is Jesus. But since America does look at celebrities like that, I want to be a positive role model and tell them the only way they can survive is through Jesus Christ."

Because he believes America is going in the wrong direction.

"If God doesn't judge America like Sodom and Gomorrah, he ought to apologize to Sodom and Gomorrah," the Reverend Reggie railed. "Abortion. Murdering children. We save whales, dolphins, everything else—but we can't allow children to live? Alcohol is not only killing our young people, it's killing innocent people. Beer commercials take ex-athletes who make it look so fun, but they never show the next-morning hangover, never show the negative parts. Our country is wicked. It's going to take Christians to stand up to the Devil. It's spiritual warfare."

These athletes obviously have thought about some key questions we all face:

• How do you balance faith, family, career, and community?

• How can you be the best in your profession if you make faith and family your top priorities?

• How do you share your testimony and money in a way that is consistent with your faith?

• How do you give back to the community?

• How, when, where, and to whom do you spread your faith?

And in our concluding chapter, they will address the contradictions and dilemmas faced when faith and sports collide.

11

Faith in Sports

Eli Herring could have been luxuriating in the lifestyle of the rich and famous. He could have been a pampered pro bringing in half a million dollars a year.

Instead, he drove an '86 Isuzu, lived in a cramped apartment, worked from daybreak to late into the night as a teacher and coach, and took care of a wife and two kids on about $21,000 a year.

All because he chose to interpret the Scriptures literally: Sunday is a day for faith and family, not football.

"Really, it came down to our faith in what the Scriptures said," said Jennifer Herring, Eli's wife of six years. "If we believe them, then we are blessed, then we are promised so many more blessings, such incredible blessings, that money from the NFL could never buy."

And so, instead of playing in the National Football League for the Oakland Raiders, Eli Herring is coaching high school football at Orem (Utah) Mountain View. The Raiders have tried to change his mind, but the NFL will change before Herring will.

"If they ever change to Saturdays, I'd be very interested," said this most devout of Mormons, one who put religion ahead of riches.

Scouts rated Herring one of the top five linemen in the 1995 draft. He stood six feet eight inches and weighed 330 pounds and displayed exceptional balance and quickness for a man his size. He was a pass-protecting tackle for pass-happy Brigham Young University. He loved the game. But after his senior season, after long hours of study and debate and reflection, he decided he must keep the Sabbath holy. He told BYU's sports information director to pass word to the pros:

Eli's not coming.

The pros approached him anyway, and he was adamant: he would not play on Sunday. The Raiders drafted him anyway, gambling a fifth-round pick and offering him late first-round money, $1.5 million for three years, with the promise of more to come. Team executive Bruce Allen flew to Utah to give him a sales pitch. Assistant coach Fred Whittingham, himself a Mormon and former player and coach at BYU, beseeched him: What about Steve Young? Why, he was the great-great-great-grandson of Mormon pioneer Brigham Young, and *he* competed on Sundays. What about Todd Christensen and all the other Mormons who have played on Sundays? What about all the Christians who have played on Sundays, on Christmas, on Easter?

"Sunday is a day to go to church, instead of a working day," Eli said. "It's a day to spend with the family. It's a day to remember the Lord. It's a day to get away from worldly things and refocus. That's what's important to me."

Eli's college line coach told Eli he was crazy to give up the cash. His father, a devout Mormon who raised seven children on a modest salary, thought it okay for Eli to play. His mother staunchly believed the Bible very clearly prohibited it. His wife and church leaders told him they would support either decision. Eli began by studying the Old Testament, and found many Scriptures about keeping the Sabbath holy. He read the Book of Mormon and the Doctrine of Covenants and found more.

"We discussed it pretty openly and tried to weigh the pros and cons of both sides," Jennifer Herring said. "Right off the top of your head, you can come up with a whole list of pros for playing in the NFL, but the more we studied and talked, the more we saw the pros for the other side, too. In the Old Testament, it actually is a very strict commandment, and that's the interpretation we followed."

Jennifer said they do not judge the Mormon and Christian athletes who choose to play in the NFL. Eli said he realized playing in the NFL could have given him a platform to spread his faith and serve as a role model.

"I think people need role models. Playing in the NFL is a good way to be a role model," Eli said. "But more important is the strict observance of the Sabbath. This was a big opportunity for me to provide security for my family, but it was not big enough for me to do something I felt was wrong in terms of the Lord."

Reaction has varied. Other members of the Church of Latter-day Saints (LDS) wrote to tell the Herrings about similar, less public decisions they had made to keep the Sabbath sacred.

"It was a little more prevalent than a lot of people thought," Jennifer said. "Most of the people were talking about decisions to not work on Sundays. A lot of them were LDS and some were not. He's received a lot of letters of support and he's received quite a few letters that told him he's crazy."

She laughed at the word "crazy." She and Eli seem totally at peace with their decision. It had been three months since they last mentioned it even in passing, and that was when a friend left for the pros, and Eli said if he had chosen to play he would be away from his family for six weeks during training camp.

On Sunday mornings, instead of heading to the locker room, Eli Herring heads to church. The afternoons and evenings he would have spent playing are instead devoted to church meetings and family gatherings at his parents' and in-laws' homes. They do not even turn on the NFL games. The families prohibit television on Sundays. They do not miss the game, the fame, the cash.

"We don't really see it as a sacrifice," Jennifer said. "The money was so unrealistic to us. Neither of us have had much money all our lives. Neither of our families ever had any. It was such an incredible amount of money, neither of us even comprehended. Actually, compared to what we were living on as students, we're feeling quite rich now."

The Raiders do not even try to sway Eli Herring anymore. "He has a huge amount of integrity," Whittingham said. "He doesn't believe you are going to buy your way into the kingdom of heaven."

Very few athletes interpret their holy books so strictly. George Foreman gave up boxing for ten years so he could preach. Muhammad Ali was stripped of his career and title and risked imprisonment when he refused to fight in the Vietnam War because of his religious convictions. Jon Schultheis was a Princeton guard drafted by the Philadelphia Eagles in 1983 who declined to play football on Sundays.

Danny O'Neil was a Rose Bowl MVP who turned down a chance to sign with the Kansas City Chiefs. They wanted him to catch the next plane out, but he said he had Bible study with his high school students scheduled for that night. He asked to wait until morning. They said no—and he said no. His commitment to God and his students was more important.

Tyce Routson, the 1997 NCAA Diver of the Year and a three-time NCAA champion, left on a two-year Mormon mission in 1997 even though it will jeopardize his lifelong goal of making the 2000 Olympics. "It's a chance I'm willing to take," said Routson, the first male diver to win both the 3-meter and platform titles in the same year since four-time Olympic gold medalist Greg Louganis. "It just feels right. It's something I have to do and want to do. I wouldn't forgive myself if I didn't do this. I want to serve my fellow man and God. I just want to help people out. By helping other people, I'm helping myself become a better person."

Sandy Koufax, the Los Angeles Dodgers' great Jewish pitcher, refused to pitch the opening game of the 1965 World Series because it was Yom Kippur. John Frank, a tight end for Ohio State and later the San Francisco 49ers, was criticized by other Jewish believers when he did play in a big game against Oklahoma University during Yom Kippur, one of Judaism's two biggest holidays. David Robinson and other Christians have decried the NBA and NFL practices of playing games on Christmas, but none has boycotted.

British favorite Eric Liddell refused to run the 100 meters on a Sunday at the 1924 Olympics. Liddell instead won the 400, helping form the basis for Oscar winner *Chariots of Fire*.

British triple jumper Jonathan Edwards took a similar stand more than sixty years later, but he did not like the comparison with Liddell. He felt faith was subject to each man's interpretation. An Anglican vicar's son, Edwards chose not to compete on Sundays for seven years because he felt the Sabbath must be kept as a day of worship and reflection.

That decision became a cause célèbre when he passed on the 1988 national Olympic trials. He struggled with the decision for years, studying the Bible, talking with his parents and wife, contemplating the pluses and minuses, and praying. Ultimately, maybe his father the vicar made the difference: he told Jonathan he had a God-given gift. Jonathan decided he should honor God by doing his absolute best, which included competing on Sundays. He finally saw *Chariots of Fire* a few months after that 1993 decision.

"The movie portrayed sports as something a religious person should not do [on Sunday]," Edwards said. "What I do in sport comes out of my dedication to God. Maybe there was a conflict for Liddell; I do not have that conflict."

Within two years, he had broken the world record three times. Within three years, he had won a gold medal at the world championships and a silver medal at the Olympics.

But Herring, Foreman, Ali, Routson, Koufax, Edwards, and Liddell are exceptions. Many devout Christians—athletes and nonathletes alike—work on Sundays and religious holidays and do not think their God asks them to sacrifice their careers.

"I'm reading Liddell's book now," the LPGA's Cris Stevens said. "I respect his decision very much. I think it's wonderful, but I think what God desires is our heart and loyalty to him. I believe it is important for people to have a Sabbath, a time of worshiping God set aside. I don't know if it has to specifically be on Sunday. We encourage players to take a Sabbath. Our church is on Tuesday night. I think the key questions are, 'Am I worshiping God? Am I growing in my faith?' and not so much what day it is. That's a tough question, and each player has to make that decision. But if they want to play out here, they have to play on Sunday."

Many faithful Muslim athletes do not fast during Ramadan because they feel they will lose strength and be put at a competitive disadvantage. Most athletes do not even view these as issues, and if they do, they figure God would rather they compete and use their sports status as an opportunity to share their faith publicly.

"That's one of the questions you get at FCA meetings," Tampa Bay Buccaneers coach Tony Dungy said. "Why play on Sundays? Isn't the Sabbath holy? Should we be involved in a game like this? Why play a game where people get hurt? Why play in an environment where drugs are prevalent? Shouldn't you divorce yourself from it?

"On the surface, they look like real good questions. But you can glorify God in all those situations. If you can glorify God, a lot of good can come out of it. Right or wrong, athletes and coaches have a tremendous platform to glorify Christ. People get hurt on the highway and I still drive."

Dr. Shirl Hoffman disagreed. "The extent to which people are willing to overlook the moral crisis in sports to have a vehicle of mass evangelism is astounding," he told Dana Scarton of the *Pittsburgh Press*. An evangelical Christian and a professor of exercise and sports science, Hoffman believes sports and religion are fundamentally opposed. "There is a psychological disposition in sports that is necessary to excel. It centers completely around your interests and it requires you to treat the opponent as, at best, a nonperson. You can't be sympathetic to that person or it is going to influence the way you approach the game. That's not a Christian attitude."

Cris Stevens agreed with Hoffman to some extent. "From a Christian perspective, our relationship with God and other people supersedes our success in the world's eyes. So how we treat people is of utmost importance. To treat someone as a nonperson is non-Christian because people are created in God's image."

So Hoffman's argument makes some sense in collision sports like football, boxing, and hockey, and even in one-on-one sports like tennis, but golfers' and runners' opponents are more the courses than each other. Hoffman is also correct that there are many athletes with moral and legal problems. The headlines second that opinion daily. None of them—or us—is perfect. But is it not better to counter the Dennis Rodmans of the sports world with the David Robinsons? Yes, a nonreligious athlete or coach with a cutthroat, workaholic attitude might have an advantage over a religious athlete who turns the other cheek and puts faith and family first. But to say you cannot be true to both your sport and faith and still excel would seem to go too far; this book offers evidence of plenty of successful religious athletes.

And what would Hoffman have us do? Ban all sports? Prohibit every show of faith in sports? Neither will happen. Sport, and the mix between sport and religion, may not be perfect, but they seem to be way down the list of society's problems. To think an athlete kneeling down or pointing to the sky in a momentary celebration is going to do lasting damage to anyone's belief system is a stretch of the imagination.

Most coaches and athletes can point to Bible passages that show God asks them to not just compete in sports but to excel. They see few contradictions between their faith and their sport.

Reggie White is a Baptist minister and one of the fiercest football players ever. *Inside Sports* called him the NFL's toughest man and "ultimate warrior" in 1997. Another future Hall of Famer and devout Christian, Mike Singletary, hit so hard that he broke dozens of helmets. Andre Waters earned a reputation as a hard and often dirty hitter. He denied he played outside the rules. "When you're a Christian, you're representing the Lord. I don't think you represent the Lord very well if you hit outside the rules of the game," Waters said. "You don't try to hurt them. You just play the way the game is supposed to be played. It's a hard-hitting sport. You try to hit hard, but not hurt them. Part of the game is intimidation."

Dungy agreed. "Part of the game is physical and rough and making people feel they don't want to play or physically aren't able to play. Because it is part of the game, I have no problem teaching that. I tell them we're going to get enough guys to the ball, we're going to hit, we're going to go until the whistle blows, and we're going to make this guy want to take himself out of the game or run out of bounds. We're going to intimidate him.

"You have remorse when someone gets hurt, but you don't feel guilty if you hit within the rules. However, I think you would cross the line if you said, 'We're gonna try to hurt him. We're gonna do something outside the rules to get him out of the game.' That would be wrong."

Some will argue that football and boxing are too barbaric for a civilized society. Participants in neither sport have a hard time reconciling religion and hurting someone. They suggest the goal of football is to knock people out of the way and score touchdowns, and the goal of boxing is to outpoint and outhit the opponent, not to kill him. Plenty of participants in both sports do get injured, but rarely do they die.

Which viewpoint is correct? I write about sports because I enjoy sports, so perhaps I am biased. I favor strict adherence to rules that make the sports safe, but not abolition of the sports. I write about religious athletes because I am intrigued by successful human beings, but I try to present their stories as an objective journalist, not a crusader trying to convert anyone. I admire those who strive to live better lives, no matter what their denomination, but I endeavor to keep this book free of any personal religious bias. Because faith is a personal choice, neither for me to impose upon you or you upon me. No, the goal of this book is not to preach or pontificate; it is to present dilemmas, facts, arguments, and opinions on all sides, from all faiths, so that readers can ponder the questions and reach their own conclusions.

Take this quandary. During its national championship season, Colorado defeated Missouri only because the game officials blundered and allowed the Buffaloes five downs instead of four. They went on to score a touchdown . . . without which they would not have won the game and ultimately the mythical championship.

Does a good Christian coach accept the extra down—or does he point out the error to the officials and let them correct it instantly? Bill McCartney, the coach who went on to form the Promise Keepers evangelical movement, said the mistake was not his, so he had no moral obligation to decline the extra play.

"If I knew they were wrong, that would be difficult," Dungy said. "My sense is that you take the extra down and you don't become the official. It's not your position to officiate."

But, Dungy said, a Christian coach should not bend the rules. He should follow not only the letter but the spirit of the rules. "Being a Christian helps because it's not really a gray line. It's pretty well defined," said Dungy, the grandson of a Baptist minister and son of a Sunday school teacher. "We try to make it gray sometimes by saying, 'I know the commissioner said this, but I think he meant this.' But as a Christian, if there's a rule, that sets your standard. Even though everybody else may be violating it, as a Christian, you just can't."

Even if that puts you at a disadvantage against the coaches who are so competitive, they are willing to bend or break the rules? "That's where your faith has to come in," Dungy replied. "You have to realize, 'No, it won't put us at a competitive disadvantage because it's never an advantage to break the rules. Eventually the shortcut will get to you.'

"For instance, the NFL has a rule that you can't make veteran players work out the ten days before camp starts. I don't know what the percentage is, but most teams probably aren't going to follow it, because who's going to regulate it? But just because everybody else is doing it, you can't have your assistant coaches say, 'Well, I know the head coach doesn't want us to, but we'll go ahead and meet and practice anyway.' You have to have people say, 'If Coach says we're not doing it, we're not doing it.' If the assistants all believe, eventually the players will believe, too.

"It's like teaching holding. You know there are certain times you can hold and get away with it because of where the officials are positioned. We know what the head linesman and umpire are looking at, and there *are* certain places you can hold. So do you teach the players, 'Now, on this play, you can hold, because no one's watching'? Or do you teach them, 'We have to do it right and move our feet and execute'? You can't teach the shortcuts. As a Christian, you've got to do things right.

"There are times you can legally go to hurt people, like with the chop block. Do you teach something because it's legal? In my opinion, you don't. Being a Christian makes it easy. There isn't a gray line as a Christian."

Golf offers chances to cheat. A lot of amateurs replace a bad shot with a "mulligan" or kick a ball to a better placement or cheat and "find" a lost ball. But pro golfers, religious or not, hold themselves to incredibly high standards. No camera or golfer could be looking, and if they realize they violated even the most technical and obscure rule, they will penalize themselves a shot or even disqualify themselves from a tournament.

Prayer in sports, like prayer in school, is another controversial topic.

Prayers are supposed to be offerings of thanks, requests for peace, for answers, for help. But does that mean it is all right to ask God to help win the big game or make the big play? Or is asking for sports success trivializing God?

Jay Wilson, the chaplain for the Pittsburgh Steelers and Pirates, says praying for victory all the time is a sign of an immature Christian or someone who is not growing in his faith. He says God is not a good-luck charm. But Cris Stevens, the LPGA Christian fellowship director, says Christians are supposed to work toward goals and pray for desires, and it is okay for athletes to ask God for victory.

The American Civil Liberties Union, the Freedom from Religion Foundation, and atheist organizations say religion has no place in sports. They do not like to see JOHN 3:16 and similar signs at stadiums. They do not like players congregating on the field or court in postgame prayer groups. They do not like athletes kneeling or crossing themselves or looking to the heavens after a big play. They do not like pregame invocations.

Sometimes not even fellow Christians like those invocations, at least not when they turn provincial. When Dr. Lee Drake gave the invocation before the big 1996 Dallas Cowboys-Miami Dolphins game, he thanked God for his "blessings, including having a healthy Dan Marino," and he urged everyone to "pray for a Dolphins win." The partisan preacher incensed the Cowboys.

"When that preacher only prayed for Dan Marino and not for Troy Aikman or anybody else on our team, that fired us up," Dallas guard Nate Newton said. "You don't pray for one quarterback's health and not the other. He's supposed to be a Christian and he only prayed for one side of the field? That just ain't right. That was a self-serving preacher."

The defending world champions drowned the Dolphins, 29–10.

Of course, most prayers are not announced to two teams and seventy-five thousand fans. Jerris McPhail, one of the Dolphins who heard that invocation, said he gets down on his knees and prays as part of his weekly pregame routine. But he does not pray for anything like touchdowns or victories.

"I think that's selfish, to be quite honest. Because if that was the case, everybody would be praying for touchdowns," McPhail said. "I pray we have a healthy game and that I keep my concentration. I just thank God for giving me ability and I ask him to just take over."

Basketball star Nancy Lieberman-Cline said she prays for both teams to give their best effort, for no one to get hurt—and for her team to win.

Olympic wrestling champion Kurt Angle prays every day. He prayed before every match, but not for victory. "I pray that God gives me the courage to give my best so I have no regrets," he said. "You're never guaranteed to be the best in the world. I always wanted to be, but I never asked for that. All I asked for is to give my best and keep improving any way I could. What society has done is say, 'You're good if you win and you're bad if you lose.' That's not true. Let's say I wrestle a guy and he beats me, 20–0. The next time, he only beats me 10–0. I've improved. The third time, if he only beats me 5–2, I've improved dramatically. That's all you can ask for."

Angle got down on his knees twice after his Olympic title match—once before he knew the result of the referee's decision

and once afterward. "Win or lose, I always thank God. I tell people that because I think they need to know I wasn't saying, 'Please
let me win.' I was praying, 'Thank you for letting me be in the
battle.'"

Mary Joe Fernandez also does not pray for victory, though she
prays every morning and evening. "On the day of the match, I
have a little devotional I read," said Fernandez, one of the world's
top twenty players. "I have a list of prayers. I've had a lot of health
problems, so I pray to stay healthy. When I was younger, I used to
pray to win. As I've gotten older, I just pray to play my best. And
whatever happens, happens."

Fernandez is a Catholic playing women's tennis. Karim Abdul-
Jabbar is a Muslim playing pro football. But they share similar
philosophies on prayer in sports. Abdul-Jabbar begins with the
same Islamic prayers that all Muslims say. Then he says personal
prayers. He prays for health, to play to his potential, to represent
Islam well. But while he will let friends and family pray for victory
or great games, he does not.

"I'm still struggling with that a little bit, because I feel like the
Creator knows what I need and so I rarely pray for what I need
and want. But I've also read that you ask the Creator what you
want because then you'll know it comes from him," Abdul-Jabbar
said.

Dungy said that point has been debated in Fellowship of Christian Athletes gatherings. "Many people say, 'God is omnipotent
and he'll do what he wants, so why does it matter if we pray?' I
can't explain everything, but I know the Bible instructs you to
pray, so that's why we do it. I think it's very reasonable as a
Christian to talk to God and let him know what you would like.

"My dad told me once that he never prayed for an A if he didn't
feel he'd done all he could do. If he had done everything, he didn't
feel guilty about praying for an A at all. I've taken that approach
too. I pray I will give every effort and when I've done that, I don't
see anything wrong with praying for victory. But if I don't put
everything into it, then right before a game, it's difficult for me to
pray, 'Lord, let us have a great game and let us win, even though I

haven't done everything I could do to get us there. Miraculously, let me be the hero and let us win.' That's a selfish prayer.

"I've had a few weeks where, because of off-field situations or whatever, I would pray and say, 'I really don't think I've given everything I can to this cause. Give me the opportunity to play as well as I can.' I don't pray for victory then. I pray somebody else picks up the slack."

A philosophical question: If a player kneels in the end zone to thank God for helping him score a touchdown, does that mean the guy he just beat was not a good Christian, does not have God on his side? Because for someone to score, someone else must have failed. For someone to win, someone else must lose. So is it a religion of works or grace? Christians are supposed to believe it is a religion of grace.

"I don't know what a person can be praying for in the end zone after a touchdown," Hoffman argued. "Are they thanking the Lord that he helped him make the touchdown? If so, because of the structure of the game, he must also be thanking the Lord for stopping the other team from tackling him. To thank the Lord for a victory is at the same time to thank the Lord for not allowing the other team to win."

He has a point there, don't you think? He does, Heisman Trophy winner Danny Wuerffel believes, only if you look at a football game and only care about the final score. Wuerffel says God does not care who wins or loses games, but sees a bigger purpose for the sport, for the people around the game and those it can influence.

Hoffman further believes prayer should remain private. "I think if the Lord were here, probably the last place he'd be is in the locker room or in the arena. I think he'd view those as the most superficial places to be. I think the Lord would be telling us to spend our time doing something a little more constructive." Donald Kaul, in an article in a Des Moines newspaper, cited Scripture from the Gospel of Matthew in which Jesus rebuked a group of people who pray in public for the sake of appearing righteous.

But that passage is referring to hypocrites, Wuerffel argued in an editorial he wrote for *Athletes in Action* magazine. "Are some athletes today ever guilty of this hypocrisy as was the group two thousand years ago? Perhaps," Wuerffel wrote. "But my readings of the Scriptures have led me to this conclusion: The Lord sees into every heart, and he alone can determine the intent of the prayer, regardless of the setting in which it is made. Some of the most beautiful prayers recorded in the Scriptures are set before large crowds of people. When Solomon prayed for the dedication of the temple, an event recorded in 2 Chronicles Chapter 6, he 'knelt down before the whole assembly of Israel and spread out his hands toward heaven.' God responded to this public prayer by filling the temple with his glory."

Wuerffel quoted Jesus from Matthew 10:32: "Whoever acknowledges me before men, I will also acknowledge him before my father in heaven." And so, the national championship quarterback concluded, "While the act of appearing righteous to garner public approval is behavior abhorrent to Jesus, it was never his intention to force his children to hide their faith and profess it only to the inside walls of their own room. With the right heart and pure motives, a public profession of faith must certainly be pleasing to the Lord."

Loren Roberts also does not think God cares who wins. "I think he cares about what the winner does with what he's won," the golfer said. "What I mean is, if I win, it's important what I do with my time, with my money, with the people I may influence because of that win. It's the ripple effect, the proverbial pebble in the pool. How am I going to glorify God with that win? Praying for a putt or a victory ends up being wrong when you pray for something you want and God doesn't want it. It's very easy to pray for the wrong thing. God doesn't grant all wishes. All prayers aren't answered, because the Lord knows what you need."

No, if all prayers were answered, there would be a lot more praying going on, from the football field to the foxhole to the bingo hall to the election hall. Still, Gary Carter is convinced God helped him get a crucial single to help the New York Mets win the 1986 World Series. Hakeem Olajuwon asked Allah to help his Houston Rockets win the final game of the 1994 NBA Finals, and they did. Boxer Evander Holyfield is convinced he "prayed away" the hole in his heart that doctors told him could not be repaired.

Golfers such as Betsy King, Suzanne Strudwick, Barb Mucha, and Barb Whitehead carry Bible verses in their yardage books, and when they are feeling tense, they repeat the verse, say a little prayer, or tell themselves their self-worth is not based upon the result of this tournament but on what God thinks of them. Roberts said he prays on the course all the time, but not just about his golf game. He likes to look around the course, at all the lush greenery, and thank God for the chance to enjoy the beauty. And yes, sometimes he prays for victory.

"I don't pray, 'Let me hole this shot from 150 yards and let me win.' I ask him to let me be calm on the course and accept the outcome," Roberts said. "I can give you two instances of this. The first tournament I won was Bay Hill in 1994, Arnold Palmer's tournament. I was on the seventy-first hole and thought I needed a birdie to win. I ran my first putt sixty feet—eight feet past the hole. As I lined up over it, I said, 'Lord, I would love to make this putt, but I just ask that you give me strength to hit it to the best of my ability.' I made it, parred the last hole, and won my first tournament. Next I'm at the seventy-second hole at the 1994 U.S. Open at Oakmont. I had a five-foot uphill putt to win the U.S. Open. I said the exact same prayer—and it didn't go in. So there are two exact opposites to draw from.

"My faith helped me with disappointments like the U.S. Open. I really have not regretted one minute of what happened at the U.S. Open. I have not sat and brooded. Oh, the next day I was disappointed, but I can't say I was emotionally depressed. I wasn't mired in self-pity. I was able to put it in the right perspective and accept it. Instead of thinking, 'I missed a putt to win the U.S. Open' and dwelling on the negative, I thought, 'I putted great all week to get there.' That Friday afternoon after twenty-six holes, I was six over and teeing off on the ninth hole needing to go two under on the back nine just to make the cut. To come back and shoot sixty-four on Saturday to get in position to win it, that's positive to me.

"The reason I can dwell on the positive is I know God loves me, I'm assured of eternal life, and I will go to heaven. That takes off a whole lot of pressure."

Epilogue

Watergate taught a generation of journalists to become skeptics. Our mantra: Verify everything. Assume nothing. If your mama says she loves you, check it out.

The skepticism carried over even into what "real journalists" derided as "the toy department." We baby-boomer sports writers became determined to detail not just athletes' on-field feats but their off-field foibles. We were more interested in writing about their pursuit of the almighty dollar than their pursuit of Almighty God, often dismissing the latter with a roll of the eyes and an "oh-brother-another-God-Squader" gripe.

So how did we end up with so many Faith in Sports stories filling our newsstands, our magazine racks, our bookstores in the 1990s? Certainly, some athletes are as immoral as ever and do things that are illegal. All of this bad news feeds the public craving for "the dirt" on celebrities, filling reams of newsprint and giving us cause for cynicism. But partly because of the pressures they face and the money they make, a growing number of athletes are turning the opposite way. How do they deal with adversity? What do they do when they get all the baubles they ever dreamed of and still find themselves empty? Often today they find the answers in God's teachings. So not only are there more religious athletes to write about, but the media are showcasing them more now because, among other reasons, (1) we do like human-interest stories; (2) we do like interesting how-I-overcame-adversity stories; and (3) we do prefer talking with gentlemen rather than with jerks. As more athletes become religious and convinced they should spread their faith, as our editors ask us to look for new angles, the stories are told more often.

As television, newspapers, and magazines gave more and more coverage to sports, as leagues expanded around the nation, as the sports marketers became more and more adept, sports grew in popularity. And because so many Americans became obsessed more with sports than with religion, worshiping teams and players gave them a commonality, a fellowship if you will, with their peers. Sports became another religion and its stars our gods, or at least the high priests.

This is not just limited to the children who buy into the Nike commercials and "SportsCenter" highlights and worship Michael Jordan as a deity. It permeates society, beginning at the youth level, when the top Little Leaguers are praised and coddled. It grows in the teen years, when a sport such as high school football is called Texas' religion, and a book about the Permian High School team, *Friday Night Lights,* is called "the Bible." And the college years, when even a devout Christian such as Rice coach Ken Hatfield watched one of his players make the pros and "made him out to the remaining Owls to be a god," one of them said. And now, with Title IX empowering a generation of girls, with the 1996 Olympics unveiling just how dominant American women had become, sports as religion is not just a male bastion, either.

So when faith and sports inevitably mixed, they brought together vast numbers of people with vast differences of beliefs.

Sometimes the mix has been violently combustible, sometimes just philosophically debatable.

This book has traced the outcome of mixing religion and sports, to show how many athletes are religious and how often their faith becomes part of their sports success or failure, to share some athletes' beliefs, and to explore the issues they face. It does not attempt to provide definitive answers. It is neither a textbook nor a theological treatise. I am a sports writer, not a biblical scholar, and like several of the athletes mentioned earlier, I feel it would be presumptuous and self-righteous to dictate my beliefs, close-minded to dismiss or embrace athletes just because they call themselves Christians or Muslims or Buddhists or Jews. The point is to open minds, not close them. The idea is to let readers reflect and reach their own conclusions, based on their own understanding and beliefs.

But writing and researching this book has been a journey of discovery and introspection for me, and I hope reading it has been enlightening and reflective for you too. Years ago I got to spend time with men like Reggie White and Dave Dravecky, and was moved by their passion, their conviction, their courage. And then, in 1995, I spent time with David Robinson and his family while writing two books with them. The whole family told very moving stories about the development of their faith, about the adversities they had overcome, about the fulfillment they had found. And I spent enough time with them that I didn't have to assume they were telling the truth. I could verify it. Their conversations spawned the idea for this book.

I had spent thousands of hours talking to sports celebrities, watching them, reading about them, and did not realize how many were religious, nor why, until I really began to ask them and listen. Some of these coaches and athletes I had known for years, had admired as human beings throughout their careers, but I had not known much or anything about their faith. As I dug deeper, I found a lot of people who were at peace with the world, who had found fulfillment not in their riches but in everyday life. They found it in their faith, whether they were Christians or Muslims or Mormons or whatever.

I think David Robinson's story says it as well as any, and so that is how I would like to leave you.

David Robinson had it all—or so it seemed.

He had five luxury cars, two beautiful homes, and more money than he ever could have imagined. He was maybe the best center—certainly one of the top two or three—in all of professional basketball. He was named College Player of the Year for the Navy Midshipmen and an NBA All-Star for the San Antonio Spurs, and everyone loved him and pampered him and praised him. His job was a game, and he was great at it.

He was tall and handsome and healthy, a consummate naval officer and a gentleman. He had a math degree from the Naval Academy and could learn anything he picked up. Not only was he an expert in computers and electronics and engineering, he played the piano, portable keyboards, saxophones, and guitars. He composed his own songs and jammed with Grover Washington and Branford Marsalis, his jazz heroes. He averaged in the 190s in bowling and in the 80s in golf, and even was a whiz at table tennis and gymnastics. He flew first class and stayed in the most elegant hotel suites in the country. He was living the high life.

His younger brother Chuck came to visit and marveled at his lifestyle. Everyone did.

"Boy, you've got it made," they said. "Man alive, you should really be enjoying this."

And yet he was not.

"I wouldn't say I was unhappy, but my life was unsatisfying," the Spurs' seven-foot-one center said. "And it was peculiar it was unsatisfying because I had so much. It was nice, but it wasn't satisfying, it wasn't fulfilling."

A hollow feeling nagged at him for some time, until a visiting minister asked him some hard questions that led him to introspection and insight.

"David, do you love God?" asked Greg Ball, an evangelist from the group Champions for Christ.

"Of course I love God," Robinson said.

"How much time do you spend praying?" Ball asked.

"Every once in a while," Robinson replied. "I eat three times a day, and I pray then."

"How much time do you spend reading your Bible?" the minister asked.

"There's one around here somewhere," Robinson said. "I've got one. I just don't understand it. It doesn't make a lot of sense to me."

"When you love someone," the minister said, "don't you usually take time to get to know that person? Don't you want to know that certain person better?"

David Robinson had never seen God as a real person. He was puzzled by this question.

"The Old Testament says to set aside one day a week to honor God," Ball said. "When was the last time you spent one day, not one day a week, just one day, to praise God and thank him for what you have?"

Robinson realized he had never done that. Oh, he had gone to church every week as a child, but once he became a collegian and a pro basketball player and his mother was not there to persuade him, his worship became sporadic. Suddenly, "I felt like a spoiled brat," he recalled. "Everything was about me, me, me. How much money can I make? It was all about David's praise and David's glory. Everybody cheering David. Everybody patting David on the back. I had never stopped to honor God for all he had done for me. That really hit me and I just cried. I cried all afternoon, and I prayed and told the Lord, 'Everything you've given me, I'm giving back to you today.'

"That was a big moment in my life."

Before, he had thought the Bible was full of fairy tales. He saw no relevance to his day-to-day life. He read computer manuals because he learned something from them. Now the minister told him the Bible was as much an instruction manual as his computer books.

A manual for life.

Why, Robinson had never considered this, and this insight excited him. Here, finally, were the answers he had been looking for. He became a born-again Christian that very day in June 1991. He decided he needed God in his life. His brain and athleticism could give him all the achievements and materialistic things he wanted, but they could not satisfy his soul. His born-again faith was solidified six nights later, when he watched Michael Jordan embrace the Chicago Bulls' first NBA championship trophy as if a piece of metal could validate a life.

"Here I am with five cars, two houses and more money than I ever thought I'd have. What more could I ask for? But where am I going? Here's Michael Jordan, he has more than me, and boy, I'd like to have some of the things he has, but is the world setting a trap for us? We win the NBA championship trophy, but is winning one trophy enough? There's always something else. Twenty years from now, who really cares? Bill Russell has won eleven championships. That's really great, it really is. That's an unbelievable accomplishment. But one day it will all be over. The things Bill Russell accomplished meant far less than who he is as a person and how he affects people's lives.

"I realized all I was pursuing couldn't fulfill me," Robinson continued. "I was a successful athlete making a lot of money, but if I couldn't be happy with myself, something was wrong. Ninety-nine percent of the people in the world would want to be in my shoes, but I was still looking for more. That's what shocked me into waking up. What I had should have been plenty, but no matter how much I had, it didn't seem like enough because material things can't satisfy your deepest needs. That's when I started to realize I needed the Lord.

"(Now) I get fulfillment out of pleasing God, knowing I'm doing the things he's calling me to do. My satisfaction comes in knowing God is smiling down at me as a husband and a father. When he sees my effort on the basketball floor, he knows I'm doing it for his glory. And he's pleased with that. As long as he's in control, I'm in good shape. I don't have to know what's coming. I know that it's going to be good. That's a great feeling: not having to worry about the future. So I have a peace and satisfaction that I can't get from anywhere else."